dutch
stonewall

D0948073

by Jacob Aagaard

EVERYMAN CHESS

Published by Everyman Publishers plc, London

First published in 2000 by Gloucester Publishers plc, (formerly Everyman Publishers plc), Northburgh House, 10 Northburgh Street, London, EC1V 0AT

British Library Cataloguing-in-Publication Data
A catalogue record for this book is available from the British Library.

978 1 85744 252 6

Distributed in North America by The Globe Pequot Press, P.O Box 480, 246 Goose Lane, Guilford, CT 06437-0480.

All other sales enquiries should be directed to Gloucester Publishers plc, Northburgh House, 10 Northburgh Street, London, EC1V 0AT
tel: 020 7253 7887 fax: 020 7490 3708
email: info@everymanchess.com
website: www.everymanchess.com

EVERYMAN CHESS SERIES (formerly Cadogan Chess)

Chief Advisor: Garry Kasparov
Commissioning Editor: Byron Jacobs

Typeset and edited by First Rank Publishing, Brighton.
Production by Navigator Guides.
Cover Design by Horatio Monteverde.

Printed and bound in the UK

CONTENTS

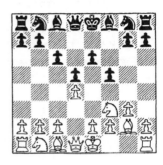

BIBLIOGRAPHY

Books
Encyclopaedia of Chess Openings Volume A (third edition), Alexander Matanovic (Sahovski Informator 1997)
Positional Play, Mark Dvoretsky (Batsford 1994)

Periodicals
Informators 1-78
New in Chess yearbooks 1-56
Chessbase Magazine

Websites
The Week in Chess

PREFACE

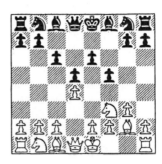

This is my third chess book for Everyman and my third book about opening theory. The two first books, *Easy Guide to the Panov-Botvinnik Attack* and *Easy Guide to the Sicilian Sveshnikov*, were produced in co-operation with Gambit, and I would like to thank Graham Burgess and Murray Chandler for giving me the opportunity to enter the world of chess books.

I would also like to thank Byron Jacobs for suggesting the title of this book to me. I admit that, initially, I did not know very much about the Stonewall and was rather apprehensive about writing a book about it, but then I remembered how little I knew of the Panov and the Sveshnikov before beginning those books, despite the fact that they were in my repertoire...

Compared to my previous books this is less loaded with theory and in all senses a more enjoyable read, and this has been my main objective. I have endeavoured to work within the format of the series in which it is part while simultaneously adding my own flavour. However, ultimately, I wanted to write a book that is fun to read as well as enabling the reader to learn about the Stonewall.

As for the practical use of this book I would like to say something about how it is structured, and how I believe the reader can most improve his experiences with the Stonewall. I am a simple player who remembers theory only if it makes sense – I know I am not the only one. In fact I remember Nigel Short writing something similar. I have around fifteen years of experience of helping friends and pupils in their quest for improvement and, thus far, my conclusion is that the actual opening phase is not very important, at least not when knowledge of the opening ends with the fifteenth move – after which one is left with little or no understanding of the position. For this reason I have devoted a considerable part of this book to non-theoretical material, with the intention of illustrating the typical themes, plans and counter-plans available to both sides in the Stonewall complex.

I compare my comprehension of the Stonewall to my understanding of the Nimzo-Indian, which I have played on and off for the last five years. These are openings which do not require learning many moves since there is no early direct contact. More important than remembering fifteen moves is to be aware of the nature of the position changing when, for example, White plays b2-b3 a move before he usually would. Or what about a2-a4 in a position where ♗b2 is almost always played? Many players could very well play something like this, believing it to be theory, only to later find that it is new and a result of mixing up the positions.

Consequently I would like to suggest that the reader will gain the most from this book by carefully reading through it and playing through all the games, as would be the idea with a collection of Ulf Andersson's games, for instance (a collection that would include many interesting draws...). If you plan to play only the Stonewall with Black and hope to have another fifty years with the King's Gambit with White, then do not skip the parts of the book where White's plans are explained! One of the main reasons why these are featured is to make Stonewall enthusiasts aware of what to look out for and what to try to prevent.

For the material in this book I have used annotations by some of the players themselves, either from Informator or Chessbase; I have taken a critical view of their analyses and found some improvements. Some of the games are heavily annotated while others are not. Normally I would like to go into all of the games in detail, but it is simply not possible with so many games to cover and with limited space. Nonetheless I have tried to annotate the best of the games in more detail, and in this way the games that are most fun and instructive can be studied deeper,

while others are also beneficial in that their presence is required to make a particular point or observation.

It has been an enjoyable learning experience working on this book and I hope that, in the future, I will have the opportunity to write more like it. Currently I am working on a book on the Kalashnikov Sicilian with my friend Jan Pinski. It will be more traditional and strict in its structure, but perhaps there will be some pages on which I can express my need for explaining ideas and plans rather than just giving games and references. I believe this is the type of book that people enjoy the most. And for me chess is about fun, and nothing else.

I would like to thank some friends for supporting me while I worked on the book during my holidays, providing me with a place to stay and not complaining when I chose to investigate the consequences of exchanging a knight for a bishop rather than go to the pub! These are Ivo Timmermans, Helen Haythornwhite and Donald Holmes. I would also like to thank my good friends Oliver Yue and Robin Waltons for their support and friendship. Finally I would like to thank Coach for helping me understand myself better as both a player and a person, and for reading through parts of the manuscript with not too many suggestions of improvement. Thank you all!

Jacob Aagaard,
Nottingham, Glasgow, Hoogoven and Bollington, January 2001.

INTRODUCTION

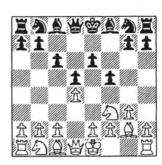

History

Unlike some systems against 1 d4, the Stonewall is not an invention of recent times, or even this century. It is interesting that in his book about the middle-game from 1964 Euwe classifies the Stonewall as a sub-variation of the Queen's Gambit, rather than the Dutch Defence. The Stonewall has been played by a number of the great players, past and present – even in World Championship matches. Among the famous names using this set-up at some time during their careers are greats such as Tarrasch, Alekhine, Botvinnik, Bronstein, Smyslov, Larsen, Korchnoi and Tal. In more recent times it has been the standard defence of such players such as Bareev, Spassky, Yusupov, Short, Nikolic, Lautier, Agdestein and, for a short period, Vladimir Kramnik.

Originally the Stonewall was known mainly for offering Black good attacking prospects, but after White found ways to deal with these attacks attention turned to the more positional aspects, thus contributing to the modern Stonewall's solid reputation.

In this section we will follow the course of the Stonewall in chess history. For convenience I have placed the beginning of the modern era at around 1960.

The first game – selected for its charm as much as strategy – is from what I would call the pre-historic period of chess.

Staunton-Saint Amant
London match (6) 1843

1 d4 f5 2 c4 c6 3 ♘c3 e6 4 ♗f4 d5 5 e3 ♘f6 6 ♘f3 ♗e7

As can be seen in Chapter Six this system is now considered rather dubious for Black.

7 ♗e2 0-0 8 0-0 ♗d6 9 ♘e5 dxc4

Back in the old days pawn structure mattered less than piece activity.

10 ♗xc4 ♘d5 11 ♗g3 ♗xe5 12 ♗xe5 ♘d7 13 ♗g3 ♘7b6 14 ♗b3 h6 15 a3 ♕e7 16 ♖c1 ♗d7

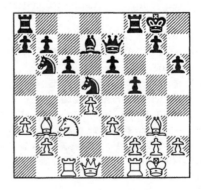

Black has nothing to compensate for his desperately weak dark squares. Although the following simplification eases the pressure for the defender, White is guaranteed an advantage.

17 ♘xd5 ♘xd5 18 ♗xd5 exd5 19 ♗e5

The point – White's bishop dominates.

19...♔h7 20 f4 a6 21 ♖f3 ♖f7 22 ♖g3

White continues to lead and, for the moment, Black continues to defend. However, while Staunton fails to make the necessary progress on the kingside, Saint Amant improves his position.

22...♖g8 23 ♕h5 ♕e6 24 ♖f1 ♗e8 25 ♕h4 ♕e7 26 ♖g5 ♕e6 27 ♖f3 ♖d7 28 ♕h3 ♖f7 29 ♖fg3 b6 30 ♕h5 ♖b7 31 ♕h4

White is getting nowhere, and now Black is ready to start aggressive operations on the other flank.

31...♖f7 32 ♕h3 c5 33 dxc5 bxc5 34 ♖h5 d4!

Black opens up the queenside for his pieces to infiltrate enter the enemy camp – a possibility for which White is unprepared.

35 exd4 cxd4 36 ♖hg5 ♕c8 37 ♖f3 ♗b5!

White's king is now in big trouble.

38 ♔f2 ♕c2+ 39 ♔g3 ♗e2 40 ♗xd4

40 ♖f2 ♕d3+ 41 ♔h4 hxg5+ 42 ♔xg5+ ♕xh3 would also win for Black.

40...♗xf3 41 gxf3 g6

Black has won the exchange and is in control, while White is unable to generate threats.

42 ♔h4 ♕d2 43 ♗e5 ♕d8 44 ♔g3 ♕d1 45 ♔h4 ♕e1+ 46 ♖g3 ♕d2 47 ♕g2 ♕d8+ 48 ♔h3 ♖d7

Black now brings his heavy pieces into play, which will shortly win the game.

49 ♕c2 ♕b6 50 a4 ♕e6 51 ♖g1 g5 52 ♖c1 g4+ 53 ♔g3 gxf3+ 54 ♔xf3 ♕g6 55 ♔e3 ♕g4 56 ♖f1 ♖gd8 57 ♗c3 ♖d3+ 58 ♔f2 ♕f3+ 0-1.

Not a very convincing game, although these were among the best players of the world at that time.

The next game, played at the end of the nineteenth century, demonstrates a higher level of positional understanding. This time more care is given to the centre, and Black's tactical skills are quite convincing.

Burn-Tarrasch
Vienna 1898

1 d4 d5 2 c4 e6 3 ♘c3 c6 4 e3 ♗d6 5 ♘f3 f5 6 ♗e2 ♘d7 7 0-0 ♕f6!?

Tarrasch exploits the stable structure in the centre to start an early kingside attack. This is as primitive as it looks, and White could have defended better, but it is still a decent approach for Black.

8 ♘e1 ♕h6 9 g3 g5 10 f3?!

The beginning of a faulty plan. Far better would have been 10 f4! followed by ♘e1-d/f3-e5 and subsequent queenside activity.

10...♘e7 11 e4 f4!

Creating weaknesses around the white king.

12 e5

White is forced to release the pressure in the centre in order to reduce the harassment of his king.

12...♗c7 13 g4 ♕g7

Preparing a quick invasion on the h-file and thus creating further defensive worries for White.

14 ♖f2 h5 15 ♖g2 ♘g6!

The prospect of the knight arriving on h4 leaves the g2-rook searching for a square.

16 gxh5 ♖xh5 17 ♗d3 ♘h4 18 ♖c2 dxc4!

Concentrating on the f5-square by distracting the bishop.

19 ♗xc4 ♘f5

The latest threat is 20...♘xd4 when 21 ♕xd4? ♗b6 pins the queen.

20 ♔h1 ♗b6!

With White's kingside looking decidedly shaky it is appropriate to instigate a tactical sequence from which Black will emerge in control.

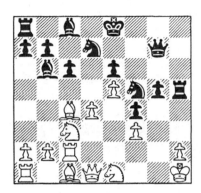

21 ♗xe6 ♘xd4 22 ♗g4 ♖h8 23 ♖d2 ♘xe5!

A nice little combination to finish the game. White can choose only the nature of his demise.

24 ♗xc8 ♖xc8 25 ♖xd4 ♗xd4 26 ♕xd4

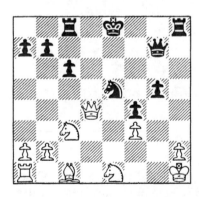

26...♖xh2+!!

This 'sacrifice', clearing away the remains of White's defensive wall, is the idea behind 23...♘xe5.

27 ♔g1

27 ♔xh2 ♘g4+ 28 fxg4 ♕xd4 29 ♔g2 ♕d7 30 ♔f3 does give White three pieces for his queen, but then Black has two healthy pawns while White lacks co-ordination and a safe haven for his king.

27...♕h8 28 ♗xf4 gxf4 29 ♘e4?!

29 ♕xf4 ♖h1+ 30 ♔f2 ♖d8 31 ♔e2 ♖h2+

32 ♔e3 prolongs the game.

29...♖h1+ 30 ♔f2 ♘g4+ 0-1

The following games are all played by one of the greatest players of the last century, Mikhail Botvinnik, a world champion who helped to promote the Stonewall as much as any player. In fact many club players approach the opening in line more with Botvinnik's concepts than with modern ideas. Moreover, I believe they have good reason to do so because it was only after White found a different set-up that Black looked for a new strategy.

Rabinovich-Botvinnik
USSR Ch. 1927

1 d4 e6 2 c4 f5 3 g3 ♘f6 4 ♗g2 ♗e7 5 ♘c3 0-0 6 ♘f3 d5 7 0-0 c6 8 ♕c2 ♕e8

This was a key theme of the Stonewall in Botvinnik's era. The queen is transferred to the kingside to take part in an offensive against the white king.

9 ♗f4

The bishop does not look well placed here. 9 ♗g5! is preferable.

9...♕h5 10 ♖ad1 ♘bd7 11 b3

Black is already doing well, for White's position looks better than it is.

11...♘e4!?

Botvinnik gets to work on his attack, although waiting with the often useful 11...♔h8 was another option. However, 11...b6! might be best, developing the traditional problem bishop.

12 ♘e5!

Finally we see action from White. 12 ♘xe4 fxe4 13 ♘e5 ♗f6 is comfortable for Black.

12...♘g5?!

As we are about to see this could and should have been punished by a swift reaction in the centre. There is no reason to believe that Black stands any worse after 12...♗f6!?, while 12...♘d6!? has also been suggested. For example 13 cxd5 cxd5 14 ♘xd5 exd5 15 ♘xd7 ♗xd7 16 ♕c7 ♕e8 17 ♗xd6 ♖c8 18 ♗xd5+ ♔h8 and Black wins a piece for a few pawns and retains an active position with good attacking prospects.

13 h4?

This weakens the whole kingside pawn structure. Instead White should strike in the centre with 13 f3!, e.g. 13...♘h3+ 14 ♗xh3 ♕xh3 15 e4 fxe4 16 fxe4 ♗b4 17 ♘b1! ♘f6 18 ♘d3 ♗e7 19 ♘f2 with a space advantage.

13...♘e4 14 ♗f3 ♕e8 15 ♘xd7 ♗xd7 16 ♔g2 ♗b4!

A strong move that forces White to make an important concession.

17 ♗xe4?!

Now Black gets the f-file and his light-squared bishop tastes freedom, so 17 ♘b1 is more circumspect.

17...fxe4 18 ♖h1 ♕h5!

Causing White another headache in view of the threatened 19...♗xc3 20 ♕xc3 ♕xe2.

19 f3 ♕g6

19...e5 has been suggested as more accurate, but White has his resources too, as the following line suggests: 20 dxe5 ♕g6 21 ♕c1! (21 ♔f1 ♖xf4 leads to the game) 21...♖xf4 (21...♗xc3 22 h5!) 22 h5 ♕g5 23 ♘xd5! cxd5 24 ♕xf4 and White comes out on top.

20 ♔f1 e5 21 dxe5?

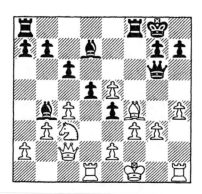

A fatal error in a demanding position. Although 21 h5! ♕f5 22 dxe5 exf3 23 e4! (23

♕xf5 ♗xf5 24 ♖c1 d4 is hopeless) 23...dxe4 24 ♘xe4 ♖ad8 must be better for Black the advantage is less clear than in the game.

21...♖xf4!

Removing a major defender.

22 gxf4 ♕g3 23 ♘xe4

23 cxd5 serves only to hasten the end in view of 23...♗c5 24 ♘xe4 ♗h3+ 25 ♖xh3 ♕g1 mate.

23...dxe4 24 ♖xd7 ♗c5!

Black should be careful here as 24...e3?? 25 ♖xg7+! turns the tables.

25 e3 ♕xf3+

Black now picks up the white rook and secures a decisive lead in the ending.

26 ♕f2 ♕xh1+ 27 ♔e2 ♕h3 28 f5 ♕g4+ 29 ♔d2 ♖f8 30 e6!?

A crafty swindle attempt.

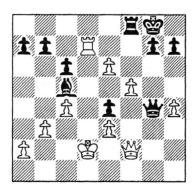

30...♕xf5

Not 30...♖xf5?? 31 ♖d8+ ♗f8 32 ♕xf5! ♕xf5 33 e7 and Black must be satisfied with perpetual check.

31 ♕xf5 ♖xf5 32 ♖xb7 ♖f2+ 33 ♔e1 ♖f6 34 b4 ♗xe3 35 ♔e2 ♗g1 36 e7 ♔f7 37 e8♕+ ♔xe8 38 ♖xg7 ♖g6 39 ♖xh7 ♗d4 40 c5 ♖g2+ 41 ♔f1 ♖f2+ 42 ♔e1 e3 0-1.

Even though this is still a young Botvinnik we are dealing with here, his handling of the Stonewall continued to be important for a long time – of course in those days a good idea could contribute to a GM's earnings over the course of a year whereas now a game is available the same day it is played, so developments in opening theory have different implications today. The following game was played six years later but, basically, little had changed. Again Black pins his hopes on a solid structure in the centre and the rapid development of an attack on the kingside.

Flohr-Botvinnik
Moscow 1933

1 d4 e6 2 c4 f5 3 g3 ♘f6 4 ♗g2 ♗e7 5 ♘c3 d5 6 ♘f3 c6 7 0-0 0-0 8 b3 ♕e8 9 ♗b2 ♘bd7 10 ♕d3 ♕h5 11 cxd5 exd5 12 ♘d2?!

Here we see what can happen if White's knights fail to concentrate on the e5-square (the c3-knight is not well placed). Better is 12 ♘e1! with the idea of 13 f4 and ♘e1-f3-e5, cementing a piece in Black's half of the board. Now Black seizes his chance.

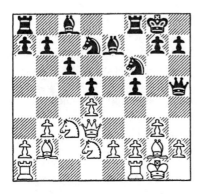

12...♘e4! 13 f3

13 f4 ♘xd2! 14 ♕xd2 ♘f6 leaves White's knight too far from e5, although the text allows Black to create a powerful initiative.

13...♘xc3

Now it is the d2-knight that has no route to e5!.

14 ♗xc3 f4!

The weakness of the dark squares around White's will soon tell.

15 ♖fe1 ♗d6 16 ♘f1 ♖f7 17 e3

17 e4? dxe4! 18 ♕xe4 ♘f6 helps Black to win the d5-square and develop his initiative.

17...fxg3 18 ♘xg3

18 hxg3 ♕g5 19 e4 transposes to the next note.

18...♕h4 19 ♘f1

White achieves nothing with the pawn sacrifice 19 e4 ♗xg3 20 hxg3 ♕xg3 21 exd5 since Black simply continues his development with 21...♘f6 22 dxc6 bxc6 with advantage.

19...♘f6 20 ♖e2

White is cramped but trying to free himself too hastily is suicidal, e.g. 20 e4? dxe4 21 fxe4 ♘g4 22 h3 (22 e5 ♖xf1+!) 22...♘f2 23 ♕e3 ♗xh3 etc.

20...♗d7 21 ♗e1 ♕g5 22 ♗g3 ♗xg3 23 ♘xg3?

Not a wise decision. Instead recapturing with the pawn at least blocks the g-file. Now Black has a decisive attack.

23...h5! 24 f4 ♕g4 25 ♖f2

25 ♖f1 h4 26 h3 ♕e6! 27 ♘h1 ♘e4 is also close to winning for Black.

25...h4 26 ♗f3?

Allowing a simple winning exchange. 26 h3! ♕e6 27 ♘f1 ♘e4 28 ♗xe4 dxe4 was necessary but nonetheless unpleasant for White.

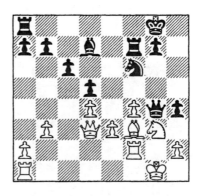

26...hxg3! 27 ♗xg4 gxf2+

White is outnumbered.

28 ♔g2 ♘xg4 29 h3 ♘f6 30 ♔xf2 ♘e4+ 0-1

White resigned as there is no reason to investigate 31 ♔g2 ♗xh3+.

Capablanca-Botvinnik
Moscow 1936

1 ♘f3 f5 2 g3 ♘f6 3 ♗g2 e6 4 c4 ♗e7 5 0-0 0-0 6 d4 d5 7 ♘c3 c6 8 ♕b3 ♔h8 9 ♘e5 ♘bd7 10 ♘xd7

White is forced to make this trade as redirecting his knight with 10 ♘d3? leaves the d4-pawn vulnerable after 10...dxc4 11 ♕xc4 ♘b6.

10...♘xd7 11 ♖d1 ♘b6!

Highlighting the drawback of White's setup. Now he is forced to make yet another unfavourable exchange.

12 cxd5 exd5 13 ♘a4 ♘c4 14 ♘c5 b6?

As is often the case this 'knee-jerk' reaction creates an unnecessary weakness on the queenside. The light-squared bishop is not necessarily best placed on b7 in positions where White has already exchanged on d5. Black has a fine game after 14...♘d6 15 ♗f4 ♖f7.

15 ♘d3 ♗f6 16 ♕c2?!

Freeing the b2-pawn so as to evict the knight. 16 e3 a5!? 17 ♕c2 a4 is roughly even, but White had another way of vacating b3, namely 16 ♕c3!, with the tactical justification 16...c5 17 ♘f4! ♗xd4 18 ♕c2 ♘d6 19 e3 ♗e5 20 ♘xd5 and White is slightly better.

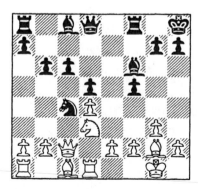

16...♗d7?

Black misses his chance. White's idea is to meet 16...♗xd4! with 17 ♘b4 ♕f6 18 ♘xc6. However this is fine for Black after 18...♗xf2+! 19 ♔xf2 ♕xc6 20 ♗xd5 (20 ♖xd5 ♗e6 does not trouble Black) 20...♕c5+ 21 e3 ♘xe3 22 ♕xc5 ♘xd1+ 23 ♔e1 bxc5 24 ♗xa8 f4 25 gxf4 ♗g4 when, if anyone, Black is better.

17 e3 ♘d6

Retreating the knight (to a decent outpost) in his own time.

18 a4 a5 19 b3 ♖e8 20 ♗a3 ♘e4?

This seems to be a mistake as the knight achieves nothing on g5. 20...♘f7 looks more appropriate.

21 f3 ♘g5 22 ♘e5 ♖c8

22...♗xe5 23 dxe5 ♖xe5 24 f4 forks e5 and g5.

23 ♖ac1 ♔g8 24 ♕d3 ♘f7 25 f4

White leads thanks to his firm grip on the centre.

25...♗e7 26 ♗xe7 ♕xe7 27 ♖c3

27 ♕a6 ♖b8!.

27...♘xe5 28 dxe5

Black has an ostensibly fine position but if he wants to free himself he has to do so with ...b6-b5. This must be the reasoning behind the following moves from Botvinnik, but in retrospect Black should have stuck to passive defence.

28...♕b4 29 ♖dc1

Another possibility was to go directly into the endgame with 29 ♕d4!? ♖b8 30 ♕xb4 axb4 31 ♖c2 b5 32 axb5 ♖xb5 33 ♖a1 with a substantial advantage to White due to his superior rooks and Black's numerous weaknesses.

29...♖b8 30 ♕d4! b5 31 ♖a1!

Now the a5-pawn is weak and the rook which was dreaming of greatness on the b-file will have to return to a8.

31...♖a8

Taking on d4 permanently fixes the pawn structure to White's advantage.

32 axb5 ♕xb5 33 ♖c5!

White now has a winning advantage,

thanks mainly to tactics involving ℤxd5.

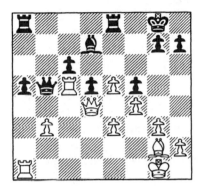

33...♛xb3

No help is 33...♛b4 34 ℤxd5! cxd5 35 ♛xb4 axb4 36 ℤxa8 ℤxa8 37 ♝xd5+ ♝e6! 38 ♝xa8 ♝xb3 39 ♚f2 ♝c4 40 ♚e1 with a healthy extra pawn in the endgame for White.

34 ℤxd5 ♝e6 35 ℤd6 c5!

A clever try. Black gives a pawn to free his pieces.

36 ♛xc5

The prophylactic 36 ♛d2!? ℤac8 37 ℤxe6 ℤxe6 38 ♝d5 ♛b6 39 ♛a2 leaves Black with problems he will find impossible to solve.

36...ℤec8 37 ♛b6?!

Missing a simple win, suggesting that White was running short of time here. 37 ♛d4 ℤc4 38 ♛d1! decides.

37...ℤab8 38 ♛xb3 ♝xb3 39 ♝c6?

The final mistake, throwing away the win. 39 ℤxa5! looks risky but is necessary if White wants to win: 39...ℤc1+ 40 ♚f2 ℤc2+ 41 ♚f3! ♝f7 (41...♝c4 42 g4 fxg4+ 43 ♚g3 also is enough for White to win) 42 ♝h3 ♝h5+ 43 g4 fxg4+ 44 ♝xg4 ♝xg4+ 45 ♚xg4 and the rook ending is winning for White.

39...a4!

Botvinnik does not miss his chance. Now the a-pawn gives Black counterplay.

40 g4

40 ♝xa4 ♝xa4 41 ℤxa4 ℤc1+ 42 ♚g2 ℤb2+ 43 ♚h3 ℤh1 leads to a draw as White can make perpetual check.

40...fxg4 41 ♚f2 ♚f8 42 ♚g3 ½-½

Despite his winning chances in this game Capablanca failed to do any damage to the reputation of the Stonewall with his set-up, so White had to find other ways of playing. The next game is in many ways nearer to the modern approach adopted by White.

Petrosian-Korchnoi
Leningrad 1946

1 d4 e6 2 ♞f3 f5 3 g3 ♞f6 4 ♝g2 d5 5 0-0 ♝d6 6 c4 c6 7 b3 0-0?

Today Black tends to make White pay a price for the thematic exchange of dark-squared bishops. Consequently 7...♛e7 is popular.

8 ♝a3 ♝xa3 9 ♞xa3 ♛e8 10 ♞c2 ♛h5 11 ♛c1 ♞e4 12 ♞ce1!

The knight is heading for d3, from where the crucial e5-square can be monitored.

12...g5?

This aggressive thrust, which creates structural weaknesses in Black's camp, ultimately falls short of troubling White.

13 ♞d3 ♞d7 14 ♞fe5

White already has a considerable positional advantage. A problem for Black here in his effort to generate a kingside attack is the absence of his 'good' bishop.

14...♚h8 15 f3 ♞d6 16 e4!

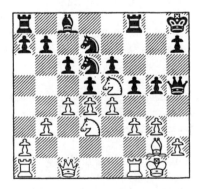

A pawn break that is tactically justified.

Since Black cannot punish this attack on his centre and he has already parted company with his best piece, he is close to losing.

16...♘f7

16...fxe4 17 fxe4 ♖xf1+ 18 ♕xf1 ♘xe4 19 ♘xd7 ♗xd7 20 ♗xe4 dxe4 21 ♘c5 ♕e8 22 ♕f6+ leads to a decisive attack for White.

17 cxd5 ♘dxe5 18 dxe5!

The knight on d3 is clearly superior to its counterpart on f7 so there is no need for further exchanges.

18...cxd5 19 exd5 exd5 20 f4!

Fixing Black's structural weaknesses. Now Black collapses but his prospects are anyway very poor.

20...♖d8 21 ♕c7 b6 22 fxg5 ♗a6 23 ♘f4 1-0

In the next game we see an example of the power of Black's kingside attack. The game also demonstrates that it is important to not only think about your own plan but also consider how the opponent might try to prevent it.

Steiner-Botvinnik
Groningen 1946

1 d4 e6 2 c4 f5 3 g3 ♘f6 4 ♗g2 ♗b4+!?

By employing this order of moves Black hopes to disrupt his opponent's development, the result here being to avoid the exchange of dark-squared bishops via a3, as in the previous game.

5 ♗d2 ♗e7 6 ♘c3 0-0 7 ♕c2

White can take time out here with the interesting 7 d5 in order to prevent the Stonewall.

7...d5 8 ♘f3 c6 9 0-0 ♕e8 10 ♗f4 ♕h5

We have reached a standard position in the Botvinnik Stonewall.

11 ♖ae1

White intends to drop his knight back to d2 to expand with f2-f3 and e3-e4, with the aim of compromising Black's centre. However, if White neglects his bishop on f4 Black

then has a target.

11...♘bd7 12 ♘d2?

12 b3 ♘e4 resembles the Rabinovich-Botvinnik game, earlier, with the only difference being that the white rook is on e1 instead of d1.

12...g5!

Black punishes White's recklessness.

13 ♗c7 ♘e8 14 ♗e5 ♘xe5 15 dxe5 f4!

Black already has the better game, and as well as his prospects of a strong attack he also has a potential prisoner in the form of the pawn on e5 (after 16...fxg3 17 hxg3 g4).

16 gxf4 gxf4 17 ♘f3

White is really struggling. He could have defended the e5-pawn with 17 e4?! (with the sneaky idea of 17...f3 18 ♕d1!), but Black would play 17...d4! 18 ♘e2 ♕xe5 19 ♘f3 ♕h5 20 ♘exd4 e5 with a strong attack.

17...♔h8 18 ♔h1 ♘g7

The knight finds and excellent outpost on f5.

19 ♕c1 ♗d7 20 a3

This is hardly appropriate. White should be more concerned about matters on the kingside.

20...♖f7 21 b4 ♖g8 22 ♖g1 ♘f5 23 ♘d1 ♖fg7!

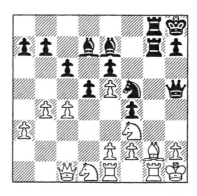

Precise calculation makes this pawn sacrifice a winning plan.

24 ♕xf4 ♖g4 25 ♕d2 ♘h4 26 ♘e3

26 ♘xh4 ♖xh4 27 h3 ♖xh3+ leads to mate.

26...♘xf3 27 exf3

27 ♗xf3 ♕xh2+!! 28 ♔xh2 ♖h4 mate(!) would have been a nice finish.

27...♖h4 28 ♘f1 ♗g5! 0-1

After the bishop comes to f4 there is no way to defend h2.

In the 1950s the Stonewall enjoyed its height of popularity. For example it was used by both Bronstein and Botvinnik in their World Championship match in 1951. In the following game, from that match, the set-up chosen by Bronstein to counter the Stonewall is not terribly threatening but it proved to trouble Black.

Bronstein-Botvinnik
World Ch. (game 22), Moscow 1951

1 d4 e6 2 c4 f5 3 g3 ♘f6 4 ♗g2 ♗e7 5 ♘c3 0-0 6 e3 d5 7 ♘ge2!?

This development takes the sting out of the queen manoeuvre ...♕d8-e8-h5 and plays a part in the fight for the e4-square, thanks to the ability to drive an enemy knight away from e4 with a timely f2-f3.

7...c6 8 b3 ♘e4

8...♘bd7 makes little sense due to 9 ♘f4, monitoring e6.

9 0-0 ♘d7 10 ♗b2 ♘df6 11 ♕d3

This intended improvement of his forces also hinders the thematic manoeuvre ♘e2-f4-d3.

11...g5!?

The soundness of this advance is not too important here. Its logic is quite understandable: White has a potential space advantage on the queenside which he will use to push his pawns with the aim of creating weaknesses in Black's camp and opening files. Black, meanwhile, hopes for the same kind of activity on the kingside, gaining space and (by ...g5-g4) cementing his grip on e4. However, perhaps this strategy, in the long term, backfires on Botvinnik. Consequently a more modern way of handling this position would

be 11...b6!? followed by either posting the bishop on b7 or – if White does not play cxd5 – even a6, with the idea of ...♘e4-d6 to pressure the c4-pawn.

12 cxd5 exd5

12...cxd5 permits White to take over the c-file and thus quickly develop an initiative.

13 f3 ♘xc3

13...♘d6 14 e4 dxe4 15 fxe4 fxe4 16 ♘xe4 ♘fxe4 17 ♗xe4 ♘xe4 18 ♕xe4 leaves Black with the bishop pair and White with an isolated pawn, but due to the open position of the black king White has the better prospects.

14 ♗xc3 g4

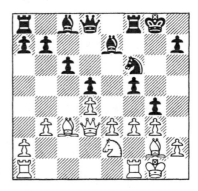

15 fxg4!

Diverting the knight away form e4 with a couple of accurate moves.

15...♘xg4 16 ♗h3! ♘h6

Black wishes to keep his knight on the board and 16...♘f6 17 ♗xf5 offers him no real compensation.

17 ♘f4

White has a definite advantage since Black has achieved nothing more from his aggressive actions on the kingside than providing White with good squares. Nevertheless with a knight on e4 here Black's position would not be too uncomfortable.

17...♗d6 18 b4 a6 19 a4 ♕e7 20 ♖ab1

The standard minority attack.

20...b5?

Black prevents White's idea of 21 b5 but

at a price, for now White is given the opportunity to operate on the a-file.

21 ♗g2 ♘g4 22 ♗d2 ♘f6 23 ♖b2! ♗d7 24 ♖a1 ♘e4

Black finally gets his knight to e4, but in the meantime White has been busy with his own plan.

25 ♗e1 ♖fe8 26 ♕b3 ♔h8 27 ♖ba2 ♕f8?

27...♗xf4 was necessary, as we are about to see.

28 ♘d3!

With this move White retains his excellent knight. The desired opening of the a-file can wait.

28...♖ab8 29 axb5 axb5 30 ♖a7 ♖e7 31 ♘e5!

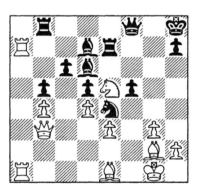

Now if Black removes this knight White will exchange on e4 and plant his remaining bishop on c3, the resultant pressure on the a1-h8 diagonal combining with the presence of the rook on the seventh rank will put White firmly in charge.

31...♗e8 32 g4!

Opening up another route for the queen's bishop.

32...fxg4 33 ♗xe4 dxe4 34 ♗h4 ♖xe5

Black is out of options and tries something desperate.

35 dxe5 ♗xe5 36 ♖f1 ♕g8 37 ♗g3!

The final blow. Black cannot now defend the position.

37...♗g7 38 ♕xg8+ 1-0

Ironically, Smyslov, the first player to take the World Championship title away from Botvinnik, gave the Stonewall his ultimate stamp of approval by using it in their 1958 World Championship match. Well, if you can play the opening when it matters most, and you can play it against the world's expert, then you must believe that it is playable...

Botvinnik-Smyslov
World Ch. (game 22), Moscow 1958

1 d4 f5 2 g3 ♘f6 3 ♗g2 e6 4 ♘f3 ♗e7 5 0-0 0-0 6 c4 c6 7 ♘c3 d5 8 ♗g5 ♘bd7 9 e3 ♕e8 10 ♕c2 ♔h8

Botvinnik's unambitious opening treatment has left him without a claim for an advantage.

11 ♘e2 h6 12 ♗xf6 ♗xf6 13 cxd5 exd5 14 ♘f4 g5

Even though this is principally a weakening of Black's king position there is no convenient way for White to exploit this.

15 ♘d3 ♖g8 16 ♕c3 ♗e7 17 ♘fe5 ♘f6

Practically forcing White to nudge his f-pawn forward and in so doing compromise the protection of his king – otherwise an enemy knight on e4 will be a nuisance. Neither choice is comfortable for White.

18 f3 ♗e6

Black has achieved equality; there is no reason why his light-squared bishop should be any worse than the one on g2.

19 ♘c5 ♗xc5 20 ♕xc5

White continues to dream of a minority attack against c6, which is why he wants to keep the c-file open. 20 dxc5 might interfere more in the development of Black's offensive.

20...♘d7 21 ♘xd7 ♕xd7 22 ♖ae1 ♖g7 23 ♖f2 b6 24 ♕c3 ♕d6 25 ♖c2 ♗d7 26 b4 h5 27 ♔h1

Black has the better position, his attack being far more dangerous. The alternative 27 e4 is punished by 27...f4! 28 e5 ♕e6 and White remains under pressure.

27...h4 28 gxh4 gxh4 29 f4 ♖ag8 30 ♗f3 ♗e8

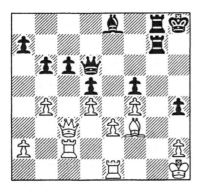

All Black's pieces have a role to play in the attack.

31 ♕d2 ♕h6 32 ♕e2 h3

In the long term an invasion on g2 looks inevitable, although White's next does nothing to address it. 33 b5!? at least tries to stir things up.

33 ♖cc1 ♖g2 34 ♗xg2 ♖xg2 35 ♕f3 ♕h4!

Ensuring the full point.

36 b5 ♗h5 37 ♕xg2 hxg2+ 38 ♔g1 c5 0-1.

The final game of this section involves a young Danish GM now known for his fantastic imagination and undogmatic style of play. Incidentally these qualities and his uncompromising attitude to chess makes him my hero.

**Johannsson-Larsen
Munich OI 1958**

1 c4 f5 2 d4 e6 3 g3 ♘f6 4 ♗g2 ♗e7 5 ♘f3 0-0 6 0-0 c6 7 ♕c2 ♕e8 8 ♘bd2 d5 9 ♘e5 ♘bd7 10 ♘d3 ♘e4 11 ♘f3

This 'new' set-up was developed after the war. It gives White good control of the dark squares in the centre, particularly e5. Black should now develop normally, which is usually the most sensible policy. Instead he

launches an attack which ultimately fails and serves only to structurally weaken his position.

11...g5? 12 ♘fe5 ♔h8 13 b3 a5 14 f3 ♘d6 15 ♗d2 ♗f6 16 ♖ae1 b5 17 c5!

White is ready to blast open the position to his advantage with 18 e4, hence Black's next attempt to create confusion with some subtle play – a plan that succeeds completely.

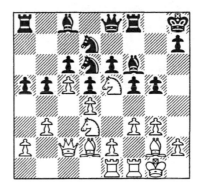

17...♗xe5!? 18 dxe5?

18 ♘xe5! ♘xe5 19 ♗xg5! Is excellent for White.

18...♘f7 19 e4 fxe4 20 fxe4 d4!

Avoiding a clearing of the centre while closing a line of defence to the vulnerable e5-pawn.

21 b4?!

White is sufficiently confused and allows his opponent active play on the a-file. Instead a slight advantage for the first player results after 21 ♖d1 b4 22 ♗c1 ♗a6 23 ♗b2.

21...axb4 22 ♕b2 ♕e7 23 ♕xd4 ♖xa2 24 ♗xb4 ♔g8 25 ♖f3 ♗b7 26 ♖ef1 ♖aa8

By now the situation is far from clear. White has weaknesses on c5, e5 and e4, but he does have a space advantage and Black's bishop is poor.

27 ♖3f2 ♖ad8 28 ♕c3 ♘h6

Black is trying to ease the pressure.

29 ♗f3 g4 30 ♗e2 ♖xf2 31 ♖xf2 ♕g5 32 ♖f4 ♘f8 33 ♕c1 ♕g7 34 ♖f6 ♘f7 35 ♕f1?!

35 ♕f4 is more active.

35...♗c8 36 ♕f4 ♘g6 37 ♕xg4 ♖xd3 38 ♗xd3 ♘fxe5

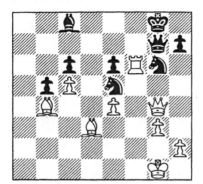

39 ♖xg6??

A terrible mistake no doubt induced by time pressure. After 39 ♕g5 ♘xd3 40 ♖xg6 hxg6 41 ♕d8+ ♕f8 42 ♕xd3 e5 a draw would be the most likely result.

39...hxg6 40 ♕e2 ♕d7 0-1

There is no defence to the double threat of ...♕xd3 and ...♕d4+.

Move orders and set-ups

The Stonewall is characterised not by specific sequences of moves – as is the case with the Najdorf variation of the Sicilian, for example – but by a particular, distinctive pawn formation that occurs in almost no other situation.

The diagram position illustrates the basic

Stonewall formation. Note that Black can deviate as well as White. He can choose to play with his knight on c6 instead of the pawn, a system that is probably a little dubious but has nevertheless seen occasional use by players as illustrious as Short and Spassky.

White's main decision concerns the posting of his king's bishop. It is not at all clear where the bishop is best placed, on g2 or d3. Some strong players even play ♗e2 in some positions, almost as if it makes little difference where this piece goes. Often Black is the one who influences whether or not the bishop takes residence on g2. This is due to the different move orders.

The player determined to play the Stonewall will most often play something like this:

1 d4 f5 2 g3 ♘f6 3 c4 e6 4 ♗g2 d5 5 ♘f3 c6 6 0-0 ♗d6

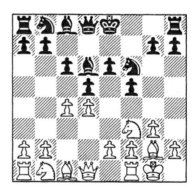

This is the most frequently seen position in the Stonewall (roughly a third of the games). Then there are many different positions which look almost the same. Black can put his bishop on e7, he can play ...b6 instead of ...c6, he can castle before playing ...c6 etc. White can play ♘h3 instead of ♘f3, b2-b3 before castling, and others. Basically, most players would select the position above if asked what characterised the Stonewall. However, this is not the only Stonewall, as we are about to see.

First, many Stonewall players do not like to face variations such as 1 d4 f5 2 ♗g5!?, which has its main justification in the line 2...h6?! 3 ♗h4 g5 4 e4 ♗g7 5 ♗g3 f4 6 ♗xf4 gxf4 7 ♕h5+ ♔f8 8 ♕f5+ ♔e8 9 ♗e2 ♘f6 10 e5 d6 11 ♕xf4 dxe5 12 dxe5 ♘d5 13 ♗h5+ ♔d7 14 ♕g4+ ♔c6 15 ♕xg7 and White wins, as in Mah-Siebrecht, London 1997. The line with 2 ♘c3 also has many followers. Therefore another common move order is the following:

1 d4 e6 2 ♘f3 f5 or 1 d4 e6 2 c4 f5

Of course this order is not without inconvenience, either. White can change direction and switch with 1 d4 e6 2 e4!?, and a player whose usual answer to 1 e4 is, for instance, 1...c5 or 1...d6 finds himself playing the French Defence! However, for Nigel Short and others who actually play the French, this specific move order is fine.

Then there are those who do not really want to play the standard Stonewall at all. A popular route comes from a declined Noteboom or Botvinnik in the Queen's Gambit: **1 d4 d5 2 c4 e6 3 ♘c3 c6 4 e3 f5!?** This has recently been tested with the sharp **5 g4!?**, which will be discussed in Chapter Six. Black can avoid this continuation with 1 d4 d5 2 c4 e6 3 ♘c3 c6 4 e3 ♘d7!? and postpone the decision of whether or not to play the Stonewall. White can then play **5 ♗d3**, still ready for **5...f5 6 g4!?**, but then he has lost the possibility to play 1 d4 d5 2 c4 e6 3 ♘c3 c6 4 e3 ♘d7 5 ♘f3 ♘gf6 6 ♕c2 (instead of 6 ♗d3) if Black plays **5...♘gf6** (players who dislike facing 6 ♕c2 in the Meran often use this order).

Some players are willing to play the Stonewall against just about anything. Many times in my junior days I played **1 d4 d5 2 c4 e6 3 ♘c3 f5?!** as White and never failed to get an advantage after **4 ♘f3 c6 5 ♗f4 ♘f6 6 e3 ♗e7 7 ♗d3 0-0 8 ♕c2 ♘e4 9 g4!**

see following diagram

I played 7 or 8 games from this position, winning them all. This line is considered in

Chapter Six. Basically Black should not allow White to develop one bishop to f4 and the other to d3, as in this line.

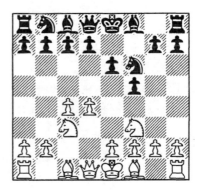

White can try to force this after **1 d4 e6 2 ♘f3 f5 3 c4 ♘f6 4 ♘c3**

The idea is to meet 4...d5 with 5 ♗f4. Black has two ways of dealing with this. The first is **4...♗b4!** with an improved version of the Nimzo-Indian, while 4...♗e7 intends 5 g3 d5 with a Stonewall with the bishop on e7. White can try (4...♗e7) 5 ♕c2!? but Black should not fear 5...0-0 6 e4 because 6...fxe4 7 ♘xe4 ♘c6! already gives him a lead in development.

Some people also play the Stonewall against the English opening. This gives White an extra possibility that probably makes the plan rather dubious for Black. The following game illustrates this nicely.

Lombardy-Soppe
Buenos Aires 1994

1 c4 e6 2 g3 d5 3 ♗g2 c6 4 ♘f3 ♗d6 5
0-0 f5?!

This is too hasty. If a Stonewall is desired
it would be better to play 5...♘d7!? with the
idea of 6 d4 ♘gf6, even though the knight
does not necessarily go to d7 in all lines.

6 d3!

The major difference – on d3 the pawn
has another role. White wants to blow the
centre apart.

6...♘f6 7 ♘c3 0-0 8 e4!

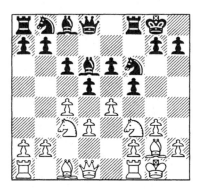

8...dxe4

8...♗c7 9 cxd5 exd5 10 e5 ♘fd7 11 d4
♘b6 12 ♘e2 ♔h8 13 h4 gave White a substantial advantage and a strong attack in Va-
ganian-Piasetski, Toronto 1990.

After 8...♗e7 9 exf5 exf5 10 ♗f4 ♘bd7
11 cxd5 ♘xd5 12 ♘xd5 cxd5 13 ♖e1 ♘c5
14 ♘d4 g5 15 ♗e5 White had much better
scope for his pieces in Szmetan-Ginzburg,
Buenos Aires 1991.

8...♘bd7 9 cxd5 exd5 10 exd5 ♘xd5 11
♘xd5 cxd5 12 ♕b3 ♘b6 13 a4 ♔h8 14 ♗g5
♗e7 15 ♗xe7 ♕xe7 16 a5 ♘d7 17 ♕xd5,
Dizdarevic-Lezcano, Gran 1990, is just another illustration of how bad things can go
for Black.

9 dxe4 e5

9...♘g4 10 ♕e2 ♘a6 11 c5 ♗b4 12 h3
♘h6 13 ♖d1 ♕e8 14 ♗xh6 gxh6 15 ♕e3

♔g7 16 ♘e2 ♗e7 17 h4 was wonderful for
White in the game Hertneck-Knaak, Pots-
dam 1988.

10 exf5 ♗xf5 11 ♕b3! ♕b6 12 ♗e3
♕xb3 13 axb3

White certainly has the superior endgame.
His bishops are better placed, the e5-pawn is
a juicy target for later and the e4-square an
attractive outpost.

13...♘a6 14 h3 ♗c7 15 g4 ♗d3 16 ♖fd1
e4 17 ♘d4 ♗b6 18 ♘xc6! ♗xe3 19 fxe3
♘c5 20 ♘a5 b6 21 b4 ♘e6 22 ♘c6
♗xc4 23 ♖xa7 ♖xa7 24 ♘xa7

Eventually precise play helped White con-
vert his extra pawn...

...1-0

Finally there are people who have fallen so
deeply in love with the Stonewall that they
want to play it always – with both colours! I
cannot fully agree with 1 d4 ♘f6 2 f4?! d5
3 e3 ♗f5, when it is already difficult to justify White's play. If you really want to play
the Stonewall with White then settle for
something like 1 d4 ♘f6 2 ♗g5 e6 3 e3
c5 4 c3 d5 5 f4!?. I do not think this is
particularly good, but at least White should
not be worse. Some players believe their
position is much better with the queen's
bishop outside the pawn chain. They are
partly right, but remember its defensive qualities can also be missed.

Recently Sokolov played a hybrid Stonewall in the Dutch Championships:

Ernst-Sokolov
Rotterdam 1998

1 ♘f3 d5 2 d4 c6 3 e3 ♗g4 4 c4 e6 5
♘c3 ♘d7 6 b3 f5 7 ♗e2 ♗d6 8 0-0
♘gf6 9 a4 ♕e7 10 ♗b2 0-0 11 h3 ♗xf3
12 ♗xf3 ♖f7 13 ♘b1 g5 14 ♗a3 ♗xa3
15 ♖xa3 ♖g7 16 g3 g4 17 hxg4 ♘xg4
18 ♗xg4 ♖xg4 19 ♔g2 ♘f6 20 ♖h1 ♘e4
21 ♖a2 ♖f8 22 ♖h3 ♕g7 23 ♕e1 f4 24
exf4 ♖gxf4 0-1

In the Exchange variation of the Slav there is a Stonewall set-up that is desirable for White. It arises after **1 d4 d5 2 c4 c6 3 cxd5 cxd5 4 ♘c3 ♘f6 5 ♗f4 e6 6 e3 ♗d6 7 ♗xd6 ♕xd6 8 f4!**

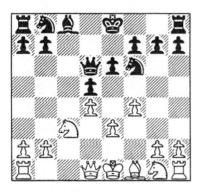

White now has good chances of starting a kingside attack after 9 ♘f3 10 ♗d3 11 0-0 and 12 ♘e5. I have seen GMs losing with Black against schoolboys in this line. Of course Black should not play 5...e6 and 6...♗d6. This is simply too passive and deserves to be punished.

It is also possible to reach the Stonewall from the Catalan Opening. After 1 d4 ♘f6 2 c4 e6 3 g3 d5 4 ♗g2 ♗e7 5 ♘f3 0-0 6 0-0 c6 7 ♕c2 Black can try 7...♘e4!? followed by ...f7-f5. This is closely related to the ...♗e7 Stonewall, which will be dealt with in Chapter Five.

There are other positions with Stonewall characteristics but we have seen the more important examples, and I do not wish to stray too far from our standard Stonewall.

Strategic Features

In this section we will investigate the options available to both sides, including those less popular ideas that nevertheless have strategic significance. I strongly recommend that the reader studies the contents of these pages in detail, for they should feature in your thought processes when playing the Stonewall.

A random position

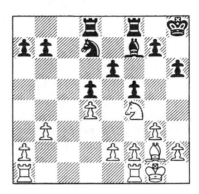

This position is from the game Petursson-Hansen, Malmo 1993. One's first impression is that White has a sizeable advantage because, for example, Black's rather rigid pawn formation has a hole on e5 and his bishop looks pathetic. In fact such an evaluation turns out to be superficial. First let us ask why White's bishop should be superior. Again this might appear obvious, since White's pawns stand mainly on dark squares while Black's centre pawns are fixed on light squares. However, when assessing positional aspects it is necessary to gauge the likelihood of weaknesses actually being exploited, and in this particular case White seems to have no practical means with which to profit from his bishop's apparent superiority. Remember also that the black bishop has potential for activity – it will not always need to protect e6. Turning to the vulnerable e5-square, how can White exploit it? Even if Black moves his knight from d7 and White transfers his own knight to e5, then Black will simply retrace his steps and challenge the horse should it become too annoying (with so few pieces on the board the knight may well prove harmless on e5). It would be logical, then, for White to eliminate the black knight for his bishop, after which White's advantages become more significant.

Does White have anything else in the diagram position? Well, there is the backward e6-pawn but, again, can this be exploited? Soon Black will transfer his king to e7, reducing the influence of the white knight, so in order to further attack e6 White needs to break in the centre with f2-f3 and e2-e4. There are disadvantages to this plan – Black can fight against it with ...♘d7-f6 and perhaps ...g7-g5 followed by ...♗f7-g6, or he can wait for the pawn to arrive on e4, meet it with ...d5xe4 and concentrate on the d4-pawn (White would also have difficulty keeping control of the c-file if his rooks were otherwise engaged in the centre).

So does White have an advantage? Yes – but it is minimal. At least he controls the action and can determine which course the game will take, while Black is really reduced to reacting to his opponent's plan – in itself not enough to worry about. The game ended in a draw after 54 moves, with White having no realistic chances to prove his advantage.

This situation illustrates an interesting practicality of chess. When you are faced with a new type of pawn structure you should try to re-evaluate the importance of different elements present in the position. Of what use is an open file, for example, if all the heavy pieces have been – or will be – exchanged? Here we investigate the concepts that I consider to be the most important in the Stonewall. These ideas do not provide a magical route to victory, of course, rather they provide the reader with something to keep in mind when faced with independent situations and problems at the board.

Black's queen's bishop

This 'problem' piece is undoubtedly the most important issue in the Stonewall, as well as the most complex. Black is naturally careful that nothing like the following should happen to him:

see following diagram

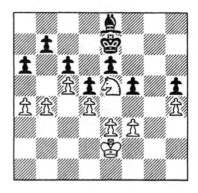

Here the knight is superior in every way, and Black has nothing but weaknesses to attend to. Put on a rook or a queen and we are in for a short and brutal kill! However, this situation is (hopefully) rather hypothetical, for Black is aware of the danger of this kind of position and consequently should endeavour to avoid exchanges that lead to such misery.

In the standard Stonewall position Black has two ways to develop his queen's bishop

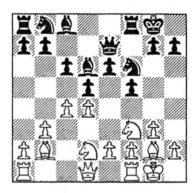

The first involves a lengthy manoeuvre to h5, reaching this outpost via d7 and e8. On h5 the bishop performs the task of a 'normal' piece, in no way restrained by its own pawns. In modern chess the weakness of the c8-bishop has been questioned. It is easy to see the downside of this bishop's existence – just take another look at the previous diagram! But what about the bishop on g2? Is it so much better? Kramnik writes: "The main idea of Black's strategy is to limit the range of the g2-bishop. In my opinion it is barely any stronger than the c8-bishop". The second option, then, is simply to develop normally with ...b7-b6 and ...♝c8-b7. In the diagram Beliavsky chose 9...♝d7 while Yusupov opted for the fianchetto with 9...b6, but most GMs playing this opening would probably prefer to have both options open for as long as possible.

Which exchanges should White make?

This is a very important question that every player should consider. Of course it concerns both sides, as both White and Black should seek/avoid certain exchanges. Due to the characteristic nature of the pawn structure in the Stonewall the first trade for White that comes to mind is that of the dark-squared bishops. This is the main reasoning behind the following moves:

1 d4 e6 2 c4 f5 3 g3 ♘f6 4 ♝g2 c6 5 ♘f3 d5 6 0-0 ♝d6

And now...

7 b3

White is ready to play 8 ♝a3 to exchange bishops and then concentrate on developing a bind on the dark squares with, typically, ♘b1-a3-c2-e1-d3, as in the instructive Petrosian-Korchnoi game in the History section.

7...♕e7!

Black avoids the exchange. This means doing without Botvinnik's old plan of ...♕d8-e8-h5 but, as shown in the History section, this eventually turned out to be favouring White due to the manoeuvre ♘f3-e5-d3-f4.

How much should White insist on the exchange of the dark-squared bishops? It is true that Black's appears to be the more useful of the two, but the real reason for desiring the trade is to win control of the dark squares in the centre.

After:

8 ♝b2 0-0

White achieves nothing special by the

time-consuming...

9 ♕c1 b6 10 ♝a3 ♝b7 11 ♝xd6 ♕xd6

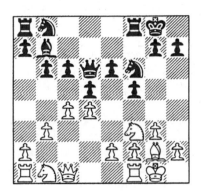

Black is now fully developed. Black has no reason to be dissatisfied with the development of the opening, and in the game Olafsson-Agdestein, Reykjavik 1987 he soon had a clear advantage after **12 ♕a3 c5 13 dxc5 bxc5 14 ♘c3 ♘bd7 15 ♖fd1?! f4!**, winning shortly thereafter: **16 ♖ac1 a6 17 ♝h3 ♖ae8 18 ♖c2 h6 19 ♘a4 ♘e4 20 cxd5 exd5 21 ♝xd7 ♕xd7 22 ♘xc5 ♘xc5 23 ♖xc5 ♖xe2 24 ♘d4 fxg3 25 fxg3 ♕f7 0-1**. Of course White did not help his cause by misplacing his queen on a3 and weakening his kingside with 15 ♖fd1?!.

It is logical to say that White would like to exchange the dark-squared bishops, but not for any price. These days White just as often plays **7 ♝f4!?** with the same aim. Here Black might as well acquiesce to the exchange because 7...♝e7 seems rather passive. In fact after **7...♝xf4! 8 gxf4** White's pawn structure has been compromised and this presents Black with something to bite on. This will be illustrated by the games in Chapter Two.

Generally White is not interested in exchanging both pairs of knights as the exploitation of weak squares in Black's camp tends to need at least one knight. Of course we should not be too dogmatic, and occasionally the removal of knights will give White extra possibilities, but as a rule White is not interested.

Remember it is important to know what kind of situation to aim for when exchanging pieces; otherwise it is difficult to decide during a game which pieces to remove and which to keep.

Again the question of Black's queen's bishop is significant. Should White exchange it? Should he prevent Black from exchanging it?

The whole subject of exchanges depends on the situation, of course. Let us examine the case of White's king's bishop against a knight. The diagram position is from the game Beliavsky-Yusupov, USSR Ch 1987.

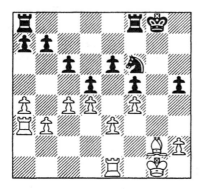

Black is clearly better, being the quicker of the two to occupy the g-file with his rooks. The ostensibly healthy bishop is inferior to the knight, which can jump to e4 at the least convenient moment for White, thus practically forcing an exchange, after which the new pawn on e4 will give Black control over f3 and d3.

Now we turn to Illescas Cordoba-Bareev, Linares 1992.

see following diagram

The position is level. Here Illescas and Zlotnik write that 33 ♗xe4 ♖xe4 would leave Black with a clear advantage. The reasons are in the pawn structures – White has a potential weakness on c5 that cannot be protected by b3-b4. The pawn ending after 34 ♖d4 ♖xd4 35 exd4 appears to be losing for

White, as Black can create a passed pawn on the h-file to keep White occupied while Black goes to the centre.

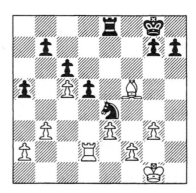

Instead White played **33 ♖c2!**, manoeuvred his bishop to e2 and prepared f2-f3 to evict the knight. Then his c5-pawn held back Black's pawns (on light squares), so Black sent his king to the queenside to achieve ...b7-b6. The game should have been drawn, but due to mishandling of the endgame by Bareev, Illescas went on to win.

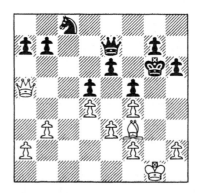

In this position, from the game Irzhanov-Agdestein, Yerevan Ol 1996, the bishop is stronger than the knight, which has no good squares to aim for, now or in the future. White will seek to nudge his f2-pawn forward – preferably after trading queens so as not to expose the king – to control the knight's traditional e4-outpost. This is the reasoning behind White's offer of a queen exchange.

30 ♕c5 ♕d8

Black declines, denying White a potential passed pawn after the recapture on c5.

31 a4 b6 32 ♕c6 ♘d6 33 b4 ♔f6 34 a5 bxa5 35 bxa5 ♔e7 36 a6 ♕c8

Now Black wants the exchange because the a7-pawn is safe from the bishop and the a6-pawn might prove vulnerable. This time White declines.

37 ♕a4 ♕c3 38 ♔g2 g5?

With careful play Black should be only slightly worse. Now his position soon falls apart:

39 fxg5 hxg5 40 h3 f4 41 exf4 gxf4 42 ♗h5 ♕c8 43 ♕a5 ♕c4 44 ♕d2 ♕xa6 45 ♕xf4 ♕a4 46 ♕g5+ ♔d7 47 ♕g7+ ♔c6 48 ♗g4 ♘b5 49 h4 ♘xd4 50 h5 ♘f5

White is happy to make this decisive trade.

51 ♗xf5 exf5 52 h6 ♕e4+ 53 ♔h2 ♕e2 54 ♕g6+ ♔c5 55 ♕xf5 ♕e8 56 h7 ♕h8 57 ♕g6 a5 58 ♔g2 a4 59 ♕g8 ♕e5 60 h8♕ ♕e4+ 61 ♔h2 1-0

I would say that in general the exchange of a white knight for Black's queen's bishop has advantages and disadvantages. They are of roughly equal value, but this could change from position to position. It is crucial for Black to avoid an endgame disaster with a terrible bishop!

Sometimes White is successful in exchanging a knight for Black's king's bishop. If the position is open this can be terrible for Black,

while a closed position could well turn out to favour the extra knight. Here are some examples:

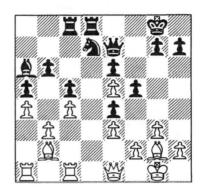

Renet-Yusupov, Dubai Ol 1986. Black has voluntarily exchanged his bishop on e5, forcing White to take back with a pawn. Having closed the a3-f8 diagonal Black is, strategically at least, close to winning.

20...♘f8 21 ♖d1 ♗b7 22 ♕c3 ♘g6 23 ♖d6 ♗c6 24 ♖ad1 ♘h8!

White is trying to profit from the e5-pawn but with this move Black forces the exchange of all the heavy pieces on the d-file, after which the difference between the knight and the bishop will tell.

25 ♔f1 ♘f7 26 ♖xd8+ ♖xd8 27 ♖xd8+ ♕xd8 28 ♔e1 g5 29 ♕d2 ♕xd2+ 30 ♔xd2 ♘h6 31 h3 ♗e8 32 ♔e1 ♗h5 33 ♗c3 ♔g7 34 ♗b2 ♘g8 35 ♔d2 ♘e7 36 ♗c3 ♗f3!

The knight's true strength is even clearer after the bishop trade, so White must decline the offer.

37 ♗f1 ♔g6 38 ♗b2 h5 39 ♗c3 ♘c6 40 ♗b2 ♘e7 41 ♗c3 f4!

White cannot succeed in keeping the position closed. The game is over.

42 exf4 gxf4 43 gxf4 ♔f5 44 ♗e2 ♗xe2 45 ♔xe2 ♘g6 46 ♔e3 ♘xf4 47 f3 exf3 48 ♔xf3 ♘xh3 49 ♔g3 ♘f4 0-1

In the next example the exchange of knight for bishop keeps the position balanced, bringing no advantage to either player.

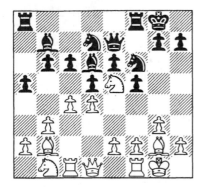

In the diagram position, from the game Tukmakov-Agdestein, Dortmund 1987, White used a common trick to gain the advantage of the two bishops.

13 cxd5 cxd5 14 ♘c4

White first exchanged on d5 in order to further open the h1-a8 diagonal in preparation for this pin. As we shall see in the next example, Black must take care not to allow this idea under the wrong circumstances.

14...b5!

With his dark-squared bishop about to go Black prepares to close the a3-f8 diagonal, ruling out the deployment of White's bishop on a3.

15 ♘xd6 ♕xd6 16 ♘c3 ♗a6 17 ♕d2 ♖fc8 18 f3 b4 19 ♘d1 a4 20 ♘e3 a3 21 ♖xc8+ ♖xc8 22 ♗c1 f4 23 gxf4 ♕xf4 24 ♖d1 ♔f7 25 ♘c2 ♕xd2 26 ♖xd2 ♗b5

The game is approximately level. White has no special reason to be fond of his two bishops and Black can protect b4.

In the following game Black was genuinely outplayed and should have lost thanks to the ♘c4 trick.

Tukmakov-Dolmatov
USSR Ch 1989

1 d4 f5 2 c4 ♘f6 3 g3 e6 4 ♗g2 c6 5 ♘f3 d5 6 0-0 ♗d6 7 b3 ♕e7 8 ♘bd2 b6 9 ♗b2 ♗b7 10 ♖c1 0-0 11 ♘e5 ♘bd7?!

12 cxd5 cxd5 13 ♘dc4!

This was a new move at the time. Compared to the previous example Black does not have time to close the a3-f8 diagonal, so his greatly reduced influence on the dark squares becomes a major factor.

13...♖fc8 14 ♘xd6 ♕xd6 15 f3 ♕e7

If 15...a5 16 ♕d2 b5 White takes over the c-file after the simple 17 ♖xc8.

16 ♘d3! ♖xc1 17 ♕xc1 ♖c8 18 ♕d2 ♕d6 19 ♖c1 ♖xc1+ 20 ♕xc1 ♕c6 21 ♕d2

White avoids the exchange of queens for now and prepares ♗b2-a3.

21...♕d6 22 ♔f2 ♘f8 23 h3

Making a later challenge with g3-g4 possible.

23...♘g6 24 ♕c1! ♘d7

After the exchange of queens with 24...♕c6 White would penetrate and dominate with his queen's bishop.

25 ♗a3 ♕b8 26 h4

White has a winning advantage, although he threw away the point in time trouble.

The conclusion regarding the exchange of Black's dark-squared bishop for knight must be that Black can allow it as long as the scope of its counterpart can be limited.

Generally Black would be more than happy to trade in both knights for White's bishops. In doing so, however, care must be taken as to whether this improves White's access to key centre squares, particularly the influential e5-square. Nonetheless the two bishops can combine to be a powerful force when employed correctly, and this can cause White considerable suffering.

As for the exchange of rooks and queens, there is no real advantage to either side here. In the typically semi-open positions that arise in the Stonewall one file is often opened, after which the major pieces tend to be exchanged. This is logical because neither player can usually afford to surrender the open file.

Manoeuvres of the white knights

One of the reasons why the Stonewall is played so differently today compared to Botvinnik's era is the way that White handles the knights. In the early days White would simply use the squares c3 and f3, whereas today White works to post the knights on d3 and f3 in order to maximize control of key dark squares in the centre (c5, e5, f4). There are a few manoeuvres that bring a knight to d3. One is ♘g1-f3-e5-d3, when the other knight travels b1-d2-f3, and the knights are in place. Another is ♘g1-h3-f4-d3, and the other knight jumps to f3 again. Finally the b1-knight can go via a3 (usually after the exchange of the dark-squared bishops) to c2-e1-d3. With numerous choices, the set-up which is today considered the strongest looks something like this:

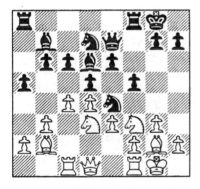

Lautier-Dolmatov, Manila 1990, is a typical Stonewall position.

Knight Exchanges on e4 and e5

Often when a knight jumps to e4 or e5 we can expect that it will be exchanged sooner or later, for it is very rare that a knight can be allowed to dominate from the middle of the arena. When these knights are exchanged they are normally recaptured with a pawn, which in turn significantly alters the pawn structure in the centre.

An important feature here is the vacation of a square that can then prove quite useful.

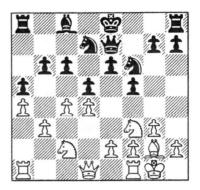

This diagram position, from the game Kharlov-Dreev, Elista 1995, is a good example of this in practice. White's next advance gives Black the opportunity to deny his opponent the facility of using the e5-square as an outpost – but there is a price to pay!

12 ♘e5 ♘xe5?

This decision seems unwise. After the recapture White has an attractive alternative for his knight on the equally central d4-square, from where e6 can be monitored as well as f5 (perhaps in conjunction with a timely g3-g4), exerting pressure on Black's pawns. Note also that the newly arrived e5-pawn controls both the d6- and f6-squares. As for Black, the c5-square is now available for a knight, but this is less valuable. Moreover, should Black transfer his remaining knight to e4, then a future ♗xe4 could well leave White with two enormous knights in an essentially closed position.

13 dxe5 ♘d7 14 cxd5 cxd5 15 f4 ♘c5 16 ♘d4 0-0 17 ♕d2 ♗d7

White is slightly better.

18 b4!?

White opens up the b-file and thereby creates strong pressure against b6. Black is already in trouble. Rather than defending for a long time he decides to sacrifice a pawn.

18...♘a6?!

It seems better to take up the challenge with 18...♘xa4 19 ♘xe6! ♗xe6 20 ♖xa4 axb4 21 ♖xb4. Perhaps Dreev did not see

that he could then play 21...罝a2! 22 豐xa2 豐xb4 and continue to fight, although 23 e3 favours White due to Black's weaknesses.
19 bxa5 bxa5 20 豐xa5 勾b4?

Here Black could have entered a tenable, albeit inferior endgame after 20...勾c5! 21 豐c7 罝fc8 22 豐d6 豐xd6 23 exd6 罝xa4 24 罝xa4 急xa4 25 罝c1, although it is an unpleasant position to defend. Note that now White can continue with 勾d4-f3-e5 at the right moment.
21 豐c7 罝fc8 22 豐b6 罝cb8 23 豐d6 豐xd6 24 exd6 勾c6 25 勾xc6 急xc6 26 a5

White has an extra pawn. The d6-pawn is doomed but it will take some time for Black to collect it and, meanwhile, White is free to improve his position further.
26...急b5 27 罝fb1 曾f7 28 a6 急c4 29 罝xb8 罝xb8 30 罝a4 急xe2 31 a7 罝a8 32 急f1 急xf1 33 曾xf1 曾e8 34 曾e2 曾d7 35 罝a6 曾c8 36 曾d3 曾b7 37 罝a4 曾c6 38 曾d4 曾xd6 39 罝a6+ 曾e7 40 曾c5 g5 41 fxg5 曾f7 42 h4 h6 43 gxh6 1-0

Although this looked bad for Black, the following 'knightmare' – from Lputian-Semkov, Yerevan 1988 – is worse.

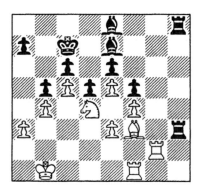

The knight has just arrived on the inviting d4-square and now completely dominates the game. Black's bishops are sitting pretty yet doing nothing, the backward e6- and c6-pawns are weak and a2-a4 is coming to exert additional pressure on Black's pawns. White went on to win this game with little effort.

When White recaptures on e5 with the f-pawn this does not necessarily produce an automatic outpost, but it does fit in well structurally. This situation occurs most often in the line with 7 急f4 急xf4! 8 gxf4, where the pawn later reaches e5. Again the (different) e5-pawn keeps enemy pieces out of d6 and f6, while here White maintains control over e5 and c5. Of course White pays a price, for ...f5-f4 is a possibility, although this advance is not as dangerous as it may seem. The following game is a good example, which also shows the downside of this advance.

Beliavsky-Karlsson
Novi Sad Ol 1990

1 d4 e6 2 勾f3 f5 3 g3 勾f6 4 急g2 d5 5 0-0 急d6 6 c4 c6 7 急f4 急xf4 8 gxf4 0-0 9 e3 曾h8 10 豐c2?!

This does not really improve White's position. Better is 10 勾e5.
10...勾e4 11 勾e5 勾d7 12 c5 a5 13 f3 勾ef6 14 勾c3 勾h5 15 罝ad1 勾xe5

Black exploits the fact that 13 f3 has weakened the dark squares around the white king.
16 fxe5 f4 17 e4!

White cannot allow an enemy piece to occupy f4.
17...豐g5 18 曾h1 急d7

18...豐h6!? seems better. Now White's bishop becomes very strong.
19 急h3! 豐h6 20 豐g2 g5!?

20...罝ad8 21 罝g1! leaves White well ahead as Black has no means of generating active play, and the knight on h5 might soon be poorly placed.
21 exd5 cxd5 22 勾xd5! 勾g3+

Forced in view of 22...exd5 23 急xd7 勾g3+ 24 曾g1 勾xf1 25 豐xf1 with advantage to White.
23 hxg3 exd5 24 g4 罝a6 25 罝f2 急b5 26

♖e1 ♖e8 27 ♕h2 ♕g7 28 ♕g1 ♖h6

Black has some but insufficient compensation.

29 ♖h2 ♖ee6 30 ♗f1 ♗xf1 31 ♕xf1 ♖xh2+ 32 ♔xh2 ♕g6 33 ♔g2 ♕c2+ 34 ♕e2 ♕g6 35 ♖c1

White has consolidated and is winning due to his extra pawn.

35...♕e8 36 ♕d3 ♔g7 37 ♖c3 h5 38 ♖b3 ♕e7 39 ♕f5 hxg4 40 fxg4 ♖h6 41 ♕c8 b6 42 cxb6 f3+ 43 ♖xf3 ♖xb6 44 b3 1-0.

When White exchanges on e4 it is often with the intention of following up with f2-f3 to challenge the centre. Black's natural recapture is with the f-pawn because this opens the f-file for the rook. However, this is not the only possibility, and it is not unusual to recapture with the d-pawn.

First we consider the classical approach.

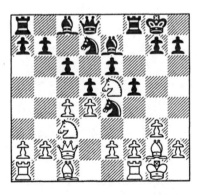

This position is from the game Smejkal-Larsen, Leningrad 1973. White has developed his knight to the slightly unusual square c3 – not within striking distance of e5 – and therefore can find no better use for it than the following exchange.

11 ♘xe4 fxe4 12 ♗f4 ♗f6 13 ♖ad1 ♗xe5!?

Note that 13...♘xe5 14 dxe5! prepares 15 ♗xe4! with the win of a pawn – hence the text. Worthy of consideration is 13...♕e8.

14 ♗xe5?!

This recapture helps Black because now either e5 becomes weak or White has to change the structure. 14 dxe5 ♕e7 15 ♕d2 h6 16 h4 ♕f7 produces a roughly level game. **14...♘xe5 15 dxe5 ♕e7 16 ♕c3 ♗d7 17 f3**

This has to be played sooner or later, and rather sooner, before Black has time for ...♗d7-e8-g6(h5).

17...exf3 18 exf3 ♕c5+ 19 ♖d4 a5 20 f4 ♕a7

The situation is balanced.

21 f5?!

The beginning of White's troubles since the e5-pawn is about to become weak, putting the onus on White to find accurate moves to avoid being worse.

21...♖ae8! 22 cxd5 cxd5 23 ♔h1 ♖c8 24 ♕d2 ♖c2!

A neat tactic that exploits White's weaknesses.

25 ♕xc2 ♕xd4

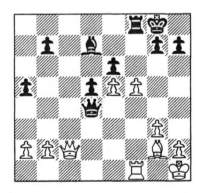

26 ♕c3?

Hoping to relieve the pressure through simplification is not always the best course, and this merely leads to a poor ending. In fact White should try his luck with 26 ♕c7! ♗c6 27 f6 gxf6 28 ♖f4!! ♕d1+ 29 ♖f1 and Black has nothing better than repeating with 29...♕d4 30 ♖f4.

26...♕xc3 27 bxc3 ♖c8 28 ♖d1 ♖c5 29 fxe6 ♗xe6 30 ♔g1 ♔f7 31 ♖d3 ♖b5 32 ♖d2 a4 33 a3?

The difficult task of defending against your opponents' numerous possibilities tends to result in a time shortage, which in turn results in mistakes. 33 ♔f2 a3 34 ♔e3 ♖b2 35 ♗f3 with the idea of ♗f3-d1-b3 is perhaps the only chance to save the game.

33...♖b3

Now Black is coasting to victory.

34 ♗xd5 ♖xa3 35 c4 ♖b3 36 ♔f2 a3 37 ♔e2 ♖b2 38 ♖xb2 axb2 39 ♗e4 ♗xc4+ 40 ♔d2 ♗a2 0-1

In the following example Black recaptures with the d-pawn. This is not natural but can afford Black certain advantages if played under the right circumstances, as was the case with the exchange of the d6-bishop for a knight.

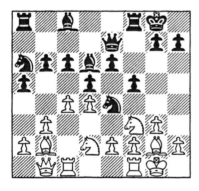

This is the game Biebinger-Volkov, Groningen 1998. White has played the opening somewhat passively, having wasted a tempo to post his queen on b1 (in fact d1 might be better). The following faulty exchange offers Black a good chance to attack the centre.

13 ♘xe4?! dxe4 14 ♘d2 ♗b7 15 e3

Unfortunately for White he is forced to play this at some point. Fortunately for Black the new possibility of ...♘a6-b4-d3 is an appealing prospect.

15...c5 16 f3?

Black's territorial superiority and more active piece placement make this challenge a definite mistake. Volkov punishes his opponent's unwise thrust with a smooth tactical demonstration.

16...cxd4! 17 ♗xd4

17 exd4 e3! would be embarrassing.

17...♗b4 18 ♕c2 e5 19 ♗c3 ♗xc3 20 ♕xc3 ♘b4 21 ♖a1 ♖ad8!

Impressive play. Black temporarily sacrifices a pawn to develop his initiative.

22 a3 ♘d3 23 fxe4 ♕g5 24 ♖f3 ♖fe8

White cannot keep his pawn and his pieces are poorly placed.

25 h4 ♕g4 26 ♔h2 fxe4 27 ♖ff1 ♕e2

Now Black invades from all sides. The final moves are a nice conclusion to a day at the office for the GM.

28 ♖a2 ♕xe3 29 b4 ♘f2! 30 ♕xe3 ♘g4+ 31 ♔g1 ♘xe3 32 ♗xe4 ♘xf1 33 ♔xf1 ♖xd2! 34 ♖xd2 ♗xe4 0-1

When both Black and White capture on e5 and e4, a special, tangled pawn structure arises. Despite the fact that the formation is hardly seen, in the Stonewall one is constantly forced to consider it as a genuine possibility.

**Yrjola-Yusupov
Mendoza 1985**

1 d4 e6 2 c4 f5 3 g3 ♘f6 4 ♗g2 d5 5 ♘f3 c6 6 0-0 ♗d6 7 b3 ♕e7 8 ♗f4 ♗xf4 9 gxf4 0-0 10 ♘e5 ♘bd7 11 e3 ♔h8 12 ♘d2 ♘xe5 13 fxe5 ♘e4 14 f4 ♗d7 15 ♘xe4 dxe4!?

An interesting decision. 15...fxe4 16 ♕g4 ♖f5 17 c5 is level.

16 ♕d2 ♗e8 17 b4

Black's decision has helped White gain a space advantage on the queenside, a factor that White tries to exploit quickly. On the other flank Black has a very simple plan. He intends to develop his bishop to h5 and push with ...g7-g5, looking to open the g-file and pressure f4 (f4xg5 invites ...f5-f4), perhaps with chances to release the e4-pawn at some point should the e3-pawn be flushed out.

The problem for White is that Black's plan is far stronger than his own.

17...Rd8 18 Rab1 g5 19 b5 gxf4 20 Rxf4

20 exf4 can be met in several ways. First Black can continue with his plan, but he can also transpose to a pleasant endgame with 20...Qc5!? 21 dxc5 Rxd2 22 Rf2 Rd3.

20...cxb5 21 cxb5 Rg8 22 b6 Bh5 23 Rf2

White's king cannot find refuge in the corner, as the following simple line demonstrates: 23 Kh1 axb6 24 Rxb6 Rg7 25 Rf2 Rdg8 26 Rb1 Rxg2 27 Rxg2 Bf3 28 Rbg1 Rxg2 29 Rxg2 Qg5 followed by ...Bxg2 and ...Qxe3 with a winning ending.

23...axb6 24 Rxb6 Bf3 25 Kf1 Qc7 26 Rb4 Qc6!

Prepares the push 27...f4! with the idea of 28 exf4 e3! and an immediate win.

27 Rb2 f4!

White is without a proper defence.

28 Kg1

Or 28 Bxf3 exf3 29 Rb3 Rc8 30 Rd3 fxe3 and White can resign.

28...Bxg2 29 Rxg2 f3!

This pawn is just too strong.

30 Rg3 Rxg3+ 31 hxg3 Rg8

White has no way of defending his four weak spots: a2, e3, g3 and h2.

32 Rc2 Qb5 33 Kf2 Qd7 34 Qc1 Qg7 35 Qg1 Qh6 36 Rc7 Ra8 37 Rc2 Ra3 0-1

On 38 Kf1 the strongest is 38...Rd3!. Black has no reason to exchange queens at this stage.

Of course Black does not normally get such a large advantage from this structure, but it can happen. Before entering these tangled pawn positions it is important to evaluate the effect on the plans available to both sides.

General Plans for White

Having considered the strategic features of the position we shall now look at general plans. In this section we will examine typical White possibilities.

White advances with b2-b4-b5

White often tries to demonstrate an advantage on the queenside in similar fashion to the Queen's Gambit Declined. This is quite natural, particularly when Black sends the bishop to d7 and e8.

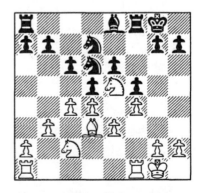

This game is Kharitonov-Guliev, Moscow 1995. White's modest opening play has left him no claim to an advantage. It is instructive to see how these two GMs handle this position, the execution of their respective plans maintaining the status quo.

16 c5 Ne4 17 b4

White begins his queenside strategy.

17...Ndf6 18 a4 a6 19 Ne1 g5!

Waiting results only in giving White a free hand with his expansion, so Black wastes no time drumming up counterplay.

20 fxg5 ♘xg5 21 ♘1f3 ♘ge4 22 ♖fc1 ♔h8

Notice how each of Black's moves is relevant.

23 ♖a2 ♖g8 24 ♖cc2 ♗h5 25 ♘d2 ♘g5 26 ♔h1 ♘g4 27 ♘xg4 fxg4!

Black switches his attack to the f-file, at the same time taking away the f3-square from White's knight.

28 b5 ♗g6 29 ♗xg6 ♖xg6 30 bxc6 bxc6 31 ♖ab2 ♖f8 32 ♖c1 ♖gf6 33 ♔g1 h5

With the plan of ...h5-h4-h3 to induce weaknesses around the white king.

34 ♖f1 ♖xf1+ 35 ♘xf1 h4 36 ♖b6 h3 37 ♘d2 a5!

Tricky!

38 ♖b7

It turns out that White must keep an eye on the first rank since after 38 ♖xc6 Black has 38...g3!! 39 hxg3 ♖f2!! in view of 40 ♔xf2 h2, when Black queens his pawn with a winning position.

38...♖f5 39 ♖b1!

White is forced to attend to his problems, allowing Black to skilfully use his resources to steer the game to a draw.

39...♖f7 40 ♖f1 ♖b7 41 ♖f4 g3 42 hxg3 ♖b2 43 ♖f2 ♖a2 44 ♘f3 ♖a1+ 45 ♔h2 hxg2 46 ♔xg2 ♘e4 47 ♖b2 ♖xa4 48 ♘e5 ♖b4 49 ♖a2 a4 50 ♘xc6 ♖b3 51 ♖xa4 ½-½

In the next game, Iskov-Malagon, Lugano Ol 1968, a GM (White) outplays a weaker opponent from a reasonably balanced position. Black fails to generate any counterplay, thus leaving White free to carry out queenside pawn-roller.

see following diagram

23 b4 a6 24 a4

White's plan is straightforward. It is imperative that Black hits back.

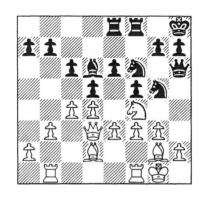

24...♘h5?

Necessary is 24...♘f7 25 c5 ♗b8 with the idea of 26...e5! and possibly a future ...g7-g5!? and ...f5-f4. Nevertheless Black is not in trouble yet.

25 b5 axb5?

25...dxc4! 26 ♕xc4 cxb5 27 axb5 ♖c8 28 ♕d3 is a lesser evil.

26 axb5 ♘xf4 27 exf4 ♘f7 28 bxc6 bxc6 29 ♖fe1

White has a substantial advantage thanks to Black's inaccurate play since we joined the game. Add the new weakness on e6 to the backward c6-pawn and the coming queenside infiltration, and Black faces severe difficulties.

29...♕f6 30 ♖b6 ♘d8 31 ♖a6 ♔g8 32 ♖b1 ♖f7 33 c5 ♗c7 34 ♖a8 ♔f8 35 ♖ba1 h6 36 ♖1a7 ♖fe7 37 ♖c8 ♕f7 38 ♖aa8 ♕f6 39 ♗f1 g5?

A mistake in an anyway hopeless position.

40 ♖a7 ♕g7 41 fxg5 hxg5 42 ♗xg5 1-0

White wins a pawn and the game.

In the following clash between two former Dvoretsky pupils, prophylactic play forms a major part of the strategy.

Chekhov-Yusupov
Germany 1993

1 d4 e6 2 c4 f5 3 ♘f3 ♘f6 4 g3 d5 5 ♗g2 c6 6 0-0 ♗d6 7 ♕c2 0-0 8 ♘c3!?

♘e4

8...♕e8 9 ♗g5 ♕h5, as one would have played in the old days with the bishop on e7, here fails due to 10 ♗xf6 ♖xf6 11 cxd5 exd5 12 ♘xd5! and White wins a pawn.

9 ♖b1 ♗d7 10 b4 ♗e8

10...a6 11 c5 ♗c7 12 ♘a4 ♗e8 13 ♗f4 ♗xf4 14 gxf4 ♘d7 15 ♘e5 is given by Chekhov as slightly better for White.

11 b5 ♘d7?

Allowing White to dictate what happens to the pawn formation is far too accommodating. Chekhov offers 11...♘xc3 12 ♕xc3 cxb5 13 cxb5 ♘d7 14 ♗a3 ♖c8 15 ♕e3 with an edge to White, although I don't see one after 15...♗xa3 16 ♕xa3 ♕b6 17 ♖fc1 ♗h5. In any case 13...♗h5!? 14 ♗a3 f4 gives Black good counterplay.

12 bxc6 bxc6 13 ♘xe4!

With this exchange White gains time to build a positional bind, gaining on the queenside as well as nipping in the bud Black's hopes of annoying distractions on the kingside. Compare this to the Kharitonov-Guliev game, above, where White was kept too busy defending his king.

13...fxe4

13...dxe4 14 ♘g5 ♖f6 15 c5 ♗c7 16 ♕c4 ♘f8 17 f4! (Chekhov) is very good for White.

14 ♘g5 ♖f6 15 c5 ♗c7 16 f4!

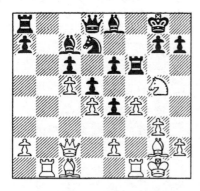

This is the key idea upon which White's play is based. The usual active plans for Black

(...e6-e5 and ...g7-g5) are unavailable, while White is free to return to business on the queenside.

16...h6 17 ♘h3 ♗h5 18 ♗e3?

Inconsistent. 18 ♖b2! ♖b8 19 e3, intending ♖f2 and ♕a4, would have put White firmly in charge according to Chekhov. Of course White stands better, but Black could maintain some kind of defensive set-up by exchanging one set of rooks and playing ...♕a8.

18...♕c8! 19 ♖b2 ♕a6

Thanks to his opponent's inaccuracy Black has now protected c6 by preventing ♕a4.

20 ♖fb1 ♖ff8 21 ♗f1?!

Again White misses his opportunity to strike: 21 ♖b7!? ♖fc8 22 ♗f1 ♖ab8 23 ♕b2 and Black still has problems to solve.

21...♖ab8 22 ♗c1

The disadvantage of 18 ♗e3 is now clear. Besides lacking a proper role on e3, the bishop was also in the way.

22...♖xb2 23 ♖xb2 ♖b8 24 e3 ♕c8 25 ♘f2 ♘f6 26 ♗d2 ♖xb2 27 ♕xb2 ♗d8 28 ♕a3 ♕c7

Black has managed to address his problems, steering the game to a draw.

29 ♗a6 ♗f3 30 ♕b3 ♘d7 31 ♕b7 ♘b8 32 ♕xc7 ♗xc7 33 ♗c8 ♔f7 34 ♔f1 ♔e7 35 ♗c3 ½-½

White attacks the queenside with c4-c5

White also has a standard plan of action against ...♗b7. This involves pushing with c4-c5 in order to highlight the weakness on c6. If successful, White achieves a pleasant game and Black can be under prolonged pressure as he cannot afford to give up the c6-pawn.

Our first example is Romanishin-Klinger, Sarajevo 1988.

see following diagram

White has gained the advantage through the removal of Black's good bishop, he has a lead in development, the facility to evict the knight from e4 with f2-f3 and the traditionally desirable knight outpost on e5. All in all a rather promising position, but how does White exploit it?

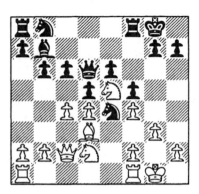

13 ♘b3!

Prevents ...♘xd2 after f2-f3 and supports c4-c5.

13...♘d7 14 f3 ♘ef6 15 c5 ♕c7

Passive, but after 15...bxc5 16 dxc5 ♕e7 17 ♖fe1 the e6-pawn is another target.

16 ♖fe1 ♖fe8 17 ♖ac1 ♘xe5 18 ♖xe5 ♘d7 19 ♖e2 b5

Positional suicide, but the pressure on the c- and e-files is very strong. Black hopes to push his a- and b-pawns and then post the bishop on a6, but this plan has no real future.

20 ♖ce1 ♔f7 21 ♖e3 g6 22 ♕e2 ♘f8 23 ♖e5 a5 24 g4

White is in full control.

24...♕d7 25 ♘d2 b4 26 ♘f1 h5 27 ♘g3 h4 28 ♘h1 ♕c8 29 ♕e3!

Just in time to keep the bishop.

29...♗a6 30 ♗b1 ♕d8 31 ♘f2 ♕d7 32 ♘h3 ♘h7 33 ♕f2 ♕d8 34 ♖1e3 ♕f6 35 ♕e1

Now Black loses material.

35...♖e7 36 gxf5 gxf5 37 ♗xf5 ♖g8+ 38 ♔h1 ♕g7 39 ♗g4 ♕g6 40 ♖xe6 ♖xe6 1-0

In the next game White is slightly better and tries to prove his advantage by c4-c5. In

this case Black exchanges on c5 but then plays wrong. White's win after this is very impressive.

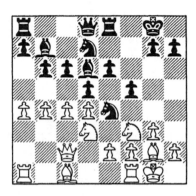

The game is Portisch-Radulov, Budapest 1969.

14 c5 bxc5 15 bxc5 ♗c7 16 ♗f4 ♗xf4 17 gxf4 ♕c7 18 ♘fe5 ♘ef6?!

This is bad judgement. Black can always try to exchange this knight with something like 18...a5!? 19 ♘xd7 ♕xd7 20 ♗xe4.

19 ♖fb1 a5 20 ♘xd7 ♘xd7 21 ♘e5 ♘xe5 22 fxe5 ♖eb8 23 ♖b6!

Had Black recognised his critical situation five moves ago, he would not have been so afraid of playing bishop against knight.

23...♗a6 24 ♖ab1 ♖b7 25 ♕d2

The a-pawn is doomed now. Black tries tactics to keep the game going.

25...♖xb6 26 cxb6 ♕b7 27 ♕xa5 ♗b5 28 ♕b4 ♖xa4 29 ♕d6 ♔f7 30 e4!!

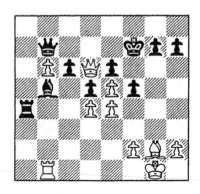

A very strong move that underlines the weak spots in the Black pawn chain.

30...♕xb6

Loses by force, but Black was already in serious trouble.

30...fxe4 31 ♗h3 ♖a8 (31...♕c8 32 ♗xe6+ ♕xe6 33 ♕xe6+ ♔xe6 34 b7) 32 ♗xe6+ ♔e8 33 ♕c7 ♖b8 34 ♖a1 ♗c4 35 ♕xb7 ♖xb7 36 ♖a8+ ♔e7 37 ♖a7 and White wins.

30...dxe4 31 d5 exd5 32 e6+ ♔e8 33 ♗f1 ♗xf1 34 ♕d7+! ♕xd7 35 exd7+ ♔xd7 36 b7 ♗d3 37 ♖b2! and White wins.

31 exf5?!

31 exd5 ♖xd4 32 ♕xe6+ ♔f8 33 ♕xf5+ ♔e8 34 dxc6 was even stronger.

31...♕a7?!

31...♕b7 32 ♕xe6+ ♔f8 33 f6 gxf6 34 exf6 is winning for White as well, but at least Black can pretend to fight on a little bit.

32 ♕xe6+ ♔f8 33 ♗xd5 cxd5 34 ♖xb5 ♖xd4 35 ♕c8+ 1-0.

In the next example Black equalizes with a timely ...e6-e5 but clearly has a bad day from then on. The game illustrates how Black can gain counterplay in the centre when White relieves the pressure on d5.

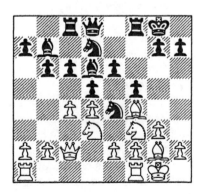

This is Burmakin-Del Rio, Ubeda 1999.

13 c5?!

13 ♗xd6 ♘xd6 14 c5 ♘e4 15 b4 secures an edge.

13...♗xf4 14 ♘xf4 ♕e7 15 b4 e5 16 ♘xe5 ♘xe5 17 dxe5 bxc5??

What a mistake! 17...♕xe5 18 ♘d3 ♕e7 followed by ....♗a6 gives Black a perfectly playable position.

18 f3 ♘g5 19 ♕xc5 ♕xc5+

19...♕xe5 is punished by simple, pawn grabbing 20 ♕xa7 with a clear plus.

20 bxc5 ♖fe8 21 h4 ♘f7 22 e6 ♘d8 23 ♗h3 g6 24 e4!

Sealing Black's fate.

24...dxe4 25 fxe4 ♘xe6 26 ♘xe6 ♖xe6 27 exf5 ♖e3 28 fxg6 ♖d8 29 gxh7+ ♔g7 30 ♖ad1 1-0.

In the final example of the c4-c5 plan two of the world's leading players clash: Shirov-Ivanchuk, Manila Ol 1992. In general when White employs the c4-c5 strategy he must expect Black to react with ....♗a6 to exploit the newly opened a6-f1 diagonal; perhaps Shirov did not consider this possibility.

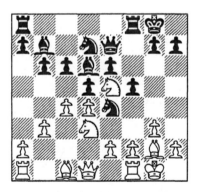

White now – perhaps unjustifiably – endeavours to prove an opening advantage.

13 ♘xd7

13 f3 meets with the clever 13...♘ec5! and is fine for Black.

13...♕xd7 14 f3?!

Premature. Preferable is 14 ♕c2!? with the idea of f2-f3 and c4-c5, after which 14...♕e7 15 ♗f4 ♗xf4 16 ♘xf4 produces a typical Stonewall position. Ivanchuk believes that White is slightly better here. Maybe, but it seems very slight.

14...♘f6 15 c5 bxc5

Black accepts the loss of the Bishop pair in return for gaining time in the centre.
16 ♘xc5

16 dxc5 ♗c7 followed by ...♕e7, ...♘d7 and ...♗a6 and Black is doing well thanks to his influence on e5.
16...♗xc5 17 dxc5 e5 18 e4??

A blunder. Better is 18 e3, planning ♗b2 and f3-f4 to fight for control over the a1-h8 diagonal. Then Ivanchuk suggests the following line as being fine for Black: 18...♗a6 19 ♖f2 d4 20 exd4 exd4 21 ♗f4 ♖fe8 22 ♗d6 d3 23 ♗f1 ♖e3 24 ♖d2 ♖ae8 25 ♗xd3 ♗xd3 26 ♖xd3 ♖xd3 27 ♕xd3 ♘d5 with compensation for the pawn.
18...♗a6! 19 ♖e1

19 ♖f2 fxe4 20 fxe4 ♘xe4! 21 ♗xe4 ♖xf2 22 ♔xf2 ♖f8+ 23 ♔g2 ♖f1 gives Black a winning attack.
19...fxe4 20 fxe4 d4

White cannot prevent an invasion down the f-file.
21 ♕d2 ♘g4 22 ♗h3 h5 23 ♗a3 ♕f7 24 ♗b4 ♖ae8 25 ♗a5 ♖e6 26 ♗f1 ♘f2 27 ♗xa6 ♕f3 0-1

White breaks out with e2-e4

Kramnik has written that when White plays f2-f3 Black can respond with ...c6-c5 to exploit the weakening of the dark squares in the centre. The following is a good illustration:

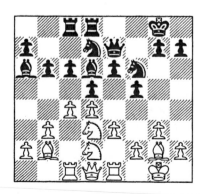

This is Ftacnik-Klinger, Dubai Ol 1986.
15 f3 c5! 16 e4 fxe4 17 fxe4 dxe4 18 ♘xe4 ♘xe4 19 ♗xe4 cxd4 20 ♗xd4 ♘c5 21 ♗d5 ♕f7 22 ♗xc5 exd5 23 ♗xd6 ♖xd6 24 ♘b4 ♗b7 25 ♘xd5 ♗xd5 26 cxd5 ♖xc1 27 ♕xc1 h6 28 ♕c8+ ♔h7 29 ♕c2+ ♔g8 30 ♕c8+ ½-½

A simple equalising game for Black. However he cannot always rely on this counterplay:

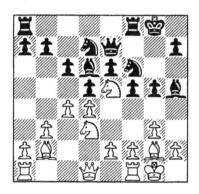

This is Kharitonov-Naumkin, Riga 1988. White prepares the e2-e4 break.
14 ♕c2 ♔h8

This practically rules out ideas of ...c6-c5 in view of dxc5, although Black is vulnerable anyway thanks to ...g7-g5.
15 ♖ae1 ♖g8

A faulty plan. The more circumspect 15...♖ae8 should be considered.
16 f3 ♖af8 17 ♘xd7 ♘xd7 18 e4 ♕g7 19 exd5 exd5 20 f4

White has a clear lead. Black tries to muddy the waters with some tactics but he fails to steal the advantage from White.
20...♘f6 21 ♘c5 gxf4 22 ♘e6 ♕g4 23 ♘xf8 ♖xf8 24 ♖e6 ♗b8 25 ♗a3 ♖f7 26 cxd5 fxg3 27 ♕xf5 ♕h4 28 hxg3 ♗xg3 29 ♕h3 ♕xh3 30 ♗xh3 ♘xd5 31 ♗d6 ♗xd6 32 ♖xf7 ♗xf7 33 ♖xd6 ♘b4 34 ♖d7 ♔g8 35 ♖xb7 ♘xa2 36 ♗g2 ♘c1 37 ♔f2 a5 38 ♗xc6 ♘xb3 39 ♖xf7 1-0

Generally Kramnik's observation is appropriate, but situations can occur in which

Black cannot afford to play ...c6-c5 against f2-f3. Remember also that it is not unusual for f2-f3 to gain time by hitting an unwelcome knight on e4. Often it is in White's interest to realise the e2-e4 break because it challenges the pawns on d5 and f5 and consequently exerts indirect pressure against e6, but there are occasions where Black is happy to see the central thrust:

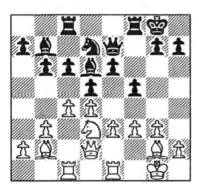

This position is from Van der Sterren-Agdestein, London 1986. The presence of a pawn on f3 suggests that e3-e4 might well be coming, so Black prepares himself rather than immediately strike with ...c6-c5.
16...♗a6 17 e4 fxe4 18 fxe4 dxc4 19 bxc4 e5 20 ♗h3 ♖cd8 21 d5 ♘c5 22 ♔g2 ♔h8 23 ♕e2 ♘xd3 24 ♕xd3 b5 25 cxb5 ♗xb5

Black is doing fine and later went on to win the game.

To conclude, this plan is generally desirable for White, but in many cases Black can either prevent it with ...c6-c5 or prepare a counter. Being insufficiently prepared for the advance can easily lead to trouble.

White exchanges on d5

The exchange cxd5 is one of the most frequent in the Stonewall, occurring in roughly fifty per cent of games at the top level. Consequently Black should know how to approach this situation. Normally Black wants to recapture with the e-pawn, as in the first two examples below. However, sometimes it also makes sense to recapture with the c-pawn, and often this is forced because the f5-pawn cannot be abandoned. Moreover the f-pawn can occasionally be sacrificed with advantage, but be careful!

The first example is from Beliavsky-Yusupov, Linares 1989

13 cxd5! exd5

This recapture is clearly natural here, as 13...cxd5 14 ♖ac1 sees White take the c-file, while the potentially vulnerable e6-pawn remains (blocking in the bishop).
14 ♗h3 ♘g4

14...g6 15 ♖g1 ♘e4 16 ♖g2 favours White according to Beliavsky.
15 ♖g1 ♘df6 16 ♖g2 ♗e6 17 ♖ag1 ♖af8 18 a3!

White has organised all his forces on the kingside, yet he suddenly switches to the other flank to launch a minority attack. Is this logical? Yes, it is. White has forced Black into a passive position on the kingside, so opening up the game on another front will then create additional problems for the defender.
18...♗d7

In reply to 18...a5 White has 19 ♘a4 followed by the journey a4-c5-d3-e5.
19 b4 ♗e8

This time 19...a5 meets with 20 ♕b2 axb4 21 axb4 ♗e8 22 b5, illustrating Black's problem with the c6-pawn.

20 ♗xg4!

Remember that in such a closed position removing an enemy knight for a bishop can be a sensible policy for White.

20...♘xg4 21 ♖g3! ♗h5 22 ♕b2 ♘f6 23 ♘e5

White dominates completely, and the half-open file on the queenside is now very useful indeed (otherwise it would be hard to attack c6 after b4-b5xc6).

23...♘g4 24 f3 ♘xe5 25 dxe5 h6 26 ♘e2

The knight sets off on a winning route to d6.

26...b6 27 ♘d4 c5 28 ♘b5 ♔h7 29 ♘d6 g5 30 ♕c2 ♕e6 31 ♖h3 ♕g6 32 fxg5 hxg5 33 e6 ♔h6 34 ♘f7+ ♖xf7 35 exf7 ♕xf7 36 bxc5 bxc5 37 ♕xc5 ♖g6 38 ♕d4 ♖g8 39 ♖c1 ♕e6 40 ♖g3 g4 41 ♕f4+ 1-0

In the following example we deal with a rather normal Stonewall position. White has no significant advantage and decides to exchange on d5, but achieves nothing. In fact it is Black – not White – who gets things going on the queenside, suggesting that White should carefully consider the implications of the trade on d5, making sure to take on his own terms.

This is from Conquest-Short, Bundesliga 1987.

14 cxd5 exd5 15 ♗h3 g6 16 ♘d3 a5 17

a4 ♗e6

The bishop might look poor here but, because Black's pawns are not permanently fixed on light squares, the bishop will come to life eventually. White now spends valuable time executing a queen exchange that, in retrospect, seems not to be in his interest.

18 ♕c1 ♘e4 19 ♕a3 ♕xa3 20 ♖xa3 b6 21 ♖c1 c5

Black has used his time well, affording him a definite initiative on the queenside.

22 e3 ♖ac8 23 ♖aa1 g5 24 ♗g2 ♔g7 25 h3 ♔f6 26 ♖ab1 g4 27 ♘fe1 h5 28 ♘f4 ♗f7 29 ♖c2 ♘b8 30 ♖bc1 ♘a6 31 ♘ed3 gxh3 32 ♗xh3 ♘b4 33 ♘xb4 axb4 34 a5 c4 35 axb6 ♖b8 36 ♖a1 ♖xb6 37 ♖a5 ♖d8 38 bxc4 b3 39 ♖b2 dxc4 40 ♖xf5+ ♔g7 41 ♔g2 c3 42 ♖xf7+ ♔xf7 43 ♖xb3 c2 44 ♖xb6 c1♕ 45 ♗e6+ ♔e8 46 ♗d5 ♘d2 47 ♔h2 ♕f1 48 ♖e6+ ♔d7 49 ♗c6+ ♔c7 50 ♘h3 ♖f8 0-1

I mentioned earlier that Black should be careful when sacrificing his f-pawn. The following nightmare should serve as a severe warning!

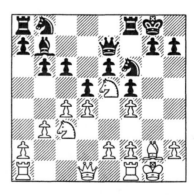

This game is Plaskett-Karlsson, Copenhagen 1985.

12 cxd5 exd5 13 ♕c2 ♘a6?!

Black simply ignores the threat to f5, believing it to be safe. Strictly speaking 13...♘e4 was more prudent.

14 ♕xf5 ♘e4??

Careless play, although this discovered attack is not uncommon. Black could still have achieved active compensation for his pawn with 14...c5! 15 dxc5 bxc5.

15 ♘xc6!! ♗xc6 16 ♘xd5 ♕b7 17 ♕xe4 ♔h8 18 ♕e7!

White has a promising position, which he converted in 55 moves.

It is true that it is more natural to recapture on d5 with the e6-pawn, thus releasing the c8-bishop and preserving the opportunity of challenging the centre with ...c7-c5. Nevertheless Black just as often recaptures with the c6-pawn. The most obvious reason, of course, is to maintain the protection of f5, but another idea is to take the sting out of White's minority attack. There is also the possibility that Black might find the c-file as useful as the e-file.

The first example is from the game Gulko-Short, Paris 1990. I have a feeling that this is a rapidplay game, a factor that has some implications in terms of quality.

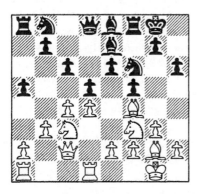

12 cxd5

Note that, thanks to b2-b3, Black can recapture with the e-pawn since 13 ♕xf5? ♘e4 hits both the queen and the unprotected knight on c3. However, because the bishop has reached e8 it already has a taste of freedom, so 12...exd5 is no longer so interesting. In fact Short decides to seek activity on the queenside.

12...cxd5!

Now we see how Black's traditional problem piece can be transformed – from the modest outpost on e8 the bishop can transfer to either side of the board.

13 ♘a4

This looks wrong. 13 ♘e5 merits consideration. Black simply has more pieces aimed at the queenside.

13...♘a6 14 ♖ac1 ♗a3 15 ♘b2 ♗b5

Black has made much progress since we joined the game.

16 ♗f1 ♘e4 17 e3 ♘b4 18 ♕b1 ♗xf1 19 ♖xf1 ♗xb2 20 ♕xb2 ♘d3

Winning.

21 ♕a3 ♘xc1 22 ♖xc1 ♖c8 23 ♗e5 ♖xc1+ 24 ♕xc1 ♕c8 25 ♕d1 ♕c3 26 ♘h4 ♖c8 27 ♔g2 ♕c2 28 ♕f3 ♕d2 0-1

Of course it is not always so easy for Black to generate such play on the c-file after the trade on d5. Often Black is content just to prevent an invasion (remember Beliavsky-Yusupov, above, where Black could not recapture with the c-pawn). The following game is a good illustration of the nature of the defensive task Black can face after ...cxd5.

Malaniuk-Vaiser
Yerevan 1996

1 d4 e6 2 c4 f5 3 g3 ♘f6 4 ♗g2 d5 5 ♘f3 c6 6 0-0 ♗d6 7 b3 ♕e7 8 a4 a5 9 ♗a3 b6 10 ♘e5 ♗b7 11 cxd5 cxd5!

This proves to be the most solid. 11...exd5 12 ♕c2 g6 13 e3 is slightly better for White.

12 ♗xd6 ♕xd6 13 ♘a3 0-0 14 ♘b5 ♕e7 15 ♖c1 ♘a6

Protecting c7.

16 ♕d2 ♖fc8 17 ♖xc8+

Not the most aggressive approach.

17...♖xc8 18 ♖c1 ♖xc1+ 19 ♕xc1 ♘e8

Freeing the knight on a6 from the defence of c7 and in turn preparing ...♗a6xb5.

20 h3 ♘b4 21 ♗f1 ♗a6 22 e3 ♗xb5 23 ♗xb5 ♕c7

Forcing White away from the c-file.

24 ♕d1 ♘f6 25 g4 g6 26 ♔g2 ♔f8 27 ♕f3 ♕c2!

A well timed infiltration.

28 ♕g3 ♕e4+ 29 ♔h2 ♔g7 30 gxf5 exf5 31 ♕g5 ♕c2 32 ♕f4 ♕e4 33 ♕xe4 fxe4 34 ♔g3 g5 35 h4 h6 36 hxg5 hxg5 ½-½

White has no way to attack the black pawns so the outcome of a draw is quite justified.

White plays a2-a4

Another plan for White is to push his a-pawn. In the first two examples White is successful, the first game being of the exceptionally high quality that one sees at the top level.

Kozul-Yusupov
Belgrade 1989

1 d4 e6 2 c4 f5 3 g3 ♘f6 4 ♗g2 d5 5 ♘f3 c6 6 0-0 ♗d6 7 ♘bd2 ♘bd7 8 ♕c2 0-0 9 b3 ♕e7 10 a4!? b6

I quite like this move, although the natural 10...a5 11 c5 ♗c7 12 ♗b2 has been suggested by Kozul as an improvement. He continues 12...e5 13 ♘xe5 ♘xe5 14 dxe5 ♗xe5 15 ♗xe5 ♕xe5 16 e3 with a small edge for White in view of ♘f3-d4, with a break on the queenside with b3-b4 and an attack against b7. Black should seriously consider 12...f4!? followed by ...e6-e5.

11 a5 ♗a6 12 ♗b2 ♖fc8 13 ♖fc1! ♘e4

This seems most natural, although Black's intentions are misguided here. 13...♗b4!? 14 axb6 axb6 15 cxd5 exd5! (15...cxd5 16 ♖xa6! is given by Kozul) 16 ♕xf5 ♗xd2 17 ♘xd2 ♕xe2 18 ♗f1 ♕xd2 19 ♖c2 ♕b4 20 ♗xa6 (20 ♕e6+ ♔h8 21 ♗xa6 ♕xb3! is better for Black) 20...♖e8 and the situation is unclear.

14 ♕d3!

With the powerful threat 15 axb6 axb6 16 ♖xa6 ♖xa6 17 c5! and Black cannot protect his rook.

14...♗b4?

14...c5! is obviously the correct move, after which the consequences are less than clear.

15 axb6 axb6 16 ♖xa6! ♖xa6 17 cxd5 ♖a2

No other move makes any sense.

18 ♖xc6! ♖ca8

After 18...♖xc6 19 dxc6 ♖xb2 we reach the diagram position, below.

It is possible that Yusupov missed that White now has 20 c7!!, e.g. 20...♕e8 (20...♘d6 21 ♘c4 wins for White) 21 ♕c4 ♕c8 22 ♕xe6+ ♔h8 23 ♘xe4 ♕xc7 24 ♘fg5!! (perhaps the only winning move here!) 24...g6 25 ♕f7 ♕c1+ 26 ♗f1 ♘f8 27 ♘f6 and Black is mated.

19 dxe6 ♘df6

19...♖xb2 20 exd7 ♕xd7 21 ♕c4+ ♔f8 22 ♘xe4 fxe4 23 ♘e5 presents White with a winning attack, while 19...♘f8!? 20 ♗c1 ♖a1 21 ♘xe4 fxe4 22 ♕xe4 ♗a3 23 ♗f1! ♗xc1 24 ♖xc1 ♖xc1 25 ♕xa8 ♕xe6 26 e4 ♕xb3 27 ♘e5 ♕e6 28 ♔g2 gives White a very promising position that looks close to winning.

20 ♕c2 ♕e8?

This loses by force. The only chance is 20...♗a3! 21 ♘c4! ♗xb2 22 ♘xb2 ♘d6 23 ♘e5 ♖a1+ 24 ♘d1, when White is better but Black has counterplay.

21 ♘xe4 fxe4 22 ♘e5 ♗a3 23 e7! b5! 24 ♗h3! ♖xb2 25 ♗e6+ ♔h8

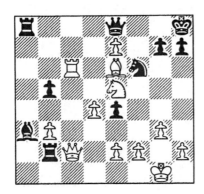

26 ♕c1?!

Here White has a convincing win with 26 ♕xb2! ♗xb2 27 ♘f7+ ♔g8 (27...♕xf7 28 ♗xf7 ♗xd4 29 e3!, with ♖xf6 to follow, wins for White) 28 ♘d6+ ♔h8 29 ♘xe8 ♘xe8 30 d5 and Black has no defence against the rolling pawns.

26...♖a2 27 ♕g5?

White could still win with 27 ♕b1! ♖b2 28 ♕xb2!.

27...♕xe7 28 ♕h4!

Probably the only move. 28 ♘f7+ ♔g8 29 ♘h6+ ♔h8 30 ♘f5 ♕b7 31 ♖b6 ♕c7 32 ♖c6 is given by Kozul as a draw, but 32...♕a7! 33 ♖a6 ♗c1!! 34 ♖xa7 ♗xg5 35 ♖xg7 h6 seems to win for Black.

28...g5! 29 ♕xg5

Also possible is 29 ♕h6 ♕g7 30 ♘f7+ ♔g8 31 ♘xg5+ ♔h8 (31...♔f8 32 ♕xf6+ ♕xf6 33 ♘xh7+ ♔e7 34 ♘xf6 ♔xf6 35 ♗d5+ ♔f5 36 ♗e6+ draws) 32 ♘f7+ with a draw.

29...♖f8 30 ♖c8??

A terrible mistake in mutual time-trouble. A draw results from 30 ♘f7+! ♖xf7 31 ♗xf7 ♕xf7 32 ♖xf6 ♗e7! (the only move as 32...♕g7? 33 ♕f5! Wins for White) 33 ♖xf7 ♗xg5 34 e3 ♖a1+ 35 ♔g2 ♖a2! etc.

30...♖xc8??

30...♕xe6! wins. Now White comes out on top.

31 ♘f7+ ♕xf7 32 ♗xf7 ♗e7 33 ♕xb5 ♔g7 34 ♗c4 ♖a7 35 ♕e5 ♖f8 36 g4! h6

37 h4 ♔h7 38 ♗e6 ♘e8 39 ♗f5+ ♔g8 40 ♕e6+ ♔g7 1-0

Obviously Black could have blocked the a-file, as Kozul points out, but could he have ignored the a-pawn's advance? Probably not. Witness the following example:

Gulko-Milov
Bern 1994

1 c4 c6 2 d4 d5 3 e3 e6 4 ♘f3 f5 5 ♗d3 ♘f6 6 0-0 ♗d6 7 b3!? ♕e7 8 a4!? 0-0

8...a5!? seems better.

9 ♗a3

9 a5!? is interesting and possibly strong.

9...♗xa3 10 ♖xa3!?

An odd recapture. I believe the usual 10 ♘xa3 is better despite the d3-bishop obstructing the manoeuvre ♘c2-e1-d3.

10...g6?

Black is not afraid of the a-pawn but it turns out he should have played 10...a5!.

11 a5! ♘bd7 12 cxd5 exd5

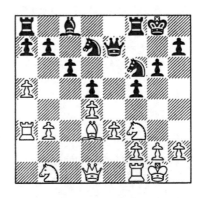

13 a6!

Black now has serious problems with the c6-pawn.

13...♘e4 14 ♕c1 ♖f6 15 axb7 ♗xb7 16 ♖a5!

Directed against ...c6-c5.

16...a6 17 ♘bd2 c5 18 ♕a3 ♕f8 19 ♕a4!

Forcing the bishop to a poor square.

19...♗c6 20 ♕a1! ♗b7 21 ♖c1 ♖c6 22 ♖a2!

With the idea of ♖ac2.

22...♕f6? 23 ♗b5! ♘xd2 24 ♘xd2 axb5 25 ♖xa8+ ♗xa8 26 ♕xa8+ ♔g7 27 ♕b7 ♕d6 28 dxc5 ♖c7 29 cxd6 ♖xb7 30 ♖c7 ♖xc7 31 dxc7

White now has a winning ending.

31...♘b6 32 ♘f3 ♔f6 33 ♘d4 b4 34 ♘c6 ♔e6 35 ♘xb4 ♔d7 36 ♘a6! ♔c6 37 ♔f1 h6 38 ♔e2 ♔b7 39 ♘b4 ♔xc7 40 ♔d3 ♔d6 41 ♔d4 g5 42 h3 ♔e6 43 ♘d3! h5 44 ♔c5 1-0

The conclusion from these two games must be that White does indeed get a good game by advancing his a-pawn, and the further the better! Black should be ready to prevent the advance and be aware of the great damage that White's a-pawn can cause when it reaches a6.

In the following game Black is more careful, meeting a2-a4 with ...a7-a5 and being rewarded with an acceptable game. See also Malaniuk-Vaiser, above, for similar concepts.

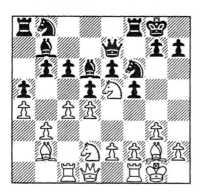

Ibragimov-Shabalov, New York 1998 (Black actually played 11...a5 to which White replied 12 a4, but the structure is the same).
12...♘a6

Black employs the knight more actively with pawns on a4 and a5, the b4-square being a perfect outpost (the more natural d7-square leaves the b7-bishop unprotected).

After the text Black is ready to compromise White's centre with ...c6-c5.
13 ♘df3 c5 14 cxd5

14 e3 ♖ac8 15 ♕e2 is more appropriate, when some observers claim White has an advantage. I see no reason why Black should be worse here; perhaps it is a matter of taste.
14...exd5

14...♗xd5 15 ♘c4 favours White.

15 ♘d3 ♘b4 16 ♖e1 ♖ac8 17 e3 ♘e4 18 ♘fe5 ♖fd8

Black is fully developed and ready for action in the centre, so White attempts to be the first to dictate matters.
19 f3 ♘xd3 20 ♘xd3 c4!

A strong intermediate move that demonstrates the potential of Black's position. White now opts for exchanges as the passed c-pawn could be very painful to watch.
21 bxc4 dxc4 22 fxe4 cxd3 23 ♕xd3?!

Stronger is 23 exf5 ♗xg2 24 ♔xg2 ♕e4+ 25 ♔g1 ♗b4 26 ♗c3 ♗xc3 27 ♕b3+ ♖d5 28 ♖xc3 ♖xc3 29 ♕xc3 ♖xf5 30 ♕c4+ ♖f7 31 ♖f1 ♕xe3+ 32 ♔h1, when Black has nothing better than perpetual check.
23...♗xe4 24 ♗xe4 ♕xe4 25 ♕xe4 fxe4 26 ♔f2 ♔f7 27 ♔e2 g6?!

Weakening the dark squares around the king. 27...♔e6 28 d5+ ♔xd5 29 ♗xg7 ♗c5 keeps up the pressure, while 27...♖b8 28 ♖f1+ ♔e8 29 ♖f5! should be avoided. Now White seizes his chance to create some activity.
28 d5! ♗b4 29 ♖f1+ ♔e8 30 ♖f4 ♖xc1 31 ♖xe4+ ♔f7 32 ♗xc1 ♖xd5 33 ♖d4 ♔e6

Black is still trying. 33...♖xd4 34 exd4 ♔e6 35 ♔d3 ♔d5 36 g4 is just a draw.
34 ♔d3 b5 35 ♖xd5 ♔xd5 36 e4+ ♔c6 37 axb5+ ♔xb5 38 ♗b2 a4 39 g4 ♗e7 40 h3 ♔b4 41 ♔d4 ♔b3 42 ♗a1 ♔a2 43 ♗c3 ♔b1 44 e5 a3 45 ♔d5 a2 46 e6

The e-pawn is as strong as the black bishop, and White's king is closer to the action, hence the coming draw.
46...♗b4 47 ♗e5 ♔c2 48 ♔c4 ♗a3 49

♗g7 h5 50 gxh5 gxh5 51 ♗a1 ♔b1 52 ♗d4 ♗b2 53 ♗xb2 ♔xb2 54 e7 a1♕ 55 e8♕ ♕f1+ ½-½

Having concentrated on White we now shift our attention to Black's aggressive strategies. I have decided to call this section...

General Plans for Black

We start by investigating the most aggressive strategies involving ...g7-g5 and ...f5-f4 – basically the ideas that generate attacking possibilities with the aim of delivering mate.

When should Black attack?

For this we follow the same criteria in practically all situations. The player with the advantage should attack, not only because since he has the advantage he can, but also because he might lose it if he does not.

In the following example the position is balanced but Black's forces might have the more potential. First Black puts his pieces on the best squares, then he attacks – an offensive generally fails when pieces have yet to enter the game!

Attacking with ...f4

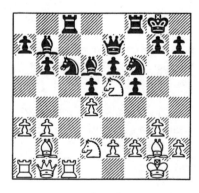

This is Dokhoian-Bareev, Rome 1990.
16 b4
White has achieved nothing special from the opening and this advance is not enough to worry Black, who is free to prepare for aggressive operations on the other flank.
16...♘e4 17 ♘f1 ♗b8!
Intending ...♘xe5 followed by ...♗a6 with a good game. White prevents this plan.
18 ♕d3 f4!
With everything in place Black can now begin to step up a gear on the kingside.
19 ♘xc6 ♗xc6 20 b5 ♗d7 21 ♖xc8 ♖xc8 22 ♖c1 ♖f8!
Of course Black is not interested in an ending, concentrating instead on creating concrete threats against the white king.
23 a4 fxg3 24 fxg3 ♘f2! 25 ♕d2 ♗d6 26 ♘e3 ♕g5
Black's set-up is quite intimidating now, but White should still be okay at this point.

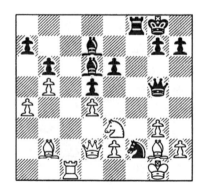

27 ♘c4?
Correct is 27 ♖f1! ♘g4 28 ♗c1 ♕xe3+ 29 ♕xe3 ♘xe3 30 ♗xe3 which is about equal, e.g. 30...♖a8 31 ♗f4 ♗xf4 32 gxf4 a6 33 f5.
27...♗e7! 28 ♘e3
Whoops.
28...♘g4 29 ♖c7 ♕h6
Even stronger is 29...♗d6!! 30 ♖xd7 ♗xg3 31 hxg3 ♕h6, when White has no other way to prevent the mate on h2 than the futile 32 ♖xg7+ ♔xg7 33 ♘f5+ ♖xf5 34 ♕xh6+ ♔xh6 with a winning ending for Black.
30 h3 ♗d6 31 ♖xd7 ♗xg3 32 ♘c4 ♕h4 33 ♗a3 ♖f2!!
A very nice move with which to win the

game. In reply to 33...♗d6 White can turn the tables with 34 e4!! ♖f2 35 ♗xd6 ♖xd2 36 ♘xd2.

34 ♕d3

The best defence is 34 ♖e7! dxc4! 35 ♖e8+ ♔f7 36 ♖f8+ ♔g6 37 ♕c2+ ♔h6 38 ♗c1+ g5 39 ♖h8 ♔g7 40 ♗xg5! ♕h5 41 ♖a8 ♕f7! 42 ♗f3 ♗h2+ and Black wins.

34...♗c7 35 ♖d8+ ♗xd8 36 hxg4 dxc4 37 ♕xc4 ♖f6 38 g5 ♕xg5 39 ♗c1 ♕g3 40 ♕c8 ♕c7 41 ♕xc7 ♗xc7 0-1

Since the kingside attack is an important aspect of Black's aggressive oriented strategy in the Stonewall we should have a look at another example.

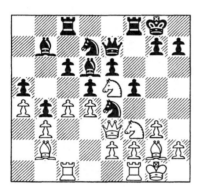

The diagram position arose in the game Ross-Tukmakov, Canada 1989. Black, if anyone, already has the better game. The queenside – where it is not unusual for Black to have problems – is closed, so Black is well placed to take action on the kingside. Facing tough opposition White tries to reduce any possible discomfort through exchanges (and repetition), but the GM manages to generate activity – and an attack!

16 ♘xd7 ♕xd7 17 ♘d2 ♘f6 18 ♘f3 ♘e4 19 ♘d2 f4!

Of course Black has no thoughts of a draw here.

20 ♕d3 ♘g5 21 gxf4 ♖xf4 22 e3 ♖h4 23 f4 ♕f7 24 c5 ♗c7 25 ♘f3 ♘xf3+ 26 ♖xf3 ♖a8!

Surprise! The queen's bishop finds a way to join the game, and f1 is suddenly unavailable for the white rook.

27 ♖h3

White tries to force matters with another trade.

27...♕h5 28 ♖xh4 ♕xh4 29 ♕f1 g5!

Black's king will be quite safe on h8, White's does not appear to be safe anywhere.

30 ♗h3 gxf4 31 ♗xe6+ ♔h8 32 e4 f3 33 e5 ♖f8 34 ♕f2 ♕h6 35 ♗g4 ♕g5 36 ♕g3 f2+ 37 ♔g2 ♗a6 0-1

These two games offer us an understanding of the ideas associated with the ...f5-f4 offensive. We have already seen other instances in which Black creates a kingside attack and, since very few examples cover only one concept, each deserves careful study.

Black plays ...g7-g5

This is another aggressive kingside attacking motif. There are several reasons why pushing the g-pawn can be desirable for Black, as the following examples demonstrate. One game will feature this or that idea that is quite different from another, but an obvious theme seen in games is, for example, extra space. In the first – from the first FIDE. World Championship Knockout tournament – Black plays ...g7-g5 not to directly attack his opponent's king, rather to eliminate the f3-pawn and thereby gain control over the e4-square for his knight.

The next example is from the game Bareev-Krasenkov, Groningen 1997. White's last move was 24 g3, inviting a thematic response.

see following diagram

24...g5!

Now that White's g-pawn no longer supports its partner on f3 Black quickly strikes, fighting for control of e4. Note that as a result White also finds his influence on the g4-

square disappearing. In fact this square tends to have some significance in the Stonewall, as is the case here.

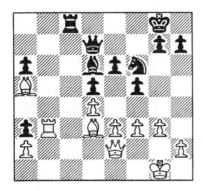

25 ♗xa6 ♖c1+ 26 ♔g2 g4 27 fxg4 ♘xg4

Black's plan is based on combining a king-side attack with pressure against the a2-pawn. The fall of this pawn will release the one on a3, so White must worry about matters on both sides of the board.

28 ♕d2 ♕c6! 29 ♖b6??

The conclusion from various analysts is that White has only one defence here, namely 29 ♗d3!, after which the game fizzles out into a drawn ending or a perpetual after 29...♖d1 30 ♕e2 ♕c1 31 ♖b1 ♖g1+! 32 ♔f3! (32 ♔h3? ♕xb1 33 ♗xb1 ♖xb1 and Black wins due to the threats ...♖b2 and ...♖h1) 32...♕xb1 33 ♗xb1 ♖xb1 34 ♗c3 ♖f1+ 35 ♔g2 ♖c1!? (more testing; 35...♖f2 draws immediately) 36 ♕a6! ♖c2+ 37 ♔g1! ♖c1+ etc.

29...♕c2!

Now Black wins.

30 ♖xd6 ♕e4+ 31 ♔h3 ♖c2 0-1

In the following game White weakens his kingside with h2-h4, in the process providing Black with a ready-made target. White does not defend terribly well but the game is nonetheless a good illustration of the manner in which Black can use the g-file.

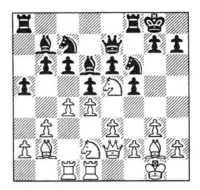

This is from Petursson-Tukmakov, Moscow 1989.

14...♗xe5!?

An interesting exchange. The key idea is to humble the b2-bishop, as seen earlier in Yrjola-Yusupov.

15 dxe5 ♘e4 16 ♘b1?

This seems to be a misunderstanding for which White will soon pay dearly. Trying to trap the e4-knight is often more trouble than it is worth.

16...c5 17 h4

White is obsessed with the intruder. By cutting off the retreat to g5 he has served only to weaken the g3-pawn, making the grand plan with f2-f3 more difficult to achieve. The immediate 17 f3 ♘g5 18 ♘c3 dxc4 19 bxc4 ♘f7 leaves White with problems with the bishop on c1 and a potentially vulnerable pawn on c4 (b6 is no easier to attack than c4, and anyway Black can try ...b6-b5!? at some point).

17...g5!

This break is very uncomfortable for White, whose aspirations on the kingside have led to his king coming under fire. Meanwhile, the knight still stands proud on e4.

18 hxg5 ♕xg5 19 ♘d2 ♖ad8 20 ♘f1 ♖d7

Preparing to launch the h-pawn, too. Once this latest foot soldier reaches h4 the defensive barrier in front of White's king will collapse. It is possible that White is already lost here, although his next reactionary try hastens the end.

21 g4?

Certainly not the best defensive policy. Now Black goes for the kill.

21...♕h4 22 cxd5 ♘xd5 23 ♖c4 ♖g7 24 gxf5 ♘f4 0-1

After 25 exf4 comes 25...♘c3!.

Now we turn to a simple idea behind Black's blatant thrust of the g-pawn – forcing the retreat of White's bishop from f4 and gaining space. Of course Black must not advance just for the sake of it, but by carefully weighing up the positional and tactical consequences it can put White under pressure. It is also interesting that ...g7-g5 is the kind of move that invites White to try, often without justification, to search for a punishing retort. This is what happened in Douven-Vaiser, Groningen 1993, with Black coming out on top. Here is the position after 23 ♕b2:

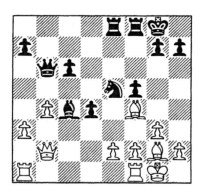

23...♘f7 24 ♖fe1 g5! 25 ♗xg5!?

25 ♗c1!? has been suggested by Kharitonov as an improvement. Now Black gains a passed pawn on the d-file and the position becomes difficult for White to defend, although many players have a problem retreating a piece back to its starting position (sometimes this feels like putting it back in the box!).

25...♘xg5 26 ♕c1 ♗xe2 27 ♕xg5+

27 ♖xe2 ♖xe2 28 ♕c4+ does not work on account of 28...♖e6!.

27...♔h8 28 ♖ac1 d3

White has problems. What should he do about 29...f4 followed by 30...d2 and wins?

29 ♗xc6?!

29 ♕d2! is given as immediately losing for White by Kharitonov, but after his 29...♕d4 White has the testing 30 ♗xc6! with the idea of 30...f4 31 ♗xe8 fxg3 32 ♖xe2!. If Black attempts 30...♖e5! White should play 31 ♕h6 (31 ♗b5?! f4!! [31...♖xb5? 32 ♖xe2 is promising for White] 32 ♗xd3 fxg3 33 ♖xe2 ♖xe2 34 ♕xe2 ♖xf2 35 ♖c8+ ♖f8+ 36 ♔g2 ♖xc8 37 hxg3 ♖d8 38 ♗c4 ♕d2 gives Black a winning endgame). Then 31...♕d8! keeps control over the dark squares, when a sample continuation is 32 ♕f4 ♖e6 33 ♕d2 f4 34 ♗g2 ♕d4 35 gxf4 ♖xf4 36 ♖c8+ ♔g7 37 ♖c7+ ♔g8 38 ♔h1 with a mess from which Black seems more likely to emerge ahead. Then again, who knows...

29...♖e6 30 ♗a4?

White is struggling thanks to the enormous d-pawn but a more stubborn defence is 30 ♗d5! ♖d6 31 ♕e7 ♕d8 32 ♕e5+ ♕f6 33 ♕xf6+ ♖fxf6 34 ♗b3! (34 ♗c4!? d2 35 ♗xe2 dxe1♕+ 36 ♖xe1 ♖fe6 37 ♔f1 ♖d2 has been suggested as clearly better for Black, but after 38 ♗g4! I don't see how Black can force an easily winning endgame). The hasty 34...d2 runs into 35 ♖c8+!, so Black has to do some more work before he can count on earning the full point. One idea is 34...f4!? 35 ♖c8+ ♔g7 36 ♖c7+ ♔h6 37 ♖xa7? (too risky) 37...d2 38 ♖a1 ♖c6 39 ♔g2 ♖c1 40 ♖a2 ♗f1+! and Black wins. After the text White is without hope.

30...f4 31 ♖c5 d2 32 ♖a1 ♕d8! 33 ♕d5 ♕f6 0-1

Our next example is Miralles-Agdestein, Lyon 1988. It does not take long to figure out that Black has a good position. He is fully developed, has no real problems with his weakness at e6, his occasionally problematic bishop has been exchanged and there is pressure against the a3-pawn – tying the rook to a1 or inducing the creation of an attractive outpost should White spend time on a3-a4. With these factors in mind Black should do something active or risk seeing his advantages disappear. For an experienced Stonewall enthusiast such as Agdestein the following sequence of moves comes with little effort.

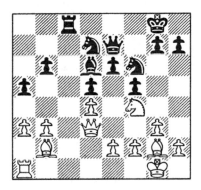

24...g5! 25 ♘h3 g4 26 ♘f4 ♗xf4!

The point. The position being mainly closed, the knights are a match for the bishops. In terms of the structure Black's agenda concerns attacking the new f4-pawn in order to force White to play e2-e3. White then has problems with f3 and e4, and we see that the difference for Black here between having the pawn on g4 instead of g7 is the control of f3.

27 gxf4 ♘f8 28 ♖c1 ♖xc1+ 29 ♗xc1 ♛c7 30 ♗d2 ♘g6 31 ♛b5

White prefers an attempt at counterplay to passivity.

31...♔f7 32 b4 axb4 33 ♛xb4 ♘e4 34 ♗xe4 fxe4 35 a4 ♛c2!

After this invasion there is little White can do.

36 a5 ♛d1+ 37 ♔g2 ♘h4+ 38 ♔g3 ♛g1+!!

An accurately calculated mating attack is a fitting culmination to Black's treatment of the position.

39 ♔xh4 ♛xh2+ 40 ♔g5 h6+ 41 ♔xg4 ♔g6 0-1

There is no defence against ...h6-h5 mate!

Black plays ...c6-c5

The Stonewall is not just a matter of Black launching a kingside attack, although many of the club players I know would like to think so! To be able to use the full potential of the Stonewall one should be acquainted with a full range of possibilities, including actions in the centre and on the queenside as well as the kingside. By now we are already familiar with the idea of ...c6-c5, but I would like to discuss the idea further and not limit ourselves to its use as a counter to White's actions.

In the first example White is unprepared for the opening of the centre and consequently pays the price.

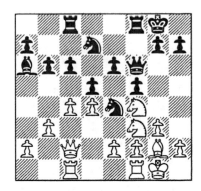

This is from Kachar-Dreev, Moscow 1988. Black should be satisfied to reach this position. There is no reason to miss the dark-squared bishop too much since the other pieces are very well placed, not least the bishop, which targets White's c4-pawn. Time to go on the offensive:

15...c5! 16 cxd5

A lesser evil is 16 dxc5!? dxc4 17 cxb6 ♘xb6 18 bxc4 ♖xc4 19 ♛b3 ♖fc8.

16...cxd4 17 ♛b2 e5!

Black achieves more than enough compensation from the coming sacrifice.

18 ♘e6 ♘c3 19 ♘xf8 ♘xf8 20 ♖c2 e4 21 ♖d2?

21 ♘e1 is forced, although it is easy to see why White did not feel comfortable about it. **21...exf3 22 ♗xf3 ♘d7 23 ♖e1 d3 24 exd3?!**

24 ♕a3! ♗b7 25 exd3 ♘e5 26 ♗g2 ♗xd5 27 d4 is less accommodating.

24...♘e5 25 ♖e3 f4!

Ruining White's kingside completely.

26 gxf4 ♘xf3+ 27 ♖xf3 ♗b7 28 d4 ♘e4 29 ♖c2

Losing by force, as does 29 ♖e2 ♕g6+ 30 ♔f1 ♕h5! 31 ♖ee3 ♕xh2 32 ♖xe4 ♗a6+ 33 ♔e1 ♕h1+.

29...♖xc2 30 ♕xc2 ♕g6+ 0-1

In the following game ...c6-c5 is a natural means to establish a suitable structure for the light-squared bishop. It also provides an opportunity for Black to gain access to the kingside for his queen's rook.

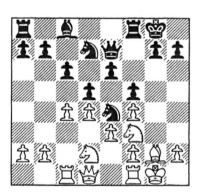

Kalinichev-Glek, Soviet Army Championships 1987. Another more or less normal situation, perhaps slightly favourable for White. This assessment is no longer relevant after the following exchange.

12 ♘xe4?! dxe4!

Kramnik does not like this exchange, but offers no convincing evidence why it should be worse than 12...fxe4, which leads to equality.

13 ♘d2?

The beginning of a poor plan. 13 ♘e5 ♘xe5 14 dxe5 ♖d8 15 ♕e2 c5 is level.

13...c5 14 ♘b3 b6 15 dxc5 ♘xc5 16 ♘xc5 bxc5 17 ♕a4 ♖b8 18 b3 ♖b6!

Preparing to swing the rook over to the kingside, a decision justified by White's failure to produce anything approaching dangerous. In fact Glek's rook manoeuvre is about to put White under tremendous pressure.

19 ♕a3 e5! 20 ♖cd1

Vacating c1 for the queen to begin a defensive manoeuvre, but Black is too quick. **20...exf4 21 exf4 ♖g6 22 ♕c1 ♕h4 23 ♕e3 ♕g4 24 ♕g3 ♕h5! 0-1**

Black will now make a decisive gain of material.

There are other ways for Black to change the structure. Originally I was going to cover something ideas with ...e6-e5 but I came to understand that, rather than being the start of an active plan, this advance tends to be part of the wrapping up process, as in the previous game. Generally Black has no real interest in pushing ...e6-e5 unless it is relevant to a particular strategy. Imagine a standard Stonewall set-up where Black plays 1...e5 and White replies 2 cxd5 cxd5 3 dxe5. This leaves Black saddled with an isolated d5-pawn and White excellent outposts on d4 and f4. When investigating 500 GM games for this book, I came across this plan only once, and Black lost in 19 moves. White was the GM! That is not to say that ...e6-e5 is always dubious (we have several examples where the opposite is true), it is simply not the appropriate way to begin an active plan.

Consequently let us move on to a more reliable policy.

Black plays ...d5xc4

There are two ways for Black to follow this capture. One is ...e6-e5, the other ...c6-c5. In the first example we consider the former option.

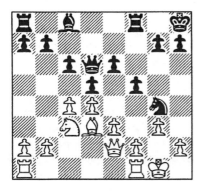

In this (typical) position, from the game Van der Sterren-Nikolic, Reykjavik 1986, White can claim no advantage. In fact Black voluntarily exchanged the dark-squared bishops, so now he alters the pawn structure to accommodate his remaining bishop.

14...dxc4! 15 ♗xc4 e5 16 ♖ad1?

16 dxe5 ♘xe5 17 ♖ad1 ♕f6 18 ♗b3 is nothing for Black to worry about but still better than what follows.

16...♕h6 17 f4?

Losing material. Forced is 17 h4, when Black's chief options feature ...f5-f4. One line leads only to perpetual, but it is illustrative of the possibilities available to Black: 17...b5 18 ♗b3 b4 19 ♘a4 f4 20 dxe5 fxg3 21 fxg3 ♗a6 22 ♕xa6 ♕xe3+ 23 ♔g2 ♕e4+ 24 ♔h3! (24 ♔g1?? ♖f3!! 25 ♖xf3 ♕xf3 26 ♕f1 ♕xg3+ 27 ♕g2 ♕e3+ 28 ♔h1 ♘f2+ 29 ♔h2 ♘xd1 30 ♗xd1 ♖f8 wins for Black) 24...♖f2! 25 ♖xf2 ♘xf2+ 26 ♔h2 ♘g4+ 27 ♔h3 ♘f2+ with a draw.

17...b5 18 ♗d3 e4 19 ♗c2 b4 20 ♘a4 ♗a6!

Thanks to the mate on h2 White has no defence.

21 ♕d2 ♗xf1 22 ♖xf1 ♕d6 23 ♗b3 h6 24 ♖c1 g5 25 ♘c5 gxf4 26 gxf4 ♘f6 27 ♕xb4 ♘d5 28 ♕d2 ♖g8+ 29 ♔h1 ♖g7 30 ♖e1 ♖ag8 31 ♕f2 ♕g6 32 ♘a4 ♕h5 33 ♕f1 ♕f3+ 0-1

In the following game the Bosnian super-GM Nikolic shows us the full positional po-

tential of ...d5xc4 followed by ...c6-c5.

**Cifuentes Parada-Nikolic
Rotterdam 1999**

This game between the South American and Balkan GMs was, strangely enough, played in the Dutch Championships! When I first saw the game I thought of boxing – this was because I had the feeling that White made no serious mistakes, he was just fighting an opponent with longer arms! I have included the entire game, which is instructive from start to finish.

1 d4 f5 2 g3 ♘f6 3 ♗g2 e6 4 ♘f3 d5 5 c4 c6 6 0-0 ♗d6 7 b3 ♕e7 8 ♕c2 0-0 9 ♘e5 ♗d7 10 ♗b2 ♗e8 11 ♘d2 ♘bd7 12 ♘d3 ♗f7!

Black's odd-looking bishop manoeuvre is logical. For the moment there is nothing for the bishop on h5, so Nikolic posts it temporarily on f7, where it protects e6 and does not obstruct the other pieces. And remember – why should the piece on g2 be stronger than the one on f7?

13 ♘f3 dxc4!

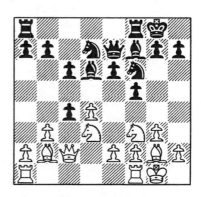

Already Black profits from his new-look bishop, as 14 ♕xc4 loses a piece to 14...e5. Consequently White must accept a weak pawn on c4.

14 bxc4 c5!

Clamping down on the c4-pawn. Black has equalized.

15 e3 ℤfc8

There is nothing happening on the king-side.

16 ♘fe5 ℤc7 17 f4 ♗e8 18 ♘xd7 ♘xd7 19 ♘e5 ♘f6 20 ℤac1 ℤac8 21 ℤfe1 b5

The conversion of advantages. Instead of attacking a weak pawn Black is now able to take advantage of the clumsiness of his opponent's pieces, finding a way for his light-squared bishop to enter the game in the process.

22 cxb5 ♗xb5 23 ♕b3 ♕e8 24 dxc5 ♗xc5 25 ♗a3 ♗a4 26 ♕d3 ♗b5 27 ♕b3 ♗a4 28 ♕d3 ♗b6 29 ℤxc7 ℤxc7 30 ℤc1

Around this point White's is only slightly worse, but he loses the thread and with it a pawn.

30...♕c8 31 ℤxc7 ♕xc7 32 ♔f2 ♗c2 33 ♕c4 ♘g4+ 34 ♔e2 ♗d1+!

35 ♔e1 ♗a5+ 36 ♗b4 ♕xc4 37 ♘xc4 ♗xb4+ 38 ♔xd1 ♘xh2

The endgame is now a matter of technique for a player of Nikolic's standard.

39 ♘e5 ♗d6 40 ♘c6 ♘g4 41 ♔e2 ♗c5 42 e4 ♔f8 43 exf5 exf5 44 ♗d5 g6 45 ♔f3 ♘f6 46 ♗e6 ♔g7 47 ♗b3 ♘e4 48 ♗d5 ♘c3 49 ♗b3 ♔f6 50 ♗g8 ♗b6 51 ♗b3 a5 52 ♘e5 ♗c7 53 ♘d7+ ♔e7 54 ♘c5 ♗d6 55 ♘d3 ♔f6 56 ♗c4 h6 57 ♘c1 ♗c5 58 ♘b3 ♗b6 59 ♘d2 a4 60 ♗g8 ♘b5 61 ♘c4 ♗c5 62 ♘e5 ♘d4+ 63 ♔g2 ♗d6 64 ♘c4 ♗f8 65 ♘b6 a3 66 ♗c4 g5 67 ♘d5+ ♔g6 68 ♗d3 g4 69

♘e3 h5 70 ♘c2 ♘f3 71 ♗e2 ♘d2 72 ♗b5 ♔f6 73 ♘e3 ♗c5 74 ♘c4 ♘e4 75 ♗a4 ♘c3 76 ♗b3 h4 77 gxh4 ♘e2 78 ♗d1 ♘c1 79 ♘e5 ♗d6 80 ♘d7+ ♔e7 81 ♘b6 ♘xa2 82 ♘d5+ ♔f7 83 ♗b3 ♘c1 84 ♗c4 ♔g6 85 ♘c3 ♗xf4 0-1

Of course this strategy has its drawbacks. For example Black should be careful not to allow White to play ♕xc4 in certain circumstances. In the two previous games Black achieved good positions, but he was also the stronger player. Here is a game in which the opening moves are more difficult to comprehend than the subsequent tactics.

**Kasparov-Petrosian
Niksic 1983**

1 d4 e6 2 c4 f5 3 g3 ♘f6 4 ♗g2 d5 5 ♘f3 ♗e7 6 0-0 0-0 7 b3 c6 8 ♕c2 ♗d7 9 ♗b2!?

I find it odd that Kasparov chooses not to exchange the dark-squared bishops – perhaps he just feels good about keeping as many pieces on the board as possible. However, I would still recommend this exchange when possible.

9...♗e8 10 ♘e5 ♘bd7 11 ♘d3 ♗h5 12 ♘c3 ♗d6 13 f3!

Limiting the activity of the busy bishop on h5.

13...♗g6

I prefer 13...♗f7, after which the position seems okay for Black.

14 e3 ℤc8 15 ♕e2

15 ♕f2!? deserves consideration.

15...ℤe8!

Forcing White to weigh up the consequences of ...e6-e5 with his queen sharing the same file as an enemy rook. Will the queen sidestep the issue?

16 ♕f2

Yes.

16...a6 17 ℤac1 ♕e7 18 ℤfe1 ♕f8

This manoeuvre looks odd to me.

19 ℤcd1

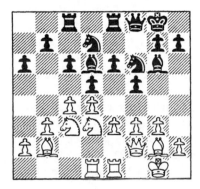

The shadow-boxing ends. Both players have finished manoeuvring and, having seen where White has decided to station his rooks, Black judges it is time for action on the queenside. A slight problem for Black is his insertion of 16...a6, as this neglects b6 and in turn reduces Black's influence on the c5-square.

19...dxc4 20 bxc4 c5 21 ♗f1 ♗f7 22 ♘a4! cxd4 23 exd4 b5 24 cxb5 axb5 25 ♘ac5 b4!?

Given the chance White would play a2-a3 to fix Black's b-pawn.

26 ♖c1 ♕e7 27 ♗h3 ♕d8 28 ♘xb4 ♕a5 29 ♘c6!

Usual Kasparov stuff!

29...♕xa2 30 ♘xd7 ♘xd7 31 d5!

Blowing apart Black's pawn structure. Since both 31...exd5 32 ♗xf5 and 31...g6 are totally unacceptable for Black he is forced to rely on tactics.

31...♕xd5 32 ♖ed1 ♗c5!

Only move.

33 ♖xd5 ♗xf2+ 34 ♔xf2 exd5 35 ♗xf5

The pin makes it possible for White to regain his exchange.

35...♘b6 36 ♗xc8 ♘xc8 37 ♗a3!

Although Black has emerged from the tactical blows without losing material – and although there is little material remaining – he is still in a lot of trouble. White has the more active forces (the isolated d5-pawn restricts Black) and therefore benefits from

the bishops of opposite colour (Black is unable to challenge on the dark squares). Consequently Black should probably try 37...d4!? in order to win himself some breathing space and a chance to regroup, although a pawn is a pawn.

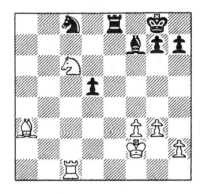

37...h6 38 ♖b1 ♖e6 39 ♘d4 ♖a6 40 ♗c5 ♘d6 41 ♖b8+ ♔h7 42 g4!

The beginning of the final attack. Clearly the target is g7.

42...♖a4 43 ♔e3 ♘c4+ 44 ♔f4 g5+ 45 ♔g3 ♖a2 46 ♖b7 ♔g6 47 ♘f5 ♖a6 48 h4 gxh4+ 49 ♘xh4+ ♔g7 50 ♘f5+ ♔g6 51 ♗d4! 1-0

I hope this game helps to illustrate the variety of possibilities in the Stonewall, being different from previous games but at the same time using and featuring themes already covered. It is not unlike pop music in that a song might sound like a hundred others but still have something unique about it.

Black gains counterplay with ...a7-a5-a4

This plan is often seen when Black has difficulty developing his knight on d7 due to the N(d2)-c4 trick discussed earlier. Instead of just ...♘a6 Black chooses to play ...a7-a5 to support the knight on b4 and sometimes to open the a-file. The latter possibility tends to make more sense when White's rook has already left the a-file, as in the following game.

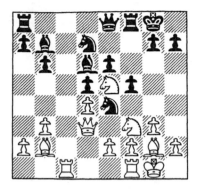

S.B.Hansen-Kristiansen, Lyngby 1989. White is a talented junior who later became a strong GM. Black is a strong IM at the height of his strength. With the centre more or less closed Black could choose to use the c-file to steer the game to a draw with the wholesale removal of heavy pieces. Instead he chooses to create counterplay on the queenside.

15...♘xe5 16 ♘xe5 a5!

As well as preparing to prise open the a-file this introduces the possibility of ...♗a6 to hit d3 and e2.

17 ♖c2 a4 18 f3?!

No better is 18 ♖fc1?! in view of 18...f4! with the main idea 19 g4 ♗xe5 20 dxe5 ♘c5 21 ♕c3 d4 22 ♕c4 ♗xg2 23 ♔xg2 f3+ 24 exf3 ♕f7 and White is being cut to pieces. 18 f4!?, on the other hand, might improve, although White must be ready to find precise moves.

18...♗xe5 19 dxe5 ♘c5 20 ♕d4?

The queen is exposed here. After 20 ♕e3 axb3 21 axb3 ♕b5 22 ♗d4! White is still fighting for equality.

20...axb3 21 axb3 ♕b5 22 b4 ♖a4 23 ♗c3

White's pieces are now poorly placed.

23...♘b3 24 ♕h4 d4!

It gets worse for White.

25 ♗e1 ♗a8 26 ♕e7?!

This sacrifice does not help. 26 ♕f4 is not quite so terrible.

26...♕xe5 27 f4 ♕f6 28 ♕d7 ♗xg2?

28...♖a1! maintains the pressure and an extra pawn.

29 ♔xg2?!

29 ♕xa4 ♗xf1 30 ♔xf1 d3 31 exd3 ♘d4 32 ♖c7 is less clear.

29...♖aa8 30 ♖c6 ♖fd8 31 ♕xe6+ ♕xe6 32 ♖xe6 ♖a2

Despite his inaccuracy Black has succeeded in keeping White under pressure.

33 ♔g1 ♔f7 34 ♖e5 g6 35 ♗f2 ♘d2 36 ♖c1 ♖d7 37 ♖d1 d3?!

Black is slightly better and believes he sees a combination.

38 ♗xb6?

The losing move. 38 ♖e3! picks up the d-pawn or forces a draw, as 38...dxe2 39 ♖xe2 leaves Black in no less than two pins. After 39...b5 40 ♔g2 ♔f6! 41 ♖e5 ♖b7 42 ♖e2 ♖d7 43 ♖e5 I doubt anything can be achieved avoiding the draw.

38...♘c4!

Winning material.

39 ♖b5 ♖xe2

And soon there is no defence to ...♘b2!

40 ♗f2 d2? 0-1

White can limit his losses to an exchange with 41 ♖a5 but instead throws in the towel. It is not unusual even at this level to see numerous mistakes, showing that there is always a chance... Of course top players are far better than the rest of us at taking their chances when they arise.

Black plays ...♘g4!?

A less popular idea for Black than posting the knight on e4 is ...♘g4 to challenge an intruding knight on e5, the point being to lodge a pawn on g4 after ♘xg4. The following game is a good illustration of the attacking chances that can be achieved in this way, and Gelfand is alert to the dangers.

Gelfand-Nikolic
Sarajevo 1991

1 d4 f5 2 c4 ♘f6 3 g3 e6 4 ♗g2 d5 5

♘f3 c6 6 0-0 ♗d6 7 ♘e5 0-0 8 ♗f4

White's set-up is not typical. Nikolic finds a way to equalize without too much effort, although his position still requires accurate play.

8...♘g4!? 9 ♘xg4 ♗xf4 10 gxf4 fxg4 11 e3 ♕h4 12 ♕e1

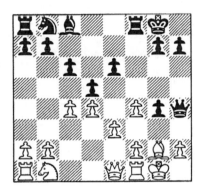

12...♖f6!

Forcing White to play f2-f3 at once, otherwise White would have time for ♘d2 to recapture with the knight. Black cannot allow this transfer to take place because the resulting structure and superior minor pieces favour White – hence the text.

13 f3 ♕xe1 14 ♖xe1 gxf3 15 ♗xf3 g5!

White is given no time to regroup.

16 ♘d2 gxf4 17 e4 ♘a6!

This active development of the knight does not disturb the c8-bishop.

18 exd5

18 a3 ♘c7 poses Black no problems.

18...cxd5 19 cxd5 ♘b4 20 ♔h1

No other move tests Black's position according to Gelfand and Kapengut.

20...♔f8!?

20...♘c2!? 21 ♖g1+ ♖g6! 22 ♖xg6+ hxg6 23 ♖g1 ♘xd4 24 ♖xg6+ ♔h7 also leads to an equal game.

21 dxe6 ♗xe6 22 ♗xb7 ♖d8!

The natural 22...♖b8 misplaces the rook after 23 ♗e4!.

23 ♘e4 ♖g6 24 ♘c5 ♗h3!

White has won a pawn but Black has ideas

such as ...♘c2, ...♖xd4 and perhaps even ...♗g2+ available, as well as a nice passed pawn.

25 ♗e4 ♖f6 26 a3 ♘d5 27 ♘b7!

Gelfand chooses to force a draw in view of 27 ♖g1 ♘e3! when Black rounds up the d-pawn. After this White has nothing to be proud of and the f-pawn looks dangerous.

27...♖d7 28 ♘c5 ♖d8 29 ♘b7 ♖d7 30 ♘c5 ♖d8 31 ♘b7 ½-½

In the following example the problem with the ...♘g4 idea becomes obvious – Black simply neglects the e4-square:

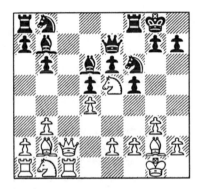

This is from Van Wely-Kveinys, Yerevan Ol 1996.

12...♘g4?

This is too optimistic. Black wants to challenge the e5-knight or have access to the f-file. This is based on White's previous move, 12 ♖c1. Unfortunately for Black the plan is not very good.

13 ♘xg4 fxg4 14 e4!

If White succeeds in pushing e4-e5 Black will be seriously short of breathing space, so the undesirable captures in the centre are forced.

14...dxe4 15 ♗xe4 ♗xe4 16 ♕xe4 ♘d7 17 ♕xg4

White nets a safe extra pawn.

17...♖f5 18 ♘c3 ♖af8 19 ♖f1 h5 20 ♕e2 ♖8f6 21 ♖ae1 ♖g6 22 ♕d3 ♕f7 23 ♘e4 ♗f8 24 f3

White has refuted Black's knight sortie and is now firmly in the driving seat.

24...♘f6 25 ♔h1 ♘d5 26 ♗c1 ♘b4 27 ♕e2 ♖a5

What good the rook is able to do out here is limited. Although Black does win back his pawn, other problems take over.

28 a3 ♘c6 29 ♕c4 ♕d7 30 ♖d1 ♗xa3 31 ♗xa3 ♖xa3 32 d5 exd5 33 ♖xd5 ♕e6 34 ♘g5 ♖xg5 35 ♖xg5 ♕xc4 36 bxc4 ♘d4 37 ♖xh5 ♖c3 38 ♖a1 a5 39 c5 bxc5 40 ♖xa5 c4 41 ♖hd5 ♖c1+ 42 ♔g2 ♖c2+ 43 ♔h3 ♘xf3 44 g4 c3 45 ♖a8+ 1-0

Black plays ...b7-b5

Sometimes Black tries to gain space on the queenside by advancing ...b7-b5 instead of nudging the b-pawn just one square. However, Kramnik has written that he has his doubts about the soundness of this more ambitious thrust. I am less sure. I understand what is behind Kramnik's opinion, namely the fact that when the pawn continues to b4 (leaving b5 in order to give the light-squared bishop more freedom) it is no better than on b6, and more susceptible to attack. This is in theory. I believe the stamp of approval from Short and Agdestein is enough for us mortals to test this different way of queenside development from time to time.

The following game is a typical illustration of the different positions Black should consider:

**Christiansen-Rodriguez
Saint John 1988**

1 d4 e6 2 c4 f5 3 g3 ♘f6 4 ♗g2 c6 5 ♘f3 d5 6 0-0 ♗d6 7 b3 ♕e7 8 ♗b2 0-0 9 ♘bd2 b5!?

Both 9...b6 and 9...♗d7 are normal.

10 ♘e5 a5 11 ♘df3

11 cxb5! is given by Christiansen as being slightly better for White. Often in openings like the Réti or the Meran the c6-square becomes Black's only – but potentially lethal – problem. I am sure that 11...cxb5 would have been answered by 12 ♖c1!, hoping to dominate.

11...♗a6 12 c5?!

A positional mistake, surrendering possible active play on the c-file and therefore facilitating Black's equalising task on the kingside.

12...♗c7 13 a3 ♖a7 14 ♗c1 ♘e4 15 h4!

White is already preparing the queenside fight.

15...♕e8?!

15...b4! provides the necessary counterplay.

16 b4!

Now the closed queenside and Black's development problems leave White in charge.

16...♗c8 17 ♗f4 a4?

Allowing the following exchange. The immediate 17...h6 and ...g7-g5 causes White more inconvenience.

18 ♘d3 h6 19 ♕c1 ♗d7 20 ♗xc7 ♖xc7 21 ♘fe5 ♕d8 22 ♘f4 ♗c8 23 h5 ♘g5 24 ♘fg6 ♖e8 25 f4 ♘e4? 26 g4 ♘d7 27 ♗xe4 dxe4 28 e3 fxg4 29 ♖a2 ♘f6 30 ♖h2 ♕d5 31 ♕d1 ♖d8 32 ♖h4 ♔h7 33 ♕c2 ♔g8 34 ♖f2 ♖e8 35 ♖g2 ♖a7 36 ♔h2 ♗d7 37 ♕f2 ♗c8 38 ♕g3 ♔h7 39 ♔g1 ♔g8 40 ♖xg4!

White has everything prepared and finishes off in style.

40...♘xg4

White also wins after 40...♘xh5 41 ♕h4 ♘f6 42 ♕xf6!! gxf6 43 ♘e7+ ♔f8 44 ♘xd5.

41 ♘xg4 ♕d8

41...♔h7 42 ♘f6+ gxf6 43 ♘f8+ ♖xf8 44 ♕g6+ ♔h8 45 ♕xh6+ mates.

42 ♘xh6+ ♔h7 43 ♘e5 ♕f6 44 ♕g6+! ♕xg6 45 hxg6+ ♔h8 46 ♘hf7+ 1-0

In the next game Black's strategy is more successful.

This is from Kavalek-Ljubojevic, Bugojno 1982.

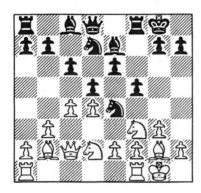

10...a5 11 ♖ad1 b5

With the knight still on f3 Black has no reason to worry about the c6-square or to fear c4xb5, although this capture is probably White's most appropriate continuation since he does not now cause Black any problems.

12 c5 ♘xd2 13 ♖xd2 b4 14 ♘e1 ♗f6 15 ♘d3 ♕e7 16 f3 ♗a6 17 ♖e1 e5! 18 dxe5 ♘xe5 19 ♘xe5 ♗xe5 20 ♗xe5 ♕xe5 21 e3 f4!

Exploiting the pin on the e-file and forcing further exchanges.

22 ♕b2 ♕xb2 23 ♖xb2 fxe3 24 ♖xe3 ♖fe8 25 ♖xe8+ ♖xe8 26 ♔f2 ♔f7 27 f4 ♔f6 28 h4 ♗b5 29 ♗f3 ♖a8 30 a4 bxa3 31 ♖a2 a4 32 ♖xa3 axb3 33 ♖xb3 ♖a5 34 ♔e3 ♔e6 35 ♗g4+ ♔e7 36 ♗f5 h6 37 g4 ♖a4 38 ♖b2 ♖a3+ 39 ♔d4 ♔f6 40 ♗b1 ♖a4+ 41 ♔e3 ♖a3+ 42 ♔d4 ♖a4+ ½-½

In the final two games of this chapter we see what happens when White takes on b5. In the first game White is successful in achieving an advantage, while in the second Black plays energetically and creates sufficient counterplay.

Ruban-Meister
Balassagyarmat 1990

1 d4 e6 2 c4 f5 3 g3 ♘f6 4 ♗g2 c6 5 ♘f3 d5 6 0-0 ♗d6 7 b3 ♕e7 8 ♘e5

♘bd7 9 ♗b2 0-0 10 ♘d2 a5 11 ♘df3 ♘e4 12 ♕c2 ♘xe5 13 ♘xe5 ♗xe5 14 dxe5 b5 15 f3 ♘g5 16 cxb5!

Opening the c-file is the logical way to play, not denying the dark-squared bishop a future.

16...cxb5 17 ♖fc1 ♗d7 18 ♕c5!

White is pressing for an ending where he has more territory, the better pieces and excellent prospects on the queenside. Notice that the text is the beginning of a campaign executed exclusively on the dark squares.

18...♕e8 19 ♕e3 ♕d8 20 ♖c2 a4?

Avoiding weak pawns on dark squares but ultimately sealing Black's fate.

21 b4 ♖c8 22 ♖xc8 ♗xc8 23 ♖c1 ♗d7 24 ♕a7 h6 25 ♖c7 ♖f7 26 ♗d4 ♗c6 27 ♖xf7 ♘xf7 28 ♔f2 ♕d7

Black now has nothing better than going for the exchange he avoided earlier.

29 ♕c5 ♘d8 30 h3 ♔f7 31 g4 fxg4 32 hxg4 ♕e7 33 ♕xe7+ ♔xe7 34 ♗c5+ ♔e8 35 f4 g6 36 e3 ♘b7 37 ♗b6 ♔f7 38 ♗f3 ♔e7 39 a3 ♘d8 40 ♗e2 1-0

Black lost on time but his position is very difficult. White will play 41 ♗d3 and force the black bishop to e8. Then perhaps 42 e4!? and an invasion by the White king from f2-c5. This can of course also happen after ♔e1-d2-c3-d4, and what should Black do? His problem is that none of his pieces is playing in the game.

This is Zak-Vaiser, Fuerteventura 1992.

From the diagram position White plays less well than his GM opponent. Natural here is something like 9 ♘d2 (observing e5 from a distance). However the game continued as follows:

9 ♗c1?

This is just too odd. Now the knight looks misplaced on h3.

9...b5!?

Black exploits his sudden lead in development – compared to normal lines – by claiming space on the queenside.

10 cxb5

In light of what happens 10 c5 might be better.

10...cxb5 11 ♘f4 ♕b6 12 ♘c3 ♔h8 13 ♕b3?

The queen is awkwardly placed here, so the prudent 13 ♖d1 is preferable.

13...♗d7 14 ♗e3 ♘a6 15 ♘d3 ♘g4 16 ♗f4

Back again!

16...b4

Not surprisingly after White's rather aimless treatment of the opening this initiation of tactics leads to a wonderful game for Black. The rest of the game, albeit not too interesting, soon goes downhill for White:

17 ♘a4 ♕xd4 18 h3 g5 19 ♗d2 ♘h6 20 ♖ac1 f4 21 e3 ♗xa4 22 exd4 ♗xb3 23 axb3 ♖ac8 24 ♖a1 ♘b8 25 gxf4 ♘f5 26 ♗e3 ♘c6 27 ♖fc1 gxf4 28 ♘xf4 ♘cxd4 29 ♖xc8 ♖xc8 30 ♖xa7 ♗d6 31 ♖d7 ♗xf4 0-1

CHAPTER ONE

White Plays 7 b3

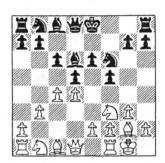

1 d4 f5 2 g3 ♘f6 3 ♗g2 e6 4 c4 c6 5 ♘f3 d5 6 0-0 ♗d6 7 b3

This is one of the two main options for White. The immediate threat is the positionally desirable 8 ♗a3. Black can prevent this idea (with 7...♕e7), after which White has alternative possibilities.

We shall first examine what happens when White insists on the bishop exchange, strategies selected in Games 1-5. The most common approach is to use b2-b3 as a simple developing move and place the bishop on b2, if not necessarily immediately. Games 6-7 feature the plan of ♗b2, ♘e5, ♘d2 and ♖c1 to exert pressure on Black's queenside (particularly c6), while in Game 8 White dispenses with ♗b2 in order to quickly settle his knights on d3 and f3. However, White's most popular and testing treatment begins with 8 ♘e5, to which Black replies with the possibly premature 8...b6 in Games 9-11. The rest of the games (12-17) in this chapter see Black play the more flexible 8...0-0.

Game 1
Arbakov-Korsunsky
Katowice 1991

1 d4 f5 2 c4 ♘f6 3 g3 e6 4 ♗g2 c6 5 ♘f3 d5 6 0-0 ♗d6 7 b3 ♕e7!

This is the natural move. The queen is better on e7 than d8 anyway, and the manoeuvre ...♕d8-e8-h5 is not too fashionable today thanks to White's knight manoeuvres involving d3 and f4. The alternative 7...0-0?! simply allows White to carry out his plan: 8 ♗a3 ♗xa3 9 ♘xa3 ♕e7 (for 9...♕e8 see Petrosian-Korchnoi in the Introduction) 10 ♕c1 ♘bd7 11 ♕b2 ♘e4 12 ♘c2 g5!? 13 ♘ce1 g4 14 ♘e5! ♘xe5 15 dxe5 ♗d7 (15...h5 16 ♘d3 h4 17 f3! ♘g5 18 gxh4 ♘h3+ 19 ♗xh3 gxh3 20 e3 ♕xh4 21 ♕f2 and White has a distinct plus) 16 ♘d3 c5!? 17 f3 gxf3 18 exf3 ♘g5 19 h4 ♘f7 was played in Chekhov-Knaak, Berlin 1989. Now 20 cxd5 exd5 21 ♖fe1 ♗e6 22 ♘f4 would have guaranteed White a healthy advantage.

8 ♗f4!?

This move is less logical than 7 ♗f4. Although we could argue that Black can no longer retreat to e7, this idea is a little dubious anyway, and Black should always trade bishops when it gives White a potentially weak pawn on f4, rather than waste time hiding. The exchange of bishops might be important but it is not crucial! There are two main differences between the text and 7 ♗f4. First, Black's queen has gained almost a free tempo as b2-b3 does little to help White. Secondly, White's dark squares on the queenside have been weakened slightly. This is highlighted chiefly in the form of the undefended knight on c3, but even in the case of ♘bd2 Black might well be given the chance to threaten to infiltrate with ...♘e4-c3. Another vulnerable point is b4, because by defending the square with a2-a3 White removes protection from the b3-pawn. These factors are not of major importance, but enough, in my opinion, to make this system harmless.

8...♗xf4 9 gxf4 0-0 10 ♘bd2

Sensible development – White remains in contact with e5. 10 ♘c3 has also been played, when 10...♘bd7 11 e3 ♔h8 12 ♘e2 b6 13 ♕c2 ♗b7 is fine for Black, e.g. 14 ♘e5 ♖ac8 15 ♖fd1 c5 etc.

10...♗d7

Developing the knight first is equally natural. 10...♘bd7!? 11 e3 ♘e4 12 ♘e5 ♘xe5 13 fxe5 ♗d7 14 ♘xe4 fxe4 15 f3 exf3 16 ♖xf3 ♖xf3 17 ♕xf3 ♗e8 18 ♖f1 ♗g6 19 ♗h3 ♗d3! 20 ♖c1 ♖f8 was equal in Grunberg-Goloshchapov, Cairo 2000.

11 e3!

Another logical choice, simply strengthening the pawn structure. 11 ♕c2 ♗e8 12 cxd5 cxd5 13 ♘e5 ♘c6 14 e3 ♖c8 15 ♕b2 ♗h5 16 f3 ♘d7 17 ♘xc6 ♖xc6 18 ♖ac1 ♘b8 19 ♖fe1 h6 20 ♘f1 ♖fc8 21 ♖xc6 ♖xc6 22 ♖c1 ♗e8 was good enough for equality in Bukic-Botvinnik, Belgrade 1969.

11...♗e8 12 ♕c2 ♘e4 13 ♘e5

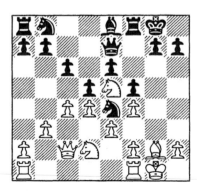

13...♘xd2?!

Releasing the tension in the centre for no particular reason. Black would do better with 13...♘d7!, with an approximately even game.

14 ♕xd2 ♘d7 15 ♘d3!

White has a small plus. Black must be careful as the traditional ...♘f6-e4 could leave him worse after ♗xe4 and ♘e5, although in parting with his bishop White should keep an eye out for counterplay involving ...♗h5-f3.

15...♖f6?!

This move also seems a little strange because the rook is poorly placed after the exchange of queens.

16 ♕b4!

Forcing a trade that instantly crushes Black's dreams of a kingside attack.

16...♕xb4 17 ♘xb4 dxc4?!

The start of a somewhat dubious plan.

18 bxc4 c5 19 ♘d3 ♖c8 20 d5 ♘b6 21 dxe6 ♗c6 22 ♗xc6 ♖xc6 23 e7 ♖g6+ 24 ♔h1 ♖ge6 25 ♘e5 ♖c8 26 ♖fd1 ♖xe7 27 a4!

Black is under severe pressure here. White has control over the d-file, targets on the queenside and an all-seeing knight enthroned on e5.

27...g6 28 a5 ♘a8 29 h4 ♘c7 30 h5 ♘e6 31 ♖d6 ♖d8 32 ♖d5 g5 33 ♖g1 h6 34 fxg5 ♖xd5 35 cxd5 ♘xg5 36 f4 1-0

Game 2
Palatnik-Dolmatov
Belgrade 1988

1 d4 e6 2 c4 f5 3 g3 ♘f6 4 ♗g2 c6 5 ♘f3 d5 6 0-0 ♗d6 7 b3 ♕e7 8 c5?!

There is some logic behind this move. The reasoning is that Black has numerous pawns on light squares, so in anticipation of the exchange of dark-squared bishops White can further improve his lot by fixing yet another enemy pawn on a light square. Unfortunately for White this argument fails to take into account the simple plan of ...b7-b6, challenging the centre and bringing the other bishop to life.

8...♗c7 9 ♗f4 b6!?

Taking on f4 is fine but Black prefers to delay the exchange, presenting White with more to think about.

10 ♕c2

10 ♗xc7 ♕xc7 11 ♕c2 bxc5 gives Black comfortable control over e5.

10...♗xf4 11 gxf4 ♘e4

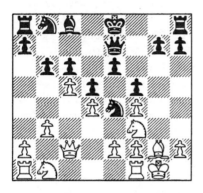

12 ♘e5?!

Instigating tactics that do not work out well for White. Better is the less stubborn 12 cxb6 axb6 13 ♘c3 with perhaps an edge to Black. Not to be recommended is 12 b4?!, when 12...a5! 13 ♘e5 axb4 14 cxb6 ♕b7 15 ♗xe4 fxe4 16 ♕c5 ♖a6 17 ♕xb4 ♖xb6 leads to a promising position for Black, as White has no development to speak of and Black has a potentially strong bishop (helped by the e4-pawn).

12...bxc5 13 f3 ♘f6 14 ♕xc5!

Forced. 14 dxc5 ♘fd7 15 ♖c1 ♘xe5 16 fxe5 f4! gives Black a large plus despite having developed only his queen! The key is Black's structural superiority. White has no easily accessible outpost for his knight – only d4 looks good, but how to get there? Then there is the e5-pawn – Black will play ...♘d7, ...0-0 and perhaps ...♖f5 and/or ...♕g5. I believe most GMs would consider that Black has a sizeable positional lead.

14...♕xc5 15 dxc5 ♘fd7 16 ♘d3

It would be logical here to consider the dark squares with 16 e3, intending 16...♘xe5

(16...♖g8!? might be stronger) 17 fxe5 ♘d7 18 f4! and the c5-pawn is safe as 18...♘xc5?! 19 ♖c1 ♘e4 20 ♗xe4 fxe4 21 ♖xc6 ♗d7 is only very slightly preferable for Black. Preparing to activate the rook with 18...g5! looks good, when 19 ♘d2 sends the knight on its way to d4.

16...♗a6 17 ♖c1 ♘f8!

This powerful manoeuvre allows both knights to enter the game, at the same time planning to hunt down the f4-pawn. From here Black remains in charge.

18 ♔f2 ♗xd3 19 exd3 ♘g6 20 ♔e3 d4+!

Cleverly denying White time to improve with 21 d4!.

21 ♔xd4 ♘xf4 22 ♗f1 ♘d7 23 ♔e3 e5 24 ♘d2 ♔e7

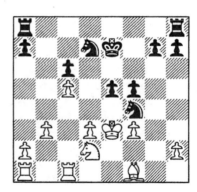

25 d4 ♘d5+ 26 ♔f2 exd4 27 ♖c4 ♘e3 28 ♖e1 ♔d8 29 ♖a4 ♔c7 30 ♖c1 ♘xf1 31 ♔xf1 d3 32 ♖d4 ♘e5 33 f4 ♘g4 34 h3 ♘e3+ 35 ♔f2 ♘d5 36 ♖cc4 h6 37 ♘f3 ♖he8 38 ♖xd3 ♖e4 39 ♘e5 g5 0-1

Game 3
I.Sokolov-Salov
New York 1996

---

1 d4 f5 2 g3 ♘f6 3 ♗g2 e6 4 ♘f3 d5 5 0-0 ♗d6 6 c4 c6 7 b3 ♕e7 8 a4

White practically insists on removing Black's good bishop. Remember also that the advance of the white a-pawn in itself can reap positional rewards, as was illustrated in the Introduction. However, in this particular line White has no chance to fight for an advantage owing to Black's no-nonsense reply.

8...a5!

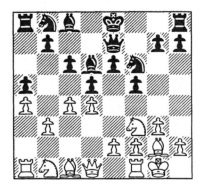

A completely natural response. Black has delayed this thrust in some games, continuing 8...0-0 9 ♗a3 ♗xa3 10 ♘xa3 a5!, but this allows the strange 9 a5!?. The insertion of the moves 8 a4 a5! affords Black several advantages. He underlines the weakness of the dark squares around White's queenside, makes it difficult for White to generate a pawn-storm and gains a very useful square on b4 for his knight.

9 ♗a3 ♗xa3 10 ♘xa3 0-0 11 ♘c2!

This is the most logical move. The knight heads for d3 via e1. Other options are:

11 ♕c2 ♘a6 12 ♘e5 ♘b4 13 ♕b2 ♘d7 14 ♘d3 b6 15 ♘c2 ♘xc2 16 ♕xc2 ♗a6 17 ♖fc1 ♖ac8 18 ♕d2 ♕f6 and, allegedly, White is slightly better, Novikov-Dreev, Manila 1992.

11 ♘e5 ♘bd7 12 ♘d3? (this seems ridiculous as the knight on a3 now has to go to f3 if White is to achieve the desired set-up with knights on f3 and d3; 12 ♘c2 is normal) 12...b6 13 cxd5?! exd5 14 ♕c2 ♗b7 15 ♘b1 ♖ae8 16 e3 ♘e4 17 ♘d2 (finally heading for f3, but it took a long time!) 17...c5 18 dxc5 bxc5 19 ♖ac1 ♖c8 and Black is better, Rajna-Dolmatov, Polanica Zdroj 1987.

11...♖d8?!

I fail to see how this move is supposed to improve Black's position. Undoubtedly Salov had some kind of idea with this move, but it still seems to be inferior to natural development with 11...b6 12 ♘ce1 ♗b7 13 ♘d3 ♘a6, when 14 e3 ♘b4 15 ♘fe5 c5 16 ♖c1 ♖ac8 was okay for Black in Tukmakov-Tseshkovsky, Sverdlovsk 1987, while 14 ♕c1 c5 15 ♕b2 ♘e4 16 ♘fe5 ♖fd8 17 e3 ♖ac8 18 ♖fd1 ♘b4 left Black no worse in Gligoric-Tukmakov, Palma de Mallorca 1989.

12 ♕c1 b6 13 ♘ce1 ♘bd7 14 ♘d3 ♗a6 15 ♘fe5 ♘xe5 16 ♘xe5 ♖ac8 17 ♕e3 ♘d7 18 ♖fc1 ♘xe5 19 ♕xe5 ♕f6!?

Salov is trying hard for the endgame – a discipline in which he is an expert – no doubt feeling confident about his ability to defend this slightly worse position.

20 ♕xf6 gxf6 21 c5

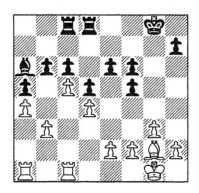

White has minimal pressure.

21...♖b8 22 e3 ♖dc8 23 ♖a3 ♗e2 24 f3 bxc5 25 ♔f2 ♗d3 26 ♖xc5 ♖b6 27 ♖xa5 ♖cb8 28 ♖c5 ♖xb3 29 ♖xb3 ♖xb3 30 g4 fxg4 31 fxg4 ♖b6 32 a5 ♖b2+ 33 ♔g3 ♗b5 34 e4 ♔g7 35 exd5 exd5 36 a6 ♖b3+ 37 ♔h4 ♗xa6 38 ♖xc6 ♗c4 39 g5 ♖b2 40 gxf6+ ♔g6 41 ♗f3 ♖xh2+ 42 ♔g3 ♖a2 43 ♗g4 ♗b5 44 ♖b6 ♗e8 45 ♔f4 ♖f2+ 46 ♔e3 ♖xf6! 47 ♗h5+ ♔xh5 48 ♖xf6 ♗g6 49 ♖d6 ♗e4 50 ♔f4 ♗h1 51 ♖f6 ♗e4 52 ♖e6 ♗h1 53 ♖e1 ♗e4 54 ♖g1 h6 55 ♖g7 ♔h4 56 ♖e7 h5 57 ♖e5 ♗g2 58 ♖g5 ♗e4 59 ♖g3 ♗h1 60 ♖e3 ♗g2 61 ♖e1 ♔h3 62 ♖e3+ ♔h4 63

Ia3 ♗e4 64 Ig3 ♗h1 65 Ig1 ♗e4 66
Ie1 ♗g2 67 Ie3 ♗h1 68 Ig3 ½-½

Game 4
Cifuentes Parada-Ulibin
Benasque 1996

**1 d4 e6 2 ♘f3 f5 3 g3 ♘f6 4 ♗g2 d5 5
c4 c6 6 0-0 ♗d6 7 b3 ♕e7 8 ♕c2**

This is played with the intention of exchanging on d5 and then trying to undermine Black's development pattern. Although resembling the 8 ♘e5! idea it merely wastes a move with the queen, a factor Black can exploit with accurate play.

8...0-0 9 ♘e5

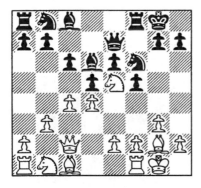

9...b6?!

This is not the best and permits White to demonstrate his idea. The correct mode of development is 9...♗d7!, featured in the game Cifuentes Parada-Nikolic in the Introduction. 9...♘bd7 10 ♗b2 ♘e4 11 e3 has also been played in this position. Then 11...g5 12 f3 ♘ef6 13 ♘d2 ♕g7 14 cxd5 cxd5 15 Iac1 gave White a small plus in Langeweg-Perez Garcia, Holland 1996. White also kept an edge in Shipov-Dyachkov, Maikop 1998, which continued 11...♘xe5 12 dxe5 ♗c5 13 ♘c3! (heading for f4!) 13...a5 14 ♘e2 b6 15 Ifd1 ♗b7 16 ♘f4.

10 cxd cxd5 11 ♘c4! ♘c6

11...♕c7 12 ♕b2 ♗b7 13 ♘xd6 ♕xd6 14 ♗f4 is also better for White.

12 ♘xd6 ♕xd6 13 ♕c3!

Taking control of the dark squares and forcing Black to lose time. The hasty 13 ♗a3 ♘b4 14 ♕d2 a5 15 ♘c3 ♗a6 is hardly any worse for Black.

13...a5 14 ♗f4 ♕d7 15 Ic1 ♗b7 16 ♘d2 ♘e4 17 ♕b2

17...♘xd2 18 ♕xd2 Iac8 19 Ic3 ♘b4 20 Iac1 Ixc3 21 Ixc3 Ic8 22 a3 Ixc3 23 ♕xc3 ♕c6 24 ♕xc6 ♘xc6 25 e3 ♗a6 26 ♗f3!

Protecting the b-pawn. 26 ♗c7 b5 27 ♗f1 b4! is only a draw!

26...♗d3 27 ♗d1 b5 28 f3 ♔f7 29 ♔f2?!

29 h4! is stronger. The text allows Black to make some breathing space on the kingside.

29...♔e7 30 ♗c7 g5! 31 ♔e1 b4 32 a4 h5 33 ♔d2 ♗f1

34 g4!

Instead 34 h4 g4 35 fxg4 hxg4! 36 h5 ♔f6 37 h6 ♔g6 38 ♗f4 ♗a6 and Black easily holds.

34...♔d7 35 ♗b6 hxg4 36 fxg4 ♗h3 37 gxf5 ♗xf5 38 ♗e2 ♔c8 39 ♗c5?!

39 ♗b5! ♔b7 40 ♗c5 is more accurate.

39...♔c7 40 ♗f8 e5?

40...♘d8! 41 ♗g7 ♘b7 42 ♗e5+ ♘d6 43 ♗b5 g4 draws as 44 ♔e2 is met with 44...♗c2!, when Black is even better!

41 ♗g7 ♔d6 42 ♗b5 g4 43 ♗f6 ♗e4 44 ♗xc6! ♔xc6 45 ♗d8 1-0.

For a strong endgame player like Cifuentes the win is just a matter of time. The annotations for this game are based on those by Cifuentes Parada in Chess Informator.

Game 5
Gabriel-Kindermann
Bundesliga 1996

---

1 d4 e6 2 ♘f3 f5 3 g3 ♘f6 4 ♗g2 d5 5 0-0 ♗d6 6 c4 c6 7 b3 ♕e7 8 ♗b2 b6 9 ♕c1?!

This idea is not convincing. White practically forces the exchange of bishops without playing a2-a4 or ♗f4 and thus avoids weakening his pawn structure. However there is a downside to this plan in that c1 is not a good square for the queen, and the bishop has already moved, so the loss of time involved leaves Black free to find counterplay.

9...♗b7 10 ♗a3 ♘bd7 11 ♗xd6 ♕xd6

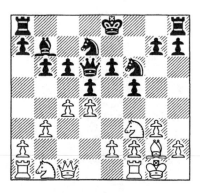

12 ♘c3

A new if unimpressive move. The knight is not going anywhere decent from c3 and there is no apparent plan in sight. Consequently Black, untroubled, is fine. Preferable and more consistent is 12 ♕a3 ♕xa3 13 ♘xa3, although after 13...♔e7! (by now the king is safe in the centre) 14 ♖ac1 ♘e4 15 ♖fd1 ♖hc8 16 ♘e1 c5 Black had equalized in Alburt-Short, Subotica 1987.

12...0-0 13 ♕b2

From here on White's play goes a little downhill.

13...♗a6

13...f4!? is another approach.

14 cxd5 cxd5 15 ♖fc1 ♖ac8 16 ♖c2

Black seems to benefit most from this. The simple 16 e3 maintains equality.

16...♖c7 17 ♖ac1 ♖fc8 18 b4 ♘e4! 19 ♘xe4 dxe4 20 ♖xc7 ♖xc7 21 ♖xc7 ♕xc7

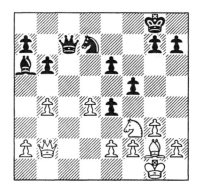

22 ♘e1?

Too passive. One should test all other options before deciding on such a move. Instead the fighting 22 ♘d2! fights for c4, and 22...♗xe2 23 ♘xe4 ♕c4 24 ♘d6 ♕d3 is only even.

22...♘f6 23 b5 ♗b7 24 ♘c2 ♘d5 25 ♘b4?

25 ♕b3 ♕c3 26 e3 is terribly uncomfortable but White might still be okay.

25...♕c3!

Winning a pawn and the game.

26 ♕xc3 ♘xc3 27 e3 ♘xb5 28 ♗f1 ♘c3
0-1

Game 6
Sturua-Vaiser
Erevan Open 1996

**1 d4 e6 2 c4 f5 3 g3 ♘f6 4 ♗g2 d5 5
♘f3 c6 6 0-0 ♗d6 7 b3 ♕e7 8 ♗b2**

I find it hard to believe that this quiet developing move should be a problem for Black.

8...b6!

Since this is possible now, without all kind of tricks, Black should take advantage of it and quietly get on with his development.

9 ♘bd2

It is also possible to play 9 ♘e5 and reach the same position after 11 moves, below. This was basically the way White played the Stonewall in the 1980s, as Black had not yet discovered his full range of resources.

9...♗b7 10 ♘e5 0-0 11 ♖c1!

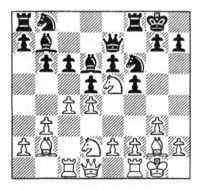

This move is designed to disturb Black's queenside development. The idea is that after 11...♘bd7 12 cxd5 Black cannot recapture with the e-pawn as c6 is then hanging. Also – of course – the rook is nicely placed on the c-file. Fortunately for Black he has other ways to develop than the strictly dogmatic.

11...a5!

The safest line, this is logical now that White has left the a-file. Black is trying to create counterplay with ...a5-a4 and supports the knight's development to a6. 11...c5!? has also been tried and is considered in the next game, but not good is 11...♘bd7? 12 cxd5 cxd5 13 ♘dc4! with a clear advantage to White, as in Tukmakov-Dolmatov in the Introduction.

12 e3

12 a4 transposes to Ibragimov-Shabalov in the Introduction. White might have a slight advantage in that line but it is nothing special.

12...♘a6 13 ♕e2 a4!?

The sharpest opportunity available to Black. The options are more solid but less interesting:

13...♘c7 14 ♖fd1 ♗xe5!? is Petursson-Tukmakov in the Introduction.

13...♗xe5 14 dxe5 ♘d7 15 ♖fd1 ♘ac5 16 ♘f3 ♖ac8 17 ♗a3 ♖fe8 18 ♕b2 g5 19 ♘e1 g4 20 ♗xc5 ♘xc5 21 ♘d3 ♘xd3 22 ♖xd3 b5 was equal in Petursson-Dolmatov, Akureyri 1988, but 13...♖ac8 14 ♖fd1 c5 15 cxd5 exd5 16 ♕b5! gave White pressure on the queenside in Tukmakov-Haba, Haifa 1989.

14 bxa4

Forced as 14 cxd5 meets with the immediate 14...a3! with the tactical point 15 dxc6? axb2 16 cxb7 bxc1N!! 17 ♖xc1 ♖a7 18 ♘c6 ♕xb7 19 ♘xa7 ♕xa7 20 ♖c6 ♖d8 21 ♘c4, and White should not have enough compensation for the piece.

14...♗xe5 15 dxe5 ♘d7

Not good is 15...♘e4?! 16 ♘b3 ♘ac5 17 f3 ♘g5 18 ♗a3 and c5 comes under heavy fire.

16 a5!

White is trying to close the a-file again. This pawn could never survive anyway, and the a2-pawn would soon become weak after a capture on a4.

16...♘ac5!

Using the open file in a tactical way to avoid closing it again.

17 ♘b3 ♗a6

Perhaps not the best option. 17...♘xb3!?

18 axb3 ♖xa5 is not unpleasant for Black.
18 ♖fd1

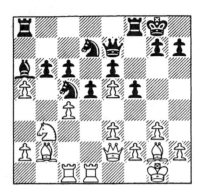

18...♗xc4?!

18...dxc4! 19 ♘xc5 ♘xc5 20 ♗a3 ♗b5! 21 ♗b4! bxa5 22 ♗a3 ♕a7 23 ♕d2! gives White compensation for his pawn, but probably no more.

19 ♖xc4 dxc4 20 ♕xc4 ♘xb3 21 axb3 ♖xa5?

21...♖ad8! 22 ♖a1! bxa5 23 ♗xc6 is better for White despite the exchange deficit. However the game continuation is even worse for Black.

22 ♕xc6 ♘b8 23 ♕xb6 ♖a6 24 ♕b5 ♕c7?

24...♖d8 25 ♖c1 ♕d7 looks awful but is nonetheless necessary.

25 ♖c1! ♖b6 26 ♕a4 ♕d7 27 ♗d4 ♕xa4 28 bxa4 ♖a6 29 ♖c4 ♖f7 30 ♔f1 g5 31 ♔e2 ♔g7 32 ♔d3 ♘d7 33 ♗b7 ♖a5 34 ♗c6 ♔g6 35 ♗b5 ♖a8 36 ♔c3 ♖b8 37 ♖c6 ♖e7 38 ♔b4 ♔f7 39 a5

There is no stopping this pawn. White's bishops and rook dominate and Black can only wait for the end.

39...♖a8 40 ♖d6 ♘b8 41 ♗c4 g4 42 ♔b5 h5 43 ♗b6 ♘d7 44 ♗d4 ♖b8+?! 45 ♔a4 ♘f8 46 a6 ♖c7 47 ♗b3 ♖a8 48 ♔a5 ♖b8 49 ♗a4 ♘g6 50 ♖d7+ ♖xd7 51 ♗xd7 ♘e7 52 a7 ♖d8 53 ♗b5 ♖a8 54 ♔a6 ♖d8 55 ♔b7 ♘d5 56 ♗a4 ♘b4 57 a8♕ ♖xa8 58 ♔xa8 ♘d3 59 e4 f4 60 ♗b5 ♘e1 61 ♗e2 1-0

Game 7
Razuvaev-Klinger
Palma de Mallorca 1989

1 d4 e6 2 c4 f5 3 ♘f3 ♘f6 4 g3 d5 5 ♗g2 c6 6 0-0 ♗d6 7 b3 ♕e7 8 ♗b2 b6 9 ♘e5 ♗b7 10 ♘d2 0-0 11 ♖c1 c5!?

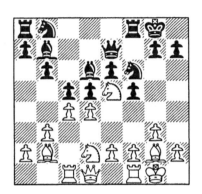

A sharp idea that still needs to be fully tested before anything conclusive can be said about it. Since the outcome of this game was positive I see no reason why it should not be tried again at this level. The diagram position is similar to those that arise after 1 d4 ♘f6 2 c4 e6 3 ♘f3 b6 4 g3 ♗a6 5 ♘bd2 – the Queen's Indian Defence. Of course the difference is the f-pawn which, in the QID, stays on f7. But – surprise, surprise – when Black plays ...♘e4 he tends to support his knight with ...f7-f5!

12 e3 ♘a6 13 ♕e2 ♖ac8 14 ♘df3 ♘b4

Black is fully developed and therefore seeks to improve the knight.

15 dxc5

White chooses to change the structure to increase the scope of his bishop. This in turn gives Black tactical options with a later ...d5-d4.

15...bxc5 16 a3 ♘c6?!

Klinger suggests the improvement 16...♘a6! with unclear play. It looks as if Black has lost two tempi but it is not that simple: the b3-pawn is a weakness.

17 ♘xc6 ♖xc6 18 ♘e5?

A grave error which invites dangerous tactics. Klinger gives 18 ♗xf6! ♕xf6 19 cxd5 exd5 20 ♖fd1 and White hits the hanging pawns.

18...♖b6 19 ♕c2 d4! 20 exd4 ♗xg2 21 ♔xg2 ♕b7+ 22 ♔g1 ♖xb3 23 ♗a1?!

23 ♘d3 offers White better chances to defend. Now his days are numbered.

23...♗xe5!

By fixing the pawn on e5 Black makes the cornered bishop look quite ridiculous.

24 dxe5 ♘e4

Suddenly the g5-square beckons.

25 h4 ♖d8

Klinger's 25...f4!? is also strong.

26 ♖cd1?

Allowing a mating attack, although the forced 26 ♖b1 ♖xb1 27 ♖xb1 ♕d7 is probably winning for Black.

26...♖xd1 27 ♖xd1

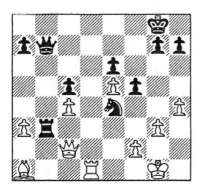

27...♘xg3!! 28 ♔h2

28 fxg3 ♖xg3+ 29 ♔h2 ♕f3 followed by ...♖h3+.

28...♕f3 29 ♕d2 ♘f1+!! 0-1

Game 8
Kazhgaleyev-Del Rio Angelis
Ubeda 1999

---

1 d4 e6 2 c4 f5 3 g3 ♘f6 4 ♗g2 c6 5 ♘f3 d5 6 b3 ♗d6 7 0-0 ♕e7 8 ♘bd2

This move does not look very worrying

for Black. It is related to 8 ♗b2 lines, except in this system White postpones the matter of the bishop's posting until later. In fact here we see White opt for ♗f4 to challenge its counterpart on d6, and in some respects this is a logical strategy. White puts his knights on d3 and f3 and exchanges bishops. That should be enough to afford him some kind of an advantage, right? No! It is true that the knights are best placed at d3 and f3, and it is true that the exchange generally suits White. Yet there are other principals that should be borne in mind. One such is, simply, development. While White's knights jump around the board Black completes his development, not being too concerned with the eventual departure of his bishop.

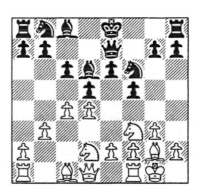

8...b6!

This avoids tricks with ♘dc4 by developing the bishop quickly.

9 ♘e5 ♗b7 10 ♘df3 ♘e4 11 ♘d3 ♘d7 12 ♗f4

By now this exchange lacks punch because Black's other pieces are doing nicely. White has no advantage.

12...0-0 13 ♗xd6 ♕xd6 14 ♖c1 ♖ac8 15 ♘fe5 ♘xe5 16 ♘xe5?!

Better is 16 dxe5 with equality.

16...c5!

With this thematic challenge to the centre Black takes over the initiative, immediately inducing White to find a faulty plan and consequently lose a pawn in a combination.

17 f3?

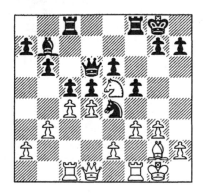

17...cxd4! 18 ♕xd4 dxc4! 19 ♕xd6 ♘xd6 20 ♖fd1

The correct continuation is 20 ♘xc4 ♘xc4 21 ♖xc4 ♖xc4 22 bxc4 when White counters 22...♖c8 with the uncompromising 23 ♖d1!, though the calm 23...♖c7! (intending ...♔f7-e7 and maybe also ...♗a6) remains excellent for Black.

20...cxb3!

Wins a pawn and the game.

21 ♖xc8 ♖xc8 22 axb3 ♗d5 23 g4 f4 24 g5 ♘f7 25 ♘d3 ♗xb3 26 ♖b1 ♗c4 27 ♘xf4 ♘xg5 28 h4 e5 29 ♘h5 ♘e6 30 ♗h3 ♖c6 31 ♔f2 ♘f4 32 ♘xf4 exf4 33 ♖d1 ♗e6 34 ♗xe6+ ♖xe6 35 ♖d7 a5 36 ♖a7 ♔f8 37 h5 ♖e7 38 ♖a6 ♖e6 39 ♖a7 h6 40 ♔e1 ♖d6 41 ♔f2 ♖d5 42 ♖a6 ♖b5 43 ♔g2 ♔f7 44 ♔h3 ♖b4 45 ♔g4 ♔f6 46 ♖a8 g6 47 ♖f8+ ♔g7 48 ♖a8 a4 49 ♖c8 gxh5+ 50 ♔f5 ♖b5+ 0-1

Game 9
Goldin-Glek
USSR 1988

---

1 d4 e6 2 c4 f5 3 g3 ♘f6 4 ♗g2 c6 5 ♘f3 d5 6 0-0 ♗d6 7 b3 ♕e7 8 ♘e5!

This is the most dangerous way of challenging Black's set-up. The knight advance is directed against natural development with ...b7-b6, unleashing the bishop on g2.

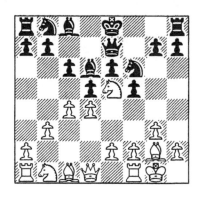

8...b6

It might be better to challenge the knight on e5 directly. This can be done with 8...♘bd7!?, which has been played in only a few games and therefore is difficult to assess. Anyway, White continues 9 ♗b2 (the only really testing move; 9 ♘d3 0-0 10 ♗f4 ♗xf4 11 ♘xf4 b6 12 ♕c1 ♗b7 13 ♕a3 ♕f7 14 ♘d2 g5 15 ♘d3 g4 16 ♕b2 ♖ae8 17 a4 c5 produced a complex game with chances for both sides in Lutz-Yusupov, Baden Baden 1992, and 9 ♗f4? loses a pawn to 9...♗xe5! 10 dxe5 ♘g4) 9...0-0 (9...♗xe5?! 10 dxe5 ♘g4 11 cxd5 exd5 12 ♕d4! gives White a clear plus) 10 ♘d2 and now the point of Black's strategy is supposed to be 10...a5!

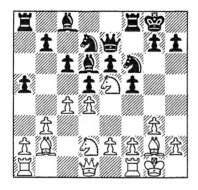

Black seeks counterplay on the queenside while leaving the bishop on c8 for the moment. Now 11 a3 has been tried (with the idea of meeting 11...a4 with 12 b4!). Then

Adorjan-Moskalenko, Balassagyarmat 1990 continued 11...♘e4 12 ♘df3 ♘xe5 13 ♘xe5 ♗xe5!? 14 dxe5 b6 and Black was okay. Another possibility is 11 ♘df3 ♘e4 (11...a4?! 12 ♘xd7! ♗xd7 13 c5 and White has the superior structure) 12 ♕c2, as played in Ruban-Meister, Balassagyarmat 1990, when Black could have maintained the balance with 12...a4! 13 ♘xd7 axb3! 14 axb3 ♗xd7 according to Ruban. For 8...0-0 see Games 12-17.

9 cxd5!

This capture seems to be the most testing. White takes advantage of the fact that Black has already decided where to put his bishop, and that 9...cxd5 favours White.

9...exd5

9...cxd5 10 ♘c4! b5 11 ♘xd6+ ♕xd6 12 ♕c2 ♘c6 13 ♖d1 is good for White, but 13 ♗f4 is less clear due to 13...♘xd4!? 14 ♕xc8+ ♖xc8 15 ♗xd6 ♘c2 16 ♘a3 ♘xa1 17 ♖xa1 a6 and Black has some compensation, although White looks a little better.

10 ♗f4

Not best. The stronger 10 ♗b2 is dealt with in the next two games. With the text White will get to exchange the bishops at some point but, since Black will play ...c6-c5 soon and create his own pressure in the centre, it is doubtful what good it will do White.

10...♗b7 11 ♕c2 g6

Black has no choice but to accept this weakening of the kingside. In the next game we will see what happens when Black decides to sacrifice the pawn.

12 ♘d2 0-0 13 ♘df3 ♘e4 14 h4!? c5

Black's kingside pawns look brittle but White has in no way organised his pieces to take any advantage of it. I believe that Black has already achieved equality.

15 e3 ♘a6 16 dxc5 bxc5 17 ♖fd1 ♘c7 18 ♘d3 ♘e6 19 ♗xd6 ♕xd6 20 ♖ac1 ♖fd8 21 ♕b2 a5 22 ♘g5!

White is under pressure as his opponent has the more active possibilities. Consequently White is forced to try to create some

play against Black's centre pawns, if only to make life more difficult. If Black had had the time he might have played ...h7-h6!? to avoid this move.

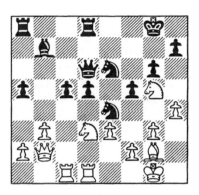

22...♘6xg5 23 hxg5 ♖ac8 24 ♘f4

24 ♕a3!? ♕b6! (with the main idea of ...d5-d4! to create a passed pawn on the d-file instead of the c-file, and to win the c3-square for the dominating knight) 25 ♗xe4 dxe4 26 ♘e5 ♗d5 and White is still struggling a little to keep Black at bay. Glek's 24...c4?! seems inferior on account of 25 ♕xd6 ♖xd6 26 ♘f4 c3 27 ♖c2!, when the black pawns have suddenly lost their potential and are difficult to protect.

24...♕e7 25 ♕a3 ♔f7! 26 ♖c2 d4! 27 exd4 ♖xd4!

27...cxd4? 28 ♖xc8! ♗xc8 29 ♕xa5 loses a pawn for no apparent reason.

28 ♖e1

28 ♖xd4 cxd4 ensures Black better chances in the endgame thanks to his dangerous d-pawn.

28...♕d7! 29 ♖ce2

With the idea of meeting 29...♘xg5 with 30 ♖e7+.

29...♖d1?!

29...a4! is more to the point, coming to the aid of the c-pawn by challenging b3. If White decides not to take the a4-pawn Black simply eliminates his own weakness and enjoys the better game.

30 ♖xd1?!

A mistake that leaves White's king exposed and hands the initiative straight back to Black. After the stronger 30 ♗xe4! ♗xe4 31 ♕xa5 White nets a pawn but Black has obvious compensation on the light squares. I'm not sure how he is able to exploit this, but there should be something.

30...♕xd1+ 31 ♔h2 h6!

This is most likely what White had failed to appreciate. The prospect of the h-file opening proves too much for White to handle.

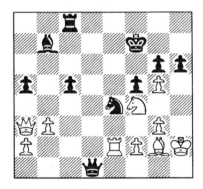

32 ♕xa5?

Glek offers a complicated alternative line as another path leading to a very promising position for Black. Unfortunately his analysis seems to be wrong: 32 ♕b2! hxg5 33 ♘h3 ♕d4! 34 ♘xg5+ ♔f6, and now instead of Glek's 35 ♘f3 ♕xb2 36 ♖xb2 ♖h8+! 37 ♔g1 ♖d8 with advantage to Black, White has 35 ♘xe4+! fxe4 36 ♕c1! (36 ♕xd4+? cxd4 37 ♗xe4 d3!! would be a real shock to the system!) 36...♖h8+ 37 ♔g1 and it is hard to see why White should be any worse, although there is a good deal of defending still to do.

32...hxg5 33 ♖e1 ♕d7! 34 ♘h3 g4!

The correct move order. 34...♖a8? 35 ♕b6 ♖a6? does not win the queen due to 36 ♘xg5+ ♔g8 (36...♔g7 37 ♖d1! ♕c8 38 ♕b5! gives White a substantial advantage) 37 ♖d1! ♕xd1 38 ♕xb7 ♕h5+ 39 ♔g1 ♕d1+ 40 ♗f1 ♘xg5 41 ♕xa6 ♘f3+ 42 ♔h1 followed by

♕e2 and White is on top.

35 ♗xe4

35 ♘f4 ♖h8+! 36 ♔g1 ♖a8 37 ♕b6 ♖a6 and Black wins.

35...♖h8! 36 ♔g1

36 ♗g2!? ♗xg2 37 ♕c3 ♖xh3+ 38 ♔xg2 ♕d5+ 39 f3 f4! 40 gxf4 ♕h5 41 ♕c4+ ♔f8 also wins for Black. Now White has no more serious checks.

36...♖xh3 37 ♕a7

37 ♗xb7 ♕xb7 is just dead and gone.

37...fxe4 38 ♕xc5 e3 39 ♕c4+ ♔g7 0-1

Game 10
Akopian-Guliev
Pula 1997

---

1 d4 f5 2 g3 ♘f6 3 ♗g2 e6 4 ♘f3 d5 5 0-0 ♗d6 6 c4 c6 7 b3 ♕e7 8 ♘e5 b6 9 cxd5 exd5 10 ♗b2!

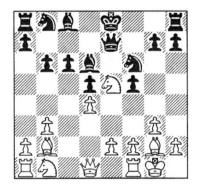

As we saw in the previous game 10 ♗f4 poses Black no problems. The reason why the bishop is better placed on b2 is simple. We know that Black is going to play ...♗b7 to continue development and that this will leave the f5-pawn exposed, which in turn should induce ...g7-g6 after ♕c2. It is also clear that ...c6-c5 is a major part of Black's counterplay, to which White does best to reply dxc5, leaving Black with hanging pawns. When this happens the a1-h8 diagonal opens up and, naturally, this is where we prefer to have our bishop! Hence 10 ♗b2!

10...♗b7 11 ♕c2 0-0?!

Black also understands why the bishop stands on b2, but this tricky attempt fails. For the correct 11...g6 see the following game.

12 ♕xf5 ♘fd7

No better is 12...♘e4 as 13 ♕h5 g6 (the only way to bother the queen) 14 ♘xg6! hxg6 15 ♕xg6+ ♔h8 16 ♗xe4 dxe4 17 d5+ ♗e5 18 ♕h5+ is a simple winning line.

13 ♕h5 g6 14 ♘xg6! hxg6 15 ♕xg6+ ♔h8 16 ♕h6+ ♔g8 17 ♕g6+ ♔h8 18 e4!

White has three pawns for his piece, but that is not the crucial factor here. Of course it is reassuring for White that he can safely enter an endgame, but what matters is the exposed king.

18...♗a6

18...dxe4 19 ♘d2 e3 20 ♕h6+ ♔g8 21 fxe3 gives White a decisive attack (22 ♘e4 is coming, as is 22 ♗h3).

19 ♖e1

White has time and does not fall for the trick 19 e5? ♗xf1 20 exd6 ♕e2!!, when there is nothing better than settle for a perpetual.

19...♕f6

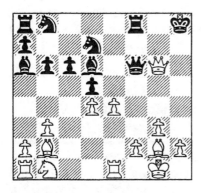

20 ♕xf6+

This is the pragmatic approach. Later Akopian analysed the following very beautiful winning line:

20 ♕h5+!? ♔g7 21 f4 ♗xf4! (the only way to put up any resistance) 22 gxf4 ♕xf4 23 ♘c3 ♕f2+ (23...♖h8 24 ♗c1!) 24 ♔h1 ♕xb2

25 ♗h3 ♖f2 26 ♖g1+ ♔f8 27 ♕h8+ ♔e7 28 ♖g7+ ♔d6 29 ♕xb8+!! and Black is mated!

20...♘xf6 21 exd5

Taking advantage of Black's susceptibility on the h1-a8 diagonal. The alternative 21 e5!? ♗b4 22 ♗c3 ♗xc3 23 ♘xc3 ♘g4 24 f4 ♗b7 25 b4 leaves Black with no real defence against the rolling pawns.

21...♗b4

21...cxd5 22 ♖e6! and Black is faced with ♖xf6.

22 ♖e6 ♗c8 23 ♖xf6!

Now White's bishops take control of the long diagonals. Black is defenceless.

23...♖xf6 24 dxc6 ♖f7! 25 ♘c3!

25 c7? ♖xc7 26 ♗xa8 ♖c2 gives Black counterplay despite White's collection of pawns.

25...♘a6 26 ♘e4?!

This wins but Akopian prefers the following winning line: 26 ♘b5! ♘c7 27 d5+ ♔h7 28 ♘xc7 ♖xc7 29 ♗e5 ♖e7 30 f4 ♖xe5 31 fxe5 ♗c3 32 ♖f1 ♗xe5 33 d6 ♗a6 34 ♖f7+ ♔g6 35 ♖e7 ♔f6 36 ♖xe5! ♔xe5 37 c7 and Black must give up his rook.

26...♗f5 27 d5+ ♔g8 28 d6

28 ♘f6+ ♔f8 29 g4 ♗e7!.

28...♗xe4 29 ♗xe4 ♗xd6 30 ♗d5 ♘b4 31 ♗xf7+ ♔xf7 32 ♖d1 ♔e6 33 h4 ♘xc6 34 ♔g2

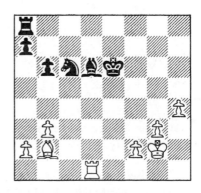

White has the better of the deal – three connected passed pawns for a piece.

34...♗e5 35 ♖e1!

35 ♗xe5 ♘xe5 36 f4 ♘g4 37 ♔f3 ♖g8 serves only to make life difficult for White.
35...♔f6

35...♔d5 36 ♗xe5 ♘xe5 37 f4 ♘d3 38 ♖e7 and White wins.
36 ♖xe5!

A nice conversion to a winning endgame.
36...♘xe5 37 f4 ♔f5 38 ♗xe5 ♔g4 39 h5!

If Black takes the pawn the white king enters and decides the game.
39...♖c8 40 h6 ♖c2+ 41 ♔g1 ♖c1+ 42 ♔f2 ♖h1 43 ♗g7 ♔f5 44 ♔g2 ♖h5 45 ♔f3 ♖h3 46 ♗f6 b5 47 b4 a6 48 ♗g7!

Black is in zugzwang.
48...♔g6 49 ♔g2 ♖h5 50 g4 ♖h4 51 ♔f3 ♖h2 52 f5+ ♔g5 53 ♔e4 1-0

Game 11
Shabalov-Vaiser
Tilburg 1993

---

1 d4 f5 2 ♘f3 e6 3 g3 ♘f6 4 ♗g2 d5 5 c4 c6 6 0-0 ♗d6 7 b3 ♕e7 8 ♘e5 b6 9 cxd5 exd5 10 ♗b2 ♗b7 11 ♕c2 g6!

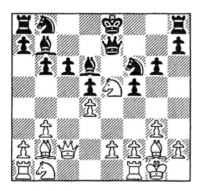

This move is unpleasant but necessary, as we saw in the previous game. White now develops normally.
12 ♘d2 0-0 13 ♖ac1 c5 14 ♘df3 ♘a6!

With the two white knights working in tandem Black is not interested in challenging e5. Instead he prepares his own forces ready for battle!

15 ♖fd1 ♖ac8 16 ♕b1
Prophylactics.
16...♘c7 17 e3 ♘e6

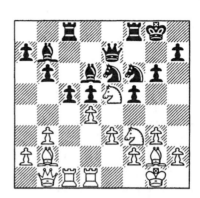

This is the ideal place for the knight. White might have a small advantage, but it is very small. During the rest of the game Black presses too hard for the full point, losing control of his pieces and pawns.
18 dxc5 bxc5 19 ♘d3 ♘e4 20 ♗a1 c4 21 ♘f4 ♘xf4 22 gxf4 ♗a3 23 ♖c2 c3 24 ♖e1 d4 25 ♘xd4 g5 26 f3 ♘d2 27 ♕d1 gxf4 28 ♖xc3 fxe3 29 ♖exe3 ♕xe3+ 30 ♖xe3 ♖c1 31 ♕xc1 ♗xc1 32 ♖e1 ♗a3 33 ♖d1 ♖c8 34 ♔f2 ♖c1 35 ♖xc1 ♗xc1 36 ♘xf5 ♘b1 37 ♗f1 ♘d2 38 ♗e2 ♗a8 39 ♗d4 a5 40 ♗e3 ♔f7 41 ♔e1 ♔f6 42 ♗xd2 ♗xd2+ 43 ♔xd2 ♔xf5 44 ♔e3 1-0

Game 12
Portisch-Van der Wiel
Amsterdam 1990

---

1 d4 e6 2 c4 f5 3 g3 ♘f6 4 ♗g2 d5 5 ♘f3 c6 6 0-0 ♗d6 7 b3 ♕e7 8 ♘e5 0-0

This is far more sensible than 8...b6. Black plans to develop his bishop over on the kingside via d7 and e8, relying on the greater solidity of his centre. White is also happy to face this form of development, for now it is harder for Black to break with ...c6-c5, and at times the bishop cannot find a better square than f7. As for Black, there is nothing to worry about – he might have to defend a position which is slightly worse but this is part of the game. Holding together an essentially solid position is not difficult to manage, and White must make concessions and commitments in order to generate winning chances, thereby presenting Black with interesting chances of his own. For example White might use his queenside pawns to concentrate on a positionally oriented offensive, but then Black has time to execute an equally dangerous plan strategy on the kingside.

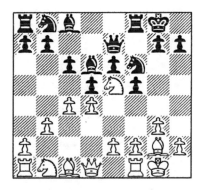

9 ♘d2

Games 14-17 deal with 9 ♗b2.

9...♗d7

For those of you who dislike this bishop manoeuvre there is always 8...♘bd7!?, as suggested in Game 9, or 9...♘e4!?.

10 ♘df3 ♗e8 11 ♘d3 ♘bd7 12 ♗f4

The more dangerous 12 ♘fe5! will be discussed in the next game.

12...♗xf4 13 ♘xf4 h6?!

Weakening the light squares unnecessarily. 13...dxc4 14 bxc4 e5 15 dxe5 ♘xe5 16 ♘xe5 ♕xe5 17 ♖b1 is only very slightly better for White according to Van der Wiel. This is actually how Portisch himself played with Black against Kallai in 1990, when White deviated with 16 ♘d4 ♘h5 17 ♘xh5 ♗xh5 18 c5, but after 18...f4 Black had no worries. 13...♗f7! is also a natural move, employed by Nigel Short.

14 cxd5! cxd5

14...exd5? loses instantly to 15 ♘h4!.

15 ♖c1

White prepares for an invasion down the c-file.

15...g5 16 ♘d3 ♘b8!

A manoeuvre well known from the Slav – the knight is better on c6 than d7. However, this does take time.

17 ♖c8

17 ♘fe5 ♘c6 18 e3, with an edge, is perhaps more prudent.

17...♗b5 18 ♖xf8+ ♕xf8?!

With the queen ideally placed on e7 – where it guards a number of weak squares – it is logical to play instead 18...♔xf8!, when 19 ♘fe5 ♔g7 restricts Black to only a slight disadvantage.

19 h4?

Portisch is in an aggressive mood throughout this game. In his annotations Van der Wiel prefers 19 ♘c5 b6 20 a4! with continued pressure.

19...♕g7?

19...gxh4! 20 ♘xh4 ♗xd3 21 ♕xd3 ♘c6 (Van der Wiel) is preferable.

20 hxg5 hxg5 21 ♘c5 ♘e4!

Black employs tactics to keep his position from falling apart.

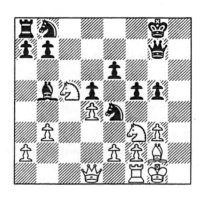

22 ♘xe6?!

Portisch embarks on an adventure. Instead the simple 22 ♕c1! ♘xc5 23 ♕xc5 ♗d7 24 ♕c7 ♘c6 25 ♕xb7 ♖b8 26 ♕c7

 c8 27 ♕d6 g4! 28 ♞e5 ♞xd4 29  e1! guarantees White a commanding position. Note that Black cannot play 29...♞xe2+? due to 30 ♚f1!, and White wins material.

22...♕h6! 23 ♕c1!

23 ♞c7?? ♞c3! and the tables are turned.

23...♕xe6 24 ♞xg5 ♕d7!

Keeping control over the most important squares.

25 ♞xe4 dxe4

25...fxe4!? 26 ♕g5+ ♚f7 27 ♕e3! ♕e7 28 f3 ♚e8 29 fxe4 ♞d7 maybe a better defence, although White is still doing very well.

26 ♕g5+ ♚f8!

Good defence. Black chooses the correct square, as 26...♚f7? 27  h3  xe2 28  xf5 ♕d6 29  e1  f3 30  xe4  xe4 31  xe4 ♞d7 32 ♕h5+! gives White a winning attack – as pointed out by John Nunn.

27 ♕f6+! ♕f7 28 ♕h8+ ♕g8 29 ♕e5  d7 30 ♕c7 ♕d5?

Black has been under pressure for so long that he misses – understandably – the best continuation. It is also possible he was running short of time. Anyway, it is a well-known fact that the attacker has the easier task, as he needs to calculate only his own creative ideas whereas the onus is on the defender to anticipate – and analyse – the next threat. The necessary defence, then, is 30... c6!, after which the situation is unclear. Now White takes control of the 8th rank and Black is left to see the irony in his material lead – he is too tied up to play.

31 ♕d8+! ♚f7 32 e3!

Threatening to prise open a crucial file or diagonal with f2-f3!.

32... c6 33 ♕h8 ♕e6

33...b6?! 34  c1! and the bishop has unwelcome attention.

34  c1 ♕f6 35 ♕c8 ♕e6 36 ♕h8 ♕f6 37 ♕h7+!

With his rook coming to c5 White targets f5.

37...♚f8

After 37...♚e8 38  c5  d7 39 ♕g8+!

♚e7 40 g4 Black's position falls apart.

38  c5  d7 39  c7! b6?

The final mistake. Black can still hope with 39...♕g7 40 ♕h4! ♚e8! 41  xb7 ♞c6, when he has finally untangled and achieved some sort of development, although White remains in the driving seat, still with his three pawns for the piece.

40  f1!

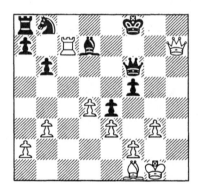

Prevents 40...♕g7, which now runs into 41 ♕xg7+ ♚xg7 42  b5. A look at the diagram position tells us that Black still suffers from an embarrassing development problem on his 40th move!

40...♕d6 41  c4 ♚e8 42 ♕g8+ ♚e7 43 ♕g5+

43 ♕c8! is even stronger!

43...♚e8 44  e2! ♞c6 45 ♕g8+ ♚e7 46  xd7+ ♕xd7 47 ♕xa8 ♞b4 48 a3 ♞d3 49 ♕g8! 1-0

Game 13
Tukmakov-Arnold
Zurich 1994

1 d4 e6 2 ♞f3 f5 3 g3 ♞f6 4  g2 d5 5 c4 c6 6 0-0  d6 7 b3 ♕e7 8 ♞e5 0-0 9 ♞d2  d7 10 ♞df3  e8 11 ♞d3 ♞bd7 12 ♞fe5!

Certainly the most dangerous move. Black could now play 12... f7 and settle for a slightly worse position. The main agenda for White is to leave his options open. The exchange of dark-squared bishops is desirable but not in itself a winning plan. However, in general Black is slightly cramped and White can adjust his development accordingly.

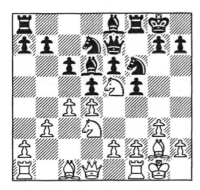

12...♘e4

Another route is 12...♔h8!? 13 ♗f4 (the beginning of a series of exchanges which in principle favours White but earns him only an edge) 13...♖d8 14 ♕c1 h6 15 ♘xd7 ♘xd7 16 ♗xd6 ♕xd6 17 ♕f4 (this is not necessary) 17...♕xf4 18 ♘xf4 ♗f7 19 cxd5 cxd5 and White's reduced forces leave him only a touch better, Petursson-Hansen, Malmö 1993. This position was discussed in the Introduction.

13 ♕c2 h6

13...♘xe5 14 dxe5 ♗c7 15 a4! is promising for White. 13...♗f7 14 ♘xd7 ♕xd7 15 c5 ♗c7 16 ♗f4 is also inadvisable for Black thanks to the bishop on f7 being genuinely lacking in potential.

14 f3 ♘g5 15 ♗d2!?

This looks rather strange but has its advantages. Also possible is 15 ♗f4! with a small plus.

15...c5!

Definitely the correct move. 15...♘xe5? 16 dxe5 ♗c7 17 cxd5! exd5 18 ♗b4 was the idea behind 15 ♗d2.

16 e3 b6

16...♖c8! is more convincing. Develop your pieces!

17 ♗c3 ♘xe5?

This is counter-productive. One should really develop all the pieces before voluntarily entering complications. Again 17...♖c8 offers decent equalising chances.

18 dxe5 ♗c7 19 cxd5 exd5 20 ♘f4 ♖d8 21 ♖ad1 d4

This seems to be forced. 21...♗xe5 22 ♘xd5 ♕e6 23 ♘f4 ♗xf4 24 ♖xd8 ♗xe3+ 25 ♔h1 promises Black little for the exchange.

22 exd4 cxd4 23 ♗xd4 ♗xe5 24 ♗xe5 ♖xd1 25 ♖xd1 ♕xe5 26 ♘d5!

White's forces dominate.

26...♕e6 27 h4 ♘h7 28 f4 ♗h5 29 ♖c1 ♔h8 30 ♕b2 ♘f6 31 ♕e5 ♕xe5 32 fxe5 ♘xd5 33 ♗xd5 ♖e8 34 e6

The endgame is close to winning for White, and the GM over-runs the amateur with ease.

34...♖e7 35 ♔f2 g6 36 ♔e3 ♔g7 37 ♔d4 ♔f6 38 ♖c8 ♗g4 39 ♖h8 ♔g7 40 ♖a8 ♔f6 41 ♖f8+ ♔g7 42 ♖f7+ ♖xf7 43 exf7 ♔f8 44 ♔e5 ♔e7 45 f8♕+! ♔xf8 46 ♔f6 g5 47 hxg5 hxg5 48 ♗e6 a5 49 ♔xg5 ♔g7 50 ♗xf5 ♗d1 51 ♔f4 b5 52 ♔e5 b4 53 ♔d4 ♔f6 54 g4 a4 55 ♔c4 1-0

Game 14
Wessman-Andrianov
New York 1990

---

1 d4 e6 2 c4 f5 3 g3 ♘f6 4 ♗g2 c6 5 ♘f3 d5 6 0-0 ♗d6 7 b3 ♕e7 8 ♘e5 0-0

9 ♗b2

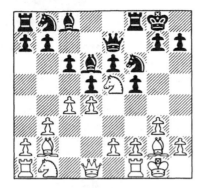

This alternative to 9 ♘d2 is probably no more dangerous but it does seem to be more popular these days. Consequently I have chosen it as the main line in this chapter. Rather than spending time securing the exchange of bishops White prefers natural development, the fianchetto adding to White's influence on the important e5-square.

9...b6?!

Not surprisingly this leads to problems on the h1-a8 diagonal and is therefore a reaction that White is happy to see. Game 16 features 9...♗d7, and 9...♘e4!? is Game 17.

10 cxd5 exd5?

Avoiding 11 ♘c4!? but presenting Black with other difficulties. For the lesser evil 11...cxd5 see the next game.

11 ♕c2 ♕c7

Another option is 11...♗xe5 12 dxe5 ♘e4 13 ♘d2. In Farago-Gleizerov, Portoroz 1993 Black played 13...c5?. This is poor but White already has the two bishops and a passed pawn on e5. Black is trying to bring his knight to c6 to justify the exchange of his bishop but, unfortunately, this gives White time to start an attack in the centre: 14 g4!! (highlighting Black's plight on the h1-a8 diagonal) 14...♕g5 15 ♖ad1 ♘c6 (15...♕xg4 drops a piece to 16 f3!) 16 ♕c1! ♕g6 17 gxf5 ♗xf5 18 ♘xe4 dxe4 19 ♖d6 ♕e8 20 ♗xe4! and White later won.

12 ♘d2 ♗e6 13 ♖ac1

Black has problems developing.

13...♖c8 14 ♘df3 a5 15 ♘g5!

Beginning an effective attack.

15...♕e7 16 f3 g6

It is symptomatic of Black's problems that he must resort to this. White now opens fire.

17 e4 dxe4 18 fxe4 ♘xe4 19 ♘xe6 ♕xe6 20 ♗xe4 fxe4 21 d5!!

A fitting finish. White's strategy has culminated in releasing his dark-squared bishop at last, exploiting Black's numerous weaknesses.

21...♕xd5 22 ♘g4 ♗c5+ 23 ♕xc5! 1-0

Game 15
Kelly-Krasenkov
Elista Ol 1998

---

1 d4 f5 2 g3 ♘f6 3 ♗g2 e6 4 ♘f3 d5 5 0-0 ♗d6 6 c4 c6 7 b3 ♕e7 8 ♘e5 0-0 9 ♗b2 b6 10 cxd5 cxd5

As we witnessed in the previous game this recapture is practically forced.

11 ♘c4

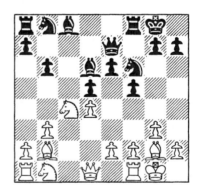

11...♘c6?

This had been played before, but might never be repeated at this level again! Much better is 11...b5!, which is necessary to avoid a later ♗a3. C.Hansen-Tisdall, Espoo 1989, went 12 ♘xd6 ♕xd6 13 ♕d3 ♗d7! (the bishop can always come to a6 later) 14 ♘d2 ♘a6 15 a3 b4 16 a4 ♖ac8 17 ♘f3 ♖c7 18 ♖ac1 ♖fc8 19 ♖xc7 ♖xc7 20 ♘e5 ♘b8 21

h3 ♗c8 22 ♖c1 ♗a6 23 ♕e3 ♖xc1+. Black
has almost equalized, there still being problems with his b-pawn as he has not had time
to play ...a7-a5.

12 ♘xd6 ♕xd6 13 ♘c3!

By threatening an invasion down the c-file
White gains time to achieve ♗a3 in favourable circumstances.

**13...♗a6 14 a4 ♖fc8 15 ♗a3 ♕d7 16
♕d2**

White has a lasting positional advantage.

**16...♘e4 17 ♘xe4 dxe4 18 ♖fd1 ♘a5
19 ♖ab1 ♕d5 20 f3 ♗b7 21 fxe4 fxe4
22 ♗b4 ♘c6 23 ♗c3 ♘e7 24 ♖f1 ♕h5
25 ♗b4 ♘f5 26 ♖f4 ♕g6 27 ♖bf1 h5 28
d5 ♖d8 29 ♗xe4 ♗xd5 30 ♗xf5 exf5 31
♖d4 1-0**

Game 16
Bareev-P.Nikolic
Groningen 1993

**1 d4 f5 2 c4 ♘f6 3 g3 e6 4 ♗g2 c6 5
♘f3 d5 6 0-0 ♗d6 7 b3 ♕e7 8 ♘e5 0-0
9 ♗b2 ♗d7!?**

As Black cannot post his bishop on b7 directly he chooses to take the longer route to
h5, from where the bishop will join the game.
This gives White some time to create a
queenside initiative, but at least Black has yet
to weaken his structure there, as happens
with ...b7-b6. For the interesting 9...♘e4!?
see the next game.

10 ♘d2!

The most challenging approach. 10 ♕c1?!
is slow: 10...♗e8 11 ♗a3 ♘bd7 12 ♘d3
♗h5 13 ♘f4 ♗f7 14 ♗xd6 ♕xd6 15 ♕a3
♕c7 16 cxd5 exd5 17 e3 ♖ae8 18 ♘d2 ♘e4
19 ♕b2 ♕d6 and Black had no problems in
Espig-Knaak, Stralsund 1988.

10...♗e8 11 ♘df3 ♘bd7 12 ♘d3 ♘g4?!

see following diagram

More consistent and better is 12...♗h5, after which the position is balanced, although
White might have an edge after 13 ♘fe5!.

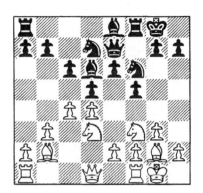

13 ♕c1!

Planning 14 ♘fe5.

**13...dxc4 14 bxc4 e5 15 c5 ♗c7 16
dxe5 ♘gxe5 17 ♘fxe5 ♘xe5 18 ♕e3
♘g6 19 ♕xe7 ♘xe7 20 ♖ab1**

White has the advantage as his pieces are
better and Black has a real weakness at b7.

20...b5?!

This creates an even weaker pawn on c6,
strengthening the potentially passed c5-pawn.
Again 20...♗h5! is necessary, finishing the
job.

21 ♖fd1! a5 22 ♗e5?!

Better to keep this bishop and still remove
its opposite number with 22 ♘f4! ♗xf4 23
gxf4, when the two strong bishops threaten
to take over. In the game the d-file turns out
to hold little promise for White.

**22...♗xe5 23 ♘xe5 ♖c8 24 ♖d6 ♖c7 25
♖bd1 g6 26 ♖1d2! ♔g7**

After 26...♗f7 White wins a pawn with 27
♗xc6! ♘xc6 28 ♖xc6 ♖xc6 29 ♘xc6.

27 f4! b4!

Intending ...a5-a4 to distract White with
the threat of creating a passed pawn. Again
27...♗f7 loses a pawn: 28 ♖d7 ♖fc8 29 ♗xc6
♘xc6 30 ♘xf7 ♘b8 31 ♖xc7 ♖xc7 32 ♘g5.

28 ♖d8 ♗f7 29 ♖2d7?!

More chances to claim an advantage come
with 29 ♖8d7, although 29...♖fc8 30 ♗xc6
♘xc6 31 ♘xf7 ♔g8! might defend. After 32
♘g5 ♖xd7 33 ♖xd7 a4 34 ♘xh7 b3 35 axb3
axb3 36 ♘f6+ ♔f8 White has nothing better

then a draw – Bareev.

29...♖xd7?

Another inaccuracy. Bareev's 29...♖xd8! 30 ♖xc7 ♔f6 31 ♘xf7 ♔xf7 32 ♗xc6 ♖d2 is not too convenient for White.

30 ♖xd7 ♖e8?

Passive. 30...♔f6 keeps the rook active.

31 ♖a7 ♔f8

31...♗xa2? runs into 32 ♗xc6.

32 ♖xa5 ♗d5 33 ♖a7 ♖d8 34 ♘d7+ ♔f7 35 ♗xd5+ ♘xd5 36 ♘e5+ ♔g8 37 ♘xc6 ♖c8 38 ♖d7 ♖xc6 39 ♖xd5 ♖a6 40 ♖d2 ♔f7 41 ♔f2 ♖a3 42 c6 1-0

Game 17
Dizdar-Schlosser
Austria 1996

---

1 d4 f5 2 ♘f3 ♘f6 3 g3 e6 4 ♗g2 d5 5 0-0 ♗d6 6 c4 c6 7 b3 ♕e7 8 ♘e5 0-0 9 ♗b2 ♘e4!?

The knight so often resides on the inviting e4-square in the Stonewall that Black opts to send it there now, the point being to keep his options open regarding the future of the c8-bishop. For example Black can still play ...b7-b6 since the h1-a8 diagonal is now effectively closed by the knight, thus ruling out the cheeky trick with ♘c4. On the other hand Black might prefer to take the other route with ....♗d7-e8 etc. Such flexibility from just one clever little move. Of course the crux of the matter is whether the knight is well placed on e4 when these developments are carried out. White can try to engineer a timely f2-f3 – with gain of tempo – and follow up with e2-e4. Perhaps this is what White was hoping for in the actual game. Anyway, he went completely wrong and Black was better after just a few additional moves!

10 f3

Too early. Black, who has not even shown his hand, now has a ready-made strategy – exerting pressure on his opponent's weak dark squares.

10...♘f6 11 ♘d2?

It is easy to see how White believes he is making progress at his opponent's expense. Bolstering the centre with 11 f4! is necessary, with a balanced game. Of course Black can then continue the dance with 11...♘e4 before deciding how best to continue.

11...c5!

The standard reaction to f2-f3, immediately undermining White's centre.

12 e3 cxd4 13 exd4 f4!

Highlighting the problems surrounding the dark squares in White's camp. Black already has the advantage.

14 ♖e1 ♘c6 15 ♗h3 dxc4 16 bxc4 ♘xe5 17 dxe5 ♗c5+ 18 ♔g2 ♘d7 19 ♘e4 b6 20 gxf4?! ♖xf4 21 ♗c1

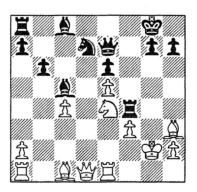

21...♖xe4!!

A very strong sacrifice. Black eliminates White's most influential piece and uses his new-found lead in development to launch an attack against the king.

22 ♖xe4 ♗b7 23 ♕e2

White decides not to keep the material. Probably a wise decision, but he is still in trouble.

23...♗xe4 24 ♕xe4 ♖d8 25 ♗f4 ♘f8 26 ♕e2 ♘g6 27 ♗g3 h5 28 ♕e4 ♕e8 29 ♔h1 ♖d4 30 ♕c2 ♕f7 31 ♖f1 h4 32 ♗f2 ♖d8 33 ♗xc5 bxc5 34 f4 ♘xf4 35 ♕f2 ♖d4 36 ♗g4 ♕e7 37 ♖b1 ♕g5 38 h3 ♕xe5 39 ♖e1 ♘d3 40 ♕e3 ♖e4! 0-1

Summary

Against 7 b3 Black should play 7...♕e7 to avoid the immediate exchange of dark-squared bishops. Of course White does have several ways of insisting on this exchange, namely 8 ♗f4, 8 c5?!, 8 a4 and 8 ♗b2 b6 9 ♕c1, but each of these has its drawbacks and allows Black to equalize. If White chooses to develop normally Black's game should never be uncomfortable, the most White can hope for being a position that he might find easier to play.

The only real test after 7 b3 ♕e7 is 8 ♘e5!, immediately aiming to disturb Black's development on the queenside. Indeed Black finds himself with a slight disadvantage after 8...b6 due to 9 cxd5 exd5 10 ♗b2!, so he must look for other replies. One way is 8...♘bd7!? (Game 9, note to Black's 8th move) to challenge the knight, but 8...0-0 is the most versatile. The traditional bishop journey with 9...♗d7-e8-h5 merits attention (Game 16), and there is also Schlosser's exciting 9...♘e4!? (Game 17), which tries to address the situation in a different way. Black should be able to cope with 7 b3 without too much effort.

**1 d4 f5 2 g3 ♘f6 3 ♗g2 e6 4 c4 c6 5 ♘f3 d5 6 0-0 ♗d6 7 b3 ♕e7
8 ♘e5**

> 8 ♗f4 – *Game 1*; 8 c5?! – *Game 2*; 8 a4 – *Game 3*; 8 ♕c2 – *Game 4*
> 8 ♗b2 b6 (D)
>> 9 ♕c1 – *Game 5*
>> 9 ♘bd2 ♗b7 10 ♘e5 0-0 11 ♖c1
>>> 11...a5 – *Game 6*; 11...c5!? – *Game 7*
> 8 ♘bd2 – *Game 8*

8...0-0

> 8...b6 9 cxd5 exd5 (D)
>> 10 ♗f4 – *Game 9*
>> 10 ♗b2 ♗b7 11 ♕c2
>>> 11...0-0?! – *Game 10*; 11...g6 – *Game 11*

9 ♗b2 (D)

> 9 ♘d2 ♗d7 10 ♘df3 ♗e8 11 ♘d3 ♘bd7
>> 12 ♗f4 – *Game 12*; 12 ♘fe5! – *Game 13*

9...♘e4!? – *Game 17*

> 9...b6?! 10 cxd5
>> 10...exd5 – *Game 14*; 10...cxd5 – *Game 15*
> 9...♗d7 – *Game 16*

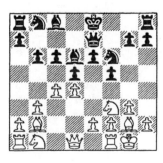

8...b6

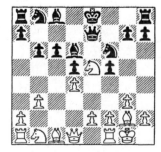

9...exd5

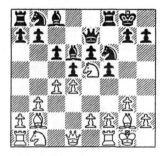

9 ♗b2

CHAPTER TWO

White Plays 7 ♗f4

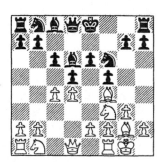

1 d4 f5 2 g3 ♘f6 3 ♗g2 e6 4 c4 c6 5 ♘f3 d5 6 0-0 ♗d6 7 ♗f4

7 ♗f4 aims for the a positionally desirable trade of bishops but, as we saw in the Introduction, it is not too worrying for Black. Consequently it makes sense to acquiesce to the exchange since 7...♗e7 wastes time. A logical move is 7...♗xf4!, getting something out of the deal by damaging White's pawn structure (unlike Game 18), even if this does strengthen White's grip on the e5-square. Then after 8 gxf4 Black should not delay castling as in Game 19, but play 8...0-0 and wait for White to choose from a range of 9th move options. The main question facing White is when to play e2-e3. 9 ♕b3 (Game 20) has more punch than 9 ♕c2 (Game 25), 9 ♘e5 (Games 23-24) plans to drop back to d3 and has more point than the simple 9 ♘bd2 (Games 21-22), and 9 ♘c3 (Game 26) lacks a point. The main move is 9 e3, when 9...♕e7 (Game 27) and 9...♗d7 (Game 28) are less popular than 9...♘e4 (Games 29-31).

Game 18
Beliavsky-Bareev
USSR 1987

---

1 d4 f5 2 c4 ♘f6 3 g3 e6 4 ♗g2 d5 5 ♘f3 c6 6 0-0 ♗d6 7 ♗f4 0-0?

This is an obvious mistake because it allows White to execute his plan without paying a price for the exchange. The rest of the games in this chapter feature ...♗xf4.

8 ♗xd6

Oddly enough it appears that the text was a new idea at the time!

8...♕xd6 9 ♕c2 b6

Beliavsky's 9...♗d7!? 10 ♘bd2 ♗e8 11 b4! ♕xb4 12 ♖ab1 favours White but is preferable to the game continuation.

10 ♘a3!

The most aggressive development. White achieves nothing with the slow 10 ♘bd2 ♗b7 11 ♖ac1 ♘bd7 12 ♖fd1 ♖ac8 13 ♕a4 ♕b8, when Black is ready for ...c6-c5 with a fine position.

10...♘a6

10...♗b7 11 cxd5 cxd5 12 ♘b5 ♕d7 13 ♕c7! ♖c8 14 ♕xd7! ♘bxd7 15 ♘d6 is also difficult for Black.

11 ♖ac1 ♗b7 12 cxd5 cxd5 13 ♘b5 ♕e7?

Choosing the natural square in view of an inevitable ♘e5, but forcing White to defend the b5-knight is necessary, when 13...♕d7 14 ♕b3 ♖fc8 15 ♘e5 retains White's lead.

14 ♕a4 ♘e8

Black's defensive task is made more difficult by being unable to contest the c-file as this leaves the a7-pawn hanging.

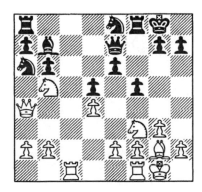

15 ♖c3 ♘ec7 16 ♘xc7

White has to play accurately to keep his advantage. For example Beliavsky gives the following line as equal: 16 ♖fc1 ♖fc8 17 ♘e5 ♘xb5! 18 ♕xb5 ♖xc3 19 ♖xc3 ♘c7 20 ♕a4 a6 21 ♕b3 ♕d6 and Black holds.

16...♘xc7 17 h3!!

With this surprisingly strong move White introduces a new challenge to Black's pawn structure and prepares to open a second front of attack, a thematic progression after softening Black up on the queenside.

17...♖fc8 18 g4 g6

Hoping to maintain his presence in the centre. The alternative 18...♘e8!? leads to a pleasant position for White after 19 gxf5 exf5 20 ♖xc8 ♗xc8 21 ♘e5, the e5-knight being difficult to dislodge after 21...♘f6 and the pressure against Black's centre quite uncomfortable.

19 gxf5 gxf5 20 ♘e5 ♘e8 21 ♖g3+

The second front of attack is now open!

21...♔h8 22 ♔h2 ♘f6 23 ♖g1 ♖c7 24 ♗f3 ♗c6

24...♘e4 runs into 25 ♗xe4 dxe4 26 ♕xa7! etc.

26 ♗h5!

White's attack is now irresistible. Every piece is promised a role in the decisive finale.

26...♕f8 27 ♖xg8+ ♘xg8 28 ♕g3 ♗b5

28...♗e8 29 ♗xe8 ♕xe8 30 ♘g6+ and White picks up the rook on c7.

29 ♕h4 ♘f6 30 ♗f7! 1-0

Game 19
Van der Sterren-Winants
Wijk aan Zee 1990

---

1 d4 f5 2 g3 e6 3 ♗g2 ♘f6 4 c4 c6 5 ♘f3 d5 6 0-0 ♗d6 7 ♗f4 ♗xf4

At least this way sees White suffer inconvenience for the removal of the dark-squared bishops in the shape of his altered kingside complex.

8 gxf4 ♘bd7

This move is slightly inaccurate but need not harm Black's prospects if followed by 9...0-0.

9 e3

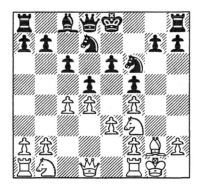

9...b6?!

One mistake often leads to another, and Black's understandable preference for immediate queenside development is not to be recommended. Black is sure to castle kingside at some point and should do so now rather than present White with an early target. This logical treatment will be considered later in this chapter. After the text White has a forcing line that prevents Black from castling and therefore makes further development awkward.

10 cxd5!

Highlighting the vulnerability of the pawns on f5 and c6 should Black recapture with the e-pawn.

10...cxd5

Of course not 10...exd5 11 ♕c2.

11 ♕a4! ♗b7

Black already has development problems with his king stuck in the centre. Note that 11...0-0 loses to 12 ♕c6!.

12 ♕a3!

Again Black's king comes under inspection, practically forcing the exchange of queens and producing a position in which Black has no prospects of genuine counterplay. One of the main reasons is that without queens on the board there is no threat of an attack from Black, and White can even remove an unwelcome knight with ♗xe4 because his remaining pieces are strong. White has certainly won the opening battle.

12...♕e7 13 ♖c1! ♕xa3 14 ♘xa3 ♔d8 15 ♘b5 ♘e8 16 ♘g5 ♔e7 17 ♘c7 ♘xc7 18 ♖xc7 ♖ab8 19 ♖ac1

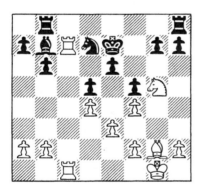

The threat of tying Black down with ♘f7! guarantees White a big lead.

19...♖hc8 20 ♘xh7

Winning a pawn and, eventually, the game.

20...♖xc7 21 ♖xc7 ♔d6 22 ♖c3 ♖c8 23 ♖xc8 ♗xc8 24 ♗f1 ♘b8 25 ♘g5 ♗a6 26 ♘f7+ ♔e7 27 ♘e5 ♗b7 28 ♗b5 ♗a8 29 ♔g2 ♔f6 30 ♔g3 ♗b7 31 ♔h4 ♗a8 32 ♔g3 ♗b7 33 ♔h4 ♗a8 34 a3 ♗b7 35 ♔h5 ♗a8 36 ♔h4 ♗b7 37 ♔h5 ♗a8 38 h3 ♗b7 39 ♔h4 ♗a8 40 ♔g3 ♗b7 41 ♔h4 ♗a8 42 ♔h5 ♗b7 43 b4 ♗a8 44 ♘d7+ ♘xd7 45 ♗xd7 ♗b7 46 b5 a6 47 a4 axb5 48 axb5 ♔e7

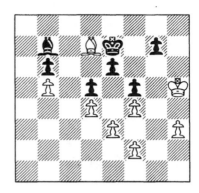

49 ♔g6 ♔xd7 50 ♔xg7 ♗c6 51 h4 1-0

Game 20
Krasenkov-Ulibin
Polish TV Knockout 1997

I have a feeling that there is something wrong with this game – probably the result. I guess that it was a quickplay game, which would help explain the strange mistakes at the end. However I find it very interesting and instructive, so here we go...

1 d4 e6 2 c4 f5 3 g3 ♘f6 4 ♗g2 c6 5 ♘f3 d5 6 0-0 ♗d6 7 ♗f4 ♗xf4 8 gxf4 0-0 9 ♕b3!?

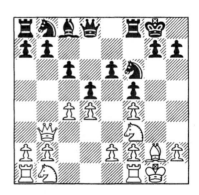

Krasenkov's pet move. The main idea is to hinder Black's queenside development. Normally in this system Black's bishop goes to h5 via d7 and e8, but now this is not possible since b7 is under fire. Another clever idea is that 9...♕b6 is answered with 10 ♕c2!, when the black queen is awkwardly placed on b6, while its opposite number is fine on c2. Not crucial, of course, but still a superior version for White than the immediate 9 ♕c2. As only two games have been played with the text at the this level it is not yet clear what we can expect from this line. Personally I believe that Black should find some comfortable way to equalize, and that this already exists in some of the major Stonewall experts' personal files.

9...♕e7

I do not think that this is less logical than 9...b6, which was the move Krasenkov met when he first tried 9 ♕b3!?. Krasenkov-Gleizerov, Poland 1993, continued 10 ♘c3 ♗b7 (not necessarily best as Black can also try to take advantage of the awkward position of White's queen with 10...♗a6!? 11 cxd5 ♘xd5! 12 ♘xd5 exd5 13 ♕c2 ♕d6 14 ♘e5 ♕e6 15 ♖fc1 ♖c8 16 ♗h3 g6 17 e3 ♘d7 with a decent position – this line deserves further investigation) 11 ♖ac1 ♘e4 12 ♘xe4?! (I agree with Gleizerov that 12 ♖fd1 gives White an edge) 12...fxe4 13 ♘g5 ♖f6 14 cxd5 cxd5 (14...exd5! seems much better, with the tactical justification evident in the variation 15 ♗xe4 h6 16 ♘h3 ♖e6 17 ♗f3 ♕h4 18 ♔g2 ♔h8 and Black has good compensation for the pawn, while 15 ♘xe4 ♖xf4 16 ♘c5 ♗c8 is unclear) 14...cxd5 15 ♗h3 ♕d7 (also possible is 15...♕d6 16 ♕a3 ♕d7 17 ♘xe6! [17 ♕g3?! Does not work out well after 17...♘c6 18 ♗xe6+ ♖xe6 19 ♕h3 ♖d6 20 ♕xh7+ ♔f8 21 ♕h8+ ♔e7 22 ♕xg7+ ♔d8] 17...♖xe6 18 ♗xe6+ ♕xe6 19 ♖c7 and White has compensation according to Gleizerov) 16 f5 exf5 17 ♘xe4 ♖h6, and now 18 ♘g5! ♘c6 19 ♕d3 ♖f6 20 f4 left White slightly better.

10 ♘bd2 ♘e4 11 e3 ♔h8 12 ♔h1 ♘d7 13 ♕c2 ♘df6

Black is too busy with his knights. 13...b6!? is a perfectly reliable alternative,

when I believe Black is doing well. It is the tactical aspect of this game that does not fit in with Black's strategy.

14 ♘xe4 fxe4 15 ♘e5 ♘d7 16 f3

White's development lead is beginning to tell, although Black should not be unduly worried just yet.

16...♘xe5 17 dxe5 exf3 18 ♖xf3 g5?

But this is simply a beginner's mistake from a strong GM, and difficult to believe. Of course Black has his reasons but he is nevertheless violating one of the most important principles of chess: do not open the position when your opponent is ahead in development.

19 ♖g3?

Hastily beginning the attack. After the accurate 19 ♖g1! White enjoys his new open file and an advantage. The impatient text affords Black an opportunity to get claim justification in his ambitious thrust of the g-pawn.

19...gxf4 20 exf4 ♖xf4!

This also seems risky but Black's reasoning is easy to follow: White will gain some time to facilitate his attack and Black lags behind in development, but this is a free pawn, and Black is not without resources. From a practical standpoint it is the familiar situation of the attacker and the defender – White needs only appreciate the idea of ♗f1-d3 in order to decide on 19 ♖g3, but Black has to search for and analyse numerous such ideas. Defending might go well for some moves but it is easier for Black to make a mistake than for White.

21 ♖g1

With the key idea ♗xd5 to clear the g-file.

21...♗d7 22 ♗f1!

The grand plan, intending to triple with 23 ♕g2.

22...♕f7

From here on things get rather weird. Instead 22...c5!? 23 ♕g2 ♕f8 24 ♗d3 ♖f7 25 ♖h3 ♕e7! 26 ♖g3 ♕f8 is a drawing line.

23 ♗d3 ♖f2 24 ♕d1 c5??

Losing valuable time. Forced is 24...dxc4! 25 ♖g7! cxd3! 26 ♖xf7 ♖xf7 27 ♕xd3 c5 with a dynamically balanced position.

25 ♖h3?! 1-0

Black must block with 25...♖f5, parting with an exchange. It seems unfair to look for an improvement on a move that results in resignation, but White has a forced win in 25 cxd5! exd5 26 ♖g7 d4 27 ♖xf7 ♗c6+ 28 ♖g2 ♗xg2+ (28...♖xg2 29 ♖xh7+ ♔g8 30 ♕b3+) 29 ♔g1 ♖xf7 30 ♔xg2 ♖g8+ 31 ♔h1.

Game 21
Meduna-Klinger
Brocco 1990

---

1 d4 e6 2 g3 f5 3 ♗g2 ♘f6 4 c4 c6 5 ♘f3 d5 6 0-0 ♗d6 7 ♗f4 ♗xf4 8 gxf4 0-0 9 ♘bd2

The logic behind the text is that it will be played anyway sooner or later, and perhaps it is more important than e2-e3. Who knows? It is not an easy question to answer. If Black plays the logical 9...♘e4 White cannot take because f4 is unprotected, so there is 10 ♘e5 ♘bd7 11 ♘d3!?, or 10 e3 with a transposition to Games 30 and 31 (and possibly Games 24 and 27).

9...♕e7!?

Not the most natural. 9...♘e4 attracts attention, but not from the games played. Also logical is 9...♗d7, as in the next game and this note. 9...♕e7 can easily transpose and

can thus be considered as a more flexible version of 9...♗d7. Browne-Christiansen, Los Angeles 1996, continued 9...♗d7 10 ♘e5 ♗e8 11 ♕b3 ♕b6 (11...♕e7 followed by 12...♘a6 or 12...♘e4 seems more appropriate; the queen has no business on b6) 12 ♕c3!? ♘bd7 13 e3 ♖d8 14 cxd5 cxd5 15 f3 h6 16 ♘b3 ♘xe5 17 fxe5 ♘d7 18 f4 ♗h5 19 ♖fc1 with a better game for White.

Black can also play 9...♘bd7. A good game to illustrate White's possibilities on the queenside is Olafsson-Chandler, Hastings 1990. White played 10 b4!, a strong pawn sacrifice that Black should consider declining. After 10...a5 11 a3 axb4 12 axb4 ♖xa1 13 ♕xa1 dxc4 14 ♘xc4 ♘d5 15 e3 ♘xb4 16 ♖b1 ♘d5 17 ♕a3 ♘7f6 18 ♘fe5 White had definite compensation and later won.

10 ♘e5 ♗d7 11 e3

11 ♕b3 ♗e8 is mentioned in the previous note; for 11 a3 see Game 23.

11...♗e8 12 ♔h1 ♔h8 13 ♖g1 ♘bd7 14 ♘df3

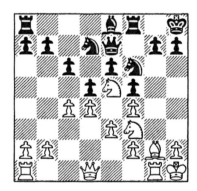

14...♘g4!

This solves Black's opening problems but is at the same time a little boring. However, it does serve to demonstrate that White has no advantage to slow in this line.

15 ♕e2 ♘dxe5 16 ♘xe5 ♕h4 17 ♘xg4 fxg4 18 f3 ♗h5 19 fxg4 ♗xg4 20 ♗f3 ♗xf3+ 21 ♕xf3 ♕f6 22 ♕h5 dxc4 23 ♖ac1 ♖ad8 24 ♖xc4 ♖d5 25 ♕g4 h6 26 ♖c2 g5 27 ♖f2 e5 28 dxe5 ♖xe5 29 h4

♖xe3 30 hxg5 ♕f5 31 ♕xf5 ♖xf5 32 gxh6 ½-½.

Game 22
Levitt-Tisdall
London 1990

---

1 d4 f5 2 ♘f3 ♘f6 3 g3 e6 4 ♗g2 d5 5 0-0 ♗d6 6 c4 c6 7 ♗f4 ♗xf4 8 gxf4 0-0 9 ♘bd2 ♗d7 10 ♕b3

This is Levitt's idea. He wants to disturb the development of Black's queenside, but this is not so serious. Now Black should not play 10...♕b6 in view of 11 ♕c2!, when White has gained half a tempo.

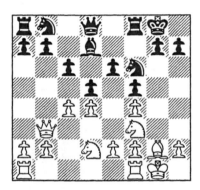

10...b5?!

A rather drastic reaction to the threat to the b-pawn, allowing White to close the queenside and subsequently be the first to create threats on the kingside. Better is the more flexible 10...♕c8 11 ♘e5 ♗e8 12 ♔h1 ♗h5 13 f3 ♘bd7 14 ♖ac1 ♔h8 15 e4 dxe4 16 fxe4 ♘xe5 17 dxe5, and a draw was agreed in Levitt-L.B.Hansen, Denmark 1990.

11 c5!

Fixing the weakness on c6, which Black will be busy protecting c6. Consequently Black will have problems finding harmony for his forces.

11...a5 12 ♘e5 ♗e8 13 ♔h1 ♖a7 14 ♖g1 ♗h5 15 ♗f3!

White is ready to launch his attack on the g-file.

15...♗xf3+ 16 ♘dxf3

The exchange brings White's other knight closer to the main battleground.

16...♘e4 17 ♖g2 ♕c8?

Levitt sees this as the losing error and considers 17...♖e7 as correct. Black's plight is uncomfortable, but after the text there is no defence.

18 ♖ag1 ♖e7

If Black had time to play ...♘d7 and snuff out the knight on e5 he might weather the storm.

19 ♘g5!

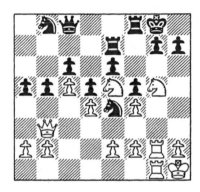

19...♘d7?

Black's defensive task is difficult and it is doubtful whether he can hold in the long-term. Levitt gives the following nice lines: 19...♘f6? 20 ♕h3 ♘bd7 21 ♘xe6! ♖xe6 22 ♖xg7+ ♔h8 23 ♕xh7+!! ♘xh7 24 ♖g8+ ♖xg8 25 ♘f7 with a fantastic mate, and 19...♖f6? 20 ♕h3 ♖h6 21 ♕xh6 gxh6 22 ♘xe4+ ♔h8 23 ♘f6 and White has an easy win. Finally, 19...♘xg5! looks best, when 20 ♖xg5 ♖f6 21 ♕g3 ♕f8 22 h4 is quite unpleasant for Black but the best hope.

20 ♘xh7!!

Not 20 ♘xe6? ♘xf2+!, and Black survives.

20...♔xh7 21 ♘g6 ♕d8 22 ♕h3+ ♔g8 23 ♕h8+ ♔f7 24 ♘xf8!

Levitt entertains us with an amusing winning line after 24 ♘e5+?! ♘xe5? (24...♔e8 is necessary) 25 ♖xg7+ ♔e8 26 ♕xf8+! ♔xf8 27 ♖g8+ ♔f7 28 ♖1g7+ ♔f6 29 dxe5 mate!

24...♞xf8 25 ♖xg7+ ♔e8 26 ♕xf8+! 1-0

Game 23
Brestian-Klinger
Austria 1989

---

1 d4 e6 2 ♞f3 f5 3 c4 ♞f6 4 g3 d5 5 ♗g2 c6 6 0-0 ♗d6 7 ♗f4 ♗xf4 8 gxf4 0-0 9 ♞e5

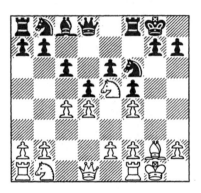

Despite not being dangerous for Black there is some logic behind this early posting. Basically the knight is coming d3 to be partnered by the other on d2, a set-up not unlike the 7 b3 variation. With control of both e4 and e5 very much part of the Stonewall this is a sensible strategy, but Black should be able to equalize with accurate play.

9...♕e7

As we will see Black should immediately challenge the knight with ...♞bd7 (and ...♞xe5), but Klinger's choice is not bad. However, I do not recommend the bizarre 9...♞fd7?! (why this knight?) from the game Beliavsky-Tseshkovsky, Cetinje 1992. After 10 ♞d2 ♞xe5 11 dxe5 ♕e7 12 ♖c1 ♞a6 13 a3 ♖d8 14 b4 ♗d7 15 ♖c3 ♗e8 16 ♕c2 White was doing well. Nevertheless Black managed to make matters worse: 16...d4 17 ♖d3 ♗h5 18 ♞b3 c5 19 b5 ♞c7 20 ♗xb7 ♖ab8 21 ♗g2 a6 22 a4 axb5 23 axb5 ♞xb5 24 cxb5 c4 25 ♕xc4 ♗xe2 26 ♞xd4 ♖dc8 27 ♞c6 ♕e8 28 ♖e1 1-0.

10 ♞d2 ♗d7

This is the idea behind 9...♕e7. On 10...♞bd7 White can play 11 ♞d3!? with an edge.

11 a3 a5?!

I do not like this move, which seems to facilitate White's queenside play, although by this stage White can already claim a slight advantage.

12 c5

Clamping down on the b7-pawn.

12...♗e8 13 b4 axb4 14 axb4 ♞a6 15 e3 ♔h8 16 ♔h1

It is not unusual to see both kings leave the g-file after the recapture gxf4.

16...♗h5 17 f3

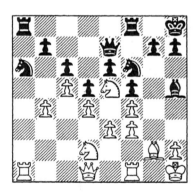

17...♞d7

17...♞xb4 18 ♖xa8 ♖xa8 19 ♕b3 ♞a6 20 ♖b1, e.g. 20...♖b8 21 ♗f1.

18 ♞d3 ♞c7 19 ♕b3 h6 20 ♖xa8 ♖xa8 21 ♕b2 g5

Played with the intention of ...g5-g4 to win back control of the e4-square.

22 ♞b3 ♞f6 23 ♞a5

It is clear that Black's opening problems remain into the middlegame. The b7-pawn is the chief worry.

23...♞b5 24 ♕f2 g4 25 ♞e5 ♖g8 26 fxg4 ♞xg4 27 ♞xg4 ♗xg4 28 h3 ♗h5 29 ♖g1 ♞c3 30 ♗f1 ♞e4

Ironically the e4-knight will prove less significant than its opposite number on a5.

31 ♖xg8+ ♔xg8 32 ♕e1 ♔h7

Black's position looks reasonably solid but

---

it is actually difficult to defend. The b7-pawn continues to be a burden requiring attention and White has plans to turn the screw on the queenside with b4-b5 and, with the exchange of bishop for knight, steer the game to a winning ending. It is understandable that Klinger failed to find a way out of this mess.

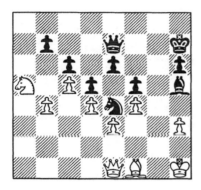

33 ♗g2 ♕g7 34 ♔h2 ♕e7 35 ♘b3 ♕f6 36 ♘c1 ♕g7 37 ♘d3 ♕f6 38 ♘e5 ♕e7 39 ♗f1 ♕d8 40 ♗d3 ♕e7 41 b5 cxb5 42 ♗xb5 ♕d8 43 ♗d3 ♕e7 44 ♗xe4

Finally reducing Black to a 'bad' bishop v. good knight ending.

44...fxe4 45 ♕a5 ♕g7 46 ♕d8 ♗f3 47 ♕d7 ♕xd7 48 ♘xd7 ♔g7 49 f5

A useful move which favourably clears the centre.

49...exf5 50 ♘b6 f4 51 ♘xd5 fxe3 52 ♘xe3 ♔g6 53 ♔g3 ♗e2 54 ♔f4 ♗b5 55 d5 ♗d7 56 ♘g4 e3 57 ♔xe3 ♔g5 58 ♔e4 h5 59 ♘f2 ♗a4 60 ♔e5 ♔h4 61 ♔f4 ♗b3 62 d6 ♗a4 63 ♘d3 ♔xh3 64 ♘e5 ♗e8 65 d7 ♗xd7 66 ♘xd7 h4 67 ♔f3 ♔h2 68 ♔f2 h3 69 ♘e5 ♔h1 70 ♘g4 1-0

Game 24
Mikhalcisin-Dreev
Pavlodar 1987

---

1 d4 d5 2 c4 e6 3 g3 c6 4 ♗g2 f5 5 ♘f3 ♘f6 6 0-0 ♗d6 7 ♗f4 ♗xf4 8 gxf4 0-0 9 ♘e5 ♘bd7!

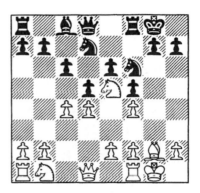

The most precise response to the new arrival. Black decides to challenge the knight immediately. As we have seen a number of times Black is no worse after the exchange of all the knights, so why not?

10 e3

10 ♘d2!? is interesting, delaying e2-e3. Now Black should not allow 10...♘e4?! 11 ♘df3! ♘df6 (11...♘xe5 12 ♘xe5 ♗d7 13 e3 ♗e8 14 ♗xe4 fxe4 15 ♕g4 is good for White according to Belov) 12 e3 ♗d7 13 ♘g5, when both 13...♘xg5 14 fxg5 ♘e4 15 h4 ♗e8 16 ♗xe4 fxe4 17 f4 (Belov) and 13...♕e7 14 f3 ♘d6 15 c5, Notkin-Gleizerov, Podolsk 1993, favour White. Instead 10...♘xe5 11 dxe5 ♘e4 and Black does not seem worse, while 11...♘g4!? is an interesting move, with the idea 12 h3 ♘h6 followed by ...♘f7 and ...g7-g5.

10...♘e4

Just as natural is the immediate 10...♘xe5. Then 11 dxe5 ♘g4! (practice has proved this to be the correct continuation) 12 h3 ♘h6 13 ♘d2 ♘f7 14 ♘b3 ♗d7 15 ♘d4 ♕b6 was no worse for Black in Mikhalcisin-Vaiser, USSR 1988, and 11 fxe5 ♘g4 12 ♘d2 ♗d7 13 h3 ♘h6 14 f4 ♗e8 15 ♔h2 ♔h8 16 ♕e2 g5 17 fxg5 ♕xg5 18 ♕f2 ♗h5, Beliavsky-Salov, Vilnius 1987, produced an equal game.

11 ♘d2

11 ♘d3 dxc4 promises White nothing so he has to accept the exchanges. 11 f3 ♘d6 12 c5 ♘xe5! 13 fxe5 ♘f7 14 ♘c3 g5! 15 ♘e2

♔h8 16 f4 g4 gave Black counterplay in Sha-balov-Glek, USSR 1987.

11...♘xe5 12 dxe5 ♗d7 13 ♕e2 ♘xd2 14 ♕xd2

The position is level.

14...♗e8 15 cxd5 cxd5 16 ♖fc1 ♗c6

Not only does the bishop block the c-file, but the a8-h1 diagonal might hold some promise for Black should he open the g-file.

17 ♖c5

In view of what soon happens to White, perhaps 17 ♔h1 is necessary, bringing his own rook(s) to the g-file.

17...♔h8 18 b4 a6 19 a4 ♖g8 20 ♔h1

Too late.

20...♕h4 21 ♖a2 g5

The inevitable push of the g-pawn. It is important to remember with this typical pawn structure that this thrust is sometimes the only available pawn break, thereby giving Black more flexibility.

22 fxg5

Having a go on the queenside with 22 b5 anyway favours Black, e.g. 22...axb5 23 axb5 ♖xa2 24 ♕xa2 ♗e8 25 fxg5 ♕xg5 26 f4 ♕e7 and the b5-pawn drops.

22...♖xg5 23 f4 ♖xg2! 24 ♕xg2

24 ♔xg2 ♖g8+ spells the end for White.

24...♕e1+ 25 ♕g1 ♕xb4 0-1

A sample continuation is 26 ♖cc2 ♕e4+ 27 ♖g2 d4 and Black can win at leisure, while 26 ♖xc6 is futile.

Game 25
Borges Mateos-Agdestein
Capablanca Mem., Havana 1998

---

1 d4 e6 2 c4 f5 3 g3 ♘f6 4 ♗g2 d5 5 ♘f3 ♗d6 6 0-0 c6 7 ♕c2 0-0 8 ♗f4 ♗xf4 9 gxf4

Note that the normal route to here is 7 ♗f4 ♗xf4 8 gxf4 0-0 9 ♕c2. In fact ♕c2 offers White's immediate prospects little or nothing, serving only to present Black with time to develop. Consequently Black has no worries.

9...♗d7

A decent alternative is 9...♘e4 10 e3 ♕e7 11 ♘c3 ♗d7 12 ♘e5 ♗e8 13 ♘xe4 fxe4 14 ♕b3 (early evidence that White has gained very little from placing his queen on c2) 14...a5 15 f3 exf3 16 ♖xf3 a4 17 ♕a3 ♕xa3 18 bxa3 ♘d7 19 ♘xd7 ♗xd7 20 ♖c1 ♖a5 with equal chances, Burmakin-Ulibin, Kstovo 1997.

10 ♘bd2 ♗e8 11 e3

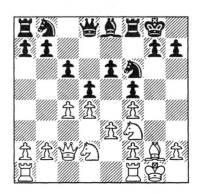

11...♘e4

Not necessarily the best move. 11...♘bd7 12 cxd5 cxd5 13 ♕b3 was preferable for White in Gausel-Dizdar, Reykjavik 1988, but consistent completion of development with 11...♗h5!? has served Black well. Lukov-Knaak, Halle 1987, went 12 b4 ♗xf3 13 ♘xf3 ♘bd7 14 c5 ♘e8 15 a4 h6 16 b5 g5 with a good game for Black. In Iljushin-Moroz, Pardubice 1995 Black replied to 12 ♘e5 with the now familiar 12...♘g4!?, and after 13 ♘xg4 ♗xg4 14 f3 ♗h5 15 ♖f2 ♘d7 16 ♗f1 ♔h8 17 ♖g2 ♖g8 18 ♔h1 ♘f6 19 ♗e2 ♖c8 20 c5 the game was dynamically balanced.

12 ♕b3 ♕b6?!

As we saw in Game 22, note to Black's 10th move, Black should prefer ...♕c8.

13 ♘xe4 fxe4 14 ♘e5!

White now has a slightly preferable pawn structure and Black's bishop lacks a future.

14...♗h5 15 f3?!

White has a very strong move in 15 ♗h3!,

activating his bishop and leaving its opposite number punching air. After 15...♖f6 16 cxd5 exd5 (16...cxd5 17 ♕xb6 axb6 18 ♖fc1 ♘a6 19 a3 might improve, although White's knight reigns and Black is struggling) 17 ♗c8 ♕xb3 18 axb3 a6 19 ♗xb7 ♖a7 20 ♗c8 it has been a worthwhile expedition for White, netting a pawn.

15...exf3 16 ♗xf3 ♗xf3 17 ♖xf3 ♕xb3 18 axb3 ♖d8

Thanks to the series of exchanges Black is close to achieving equality. Consequently, with his opponent ready to bring his knight into play, White wastes no time stepping up the pace.

19 f5! exf5 20 ♖xf5 ♘d7 21 ♘xd7 ♖xd7 22 cxd5 cxd5 23 ♖a5!

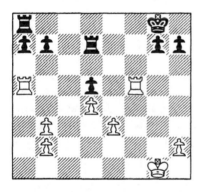

The rook ending is at best unpleasant for Black, who must either surrender a pawn or grant White two connected passed pawns. In practical terms Black has an unenviable defensive task ahead.

23...♖e8 24 ♔f2 ♖c7 25 ♖axd5 ♖c2+ 26 ♔f3 ♖xb2 27 ♖b5 b6 28 h3 ♖h2 29 ♖be5 ♖xh3+ 30 ♔e4 ♖h4+ 31 ♔d3 ♖f8 32 d5 ♖d8 33 e4 ♖h3+ 34 ♔c4 b5+ 35 ♔b4 a5+ 36 ♔xa5 ♖xb3 37 ♖e7 1-0

Game 26
Vladimirov-Dolmatov
Russia 1989

---

1 d4 e6 2 c4 f5 3 g3 ♘f6 4 ♗g2 d5 5

♘f3 c6 6 0-0 ♗d6 7 ♗f4 ♗xf4 8 gxf4 0-0 9 ♘c3

As has already been discussed elsewhere a knight on c3 tends to carry out no other function than removing a troublesome horse from e4, for from c3 it is not in contact with the important e5-square. Consequently the text is not considered to pose Black any difficulties. Moreover with stereotyped play White can easily find himself in an awkward situation.

9...b6

This is not the only way to achieve a good position. 9...♗d7 10 ♕b3 ♕b6 11 ♘e5! ♗e8 12 ♕a3! was Birnboim-Keitlinghaus, Ramat Hasharon 1987, when Black could have kept the balance with 12...♕d8!.

10 ♘e5 ♗b7 11 ♕a4

Hoping to inconvenience Black by exerting pressure on the c6-pawn. Unfortunately Black can address this matter comfortably, leaving White with insufficient pressure to justify the queen sally.

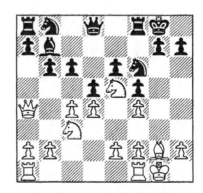

11...♘fd7!

A logical response well worth remembering. By liquidating his opponent's strongest piece Black puts an end to White's hopes of a queenside initiative. Over on the other flank, meanwhile, we must not forget that White still has compromised pawns, providing Black with a target at some stage of the game.

12 ♖ad1 ♘xe5 13 fxe5 ♔h8!

Introducing the possibility that Black might generate dangerous threats down the g-file.

14 b4?!

Clearly not in a position to throw his weight around on the kingside White must look to the queenside for activity. However, the text is not the right way to go about it because now Black can engineer some decent play for himself on this flank, too. Better is 14 cxd5 to try to open lines for the white army.

14...a6! 15 ♕b3 b5 16 cxb5?

White's queenside ambitions disappear with this capture. In fact after Black's next Dolmatov obtains the better chances on both sides of the board.

16...axb5 17 a4 bxa4 18 ♘xa4 ♘d7 19 ♖a1 ♗a6 20 ♕c2 ♗c4 21 ♕d2 h6 22 ♘b2 ♗b5 23 ♘d3 ♕e7 24 ♘f4 ♔h7 25 h4 g5! 26 ♘h3! ♔g6!

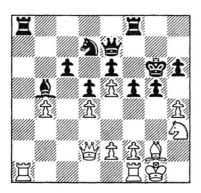

The fact that Black is free to bring his king to the third rank to join in the makings of an attack is testament to his potentially superior kingside prospects in lines where White invites a trade of bishops on f4. Notice also Black's traditionally problem bishop, now transformed on b5. There is no doubt that White is struggling in the diagram position, but after his next he is close to losing. The best policy is to wait for ...g5-g4 and then jump into f4. The opening of the h-file helps only Black.

27 hxg5? hxg5 28 f4 g4 29 ♘g5 ♖fb8! 30 ♔f2 ♘f8 31 ♖h1 ♖xa1 32 ♖xa1 ♘h7 33 ♖h1 ♘xg5 34 fxg5 ♕xg5 35 ♕xg5+ ♔xg5 36 ♖h7 ♖a8 37 e3 ♖a2+ 38 ♔g3 ♖e2 39 ♖g7+ ♔h5 40 ♖h7+ ♔g6 41 ♖e7 ♖xe3+ 42 ♔h4 f4! 43 ♖xe6+ ♔g7 44 ♔xg4 ♖g3+ 45 ♔xf4 ♖xg2 46 ♖f6 ♖f2+ 47 ♔g5 ♖f1 48 ♖g6+ ♔f7 49 ♖h6 ♖g1+ 50 ♔f4 ♖d1 51 ♔f5 ♗d3+ 52 ♔g5 ♖g1+ 53 ♔f4 ♖f1+ 54 ♔g5 ♖c1 55 ♔f4 ♔e7 56 ♖h3 ♖f1+ 57 ♔g5 ♗f5 58 ♖h6 ♗e6 59 ♖h7+ ♖f7 60 ♖h4 ♖g7+ 61 ♔f4 ♔d7 62 ♔f3 ♖f7+ 63 ♔e2 ♔c7 64 ♖h6 ♗f5 65 ♔e3 ♗e4 66 ♖h3 ♖f1 0-1

Game 27
Ziegler-Gleizerov
Gothenberg 1997

1 d4 e6 2 c4 f5 3 g3 ♘f6 4 ♗g2 c6 5 ♘f3 d5 6 0-0 ♗d6 7 ♗f4 ♗xf4 8 gxf4 0-0 9 e3

Sensibly strengthening the pawn structure – which White will almost certainly have to do in the near future – without yet committing himself to a specific continuation of development.

9...♕e7!?

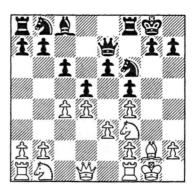

Although it does not appear to be the most natural, this is a good move, being no less logical than 9...♗d7 (Game 28) or the popular 9...♘e4 (Games 29-31). However the ostensibly feasible 9...♘bd7 has a poor history, having all but disappeared from the professional scene since Beliavsky-Yusupov, Linares 1989: 10 ♕e2 (10 ♘e5 ♘xe5 11 dxe5 ♘d7 12 ♘d2 ♕e7 13 ♖c1 ♖d8 14 ♕c2 was better for White in Beliavsky-Van der Wiel, Amsterdam 1990, but Black could have improved with 10...♘e4) 10...♔h8 11 ♘c3 ♕e7 12 ♔h1 ♖g8 13 cxd5! with advantage to White. Check out this game in the Introduction.

10 ♘bd2!

The key to White's plan is to keep in touch with the e5-square. The alternative deployment of the knight is less dangerous for Black, for after 10 ♘c3 White's lack of communication between his knights affords Black the luxury of being able to send his bishop to h5 with 10...♗d7!. Bauer-Vaiser, Cappelle 1994 continued 11 ♘e5 ♗e8 12 ♗f3 ♘e4 13 ♖c1 ♘d7 14 ♔h1 ♕h4 15 ♘xd7 ♗xd7 16 ♗xe4 fxe4 17 f3 exf3 18 ♕xf3 ♗e8 19 ♕g3 ♕e7 20 ♘d1 c5 21 cxd5 cxd4 22 exd4 exd5 23 ♘c3 ♗g6 24 ♖ce1 ♗e4+ with an equal game.

10...♘e4

Black can also try 10...♗d7!? but I have a feeling that White should achieve some kind of advantage. Nonetheless Cisneros-Vaiser, Spain 1996 saw Black earn himself a playable position after 11 ♘e5 ♗e8 12 a3 ♘bd7 13 ♘xd7 ♕xd7 14 c5 h6 15 ♘f3 ♔h8 16 ♘e5 ♕e7 17 ♔h1 ♖g8 18 ♖g1 g5.

11 ♘xe4 fxe4 12 ♘d2! ♗d7 13 f3

13...exf3 14 ♘xf3 ♗e8 15 ♕b3 dxc4 16 ♕xc4

White might have a slight edge but is eventually outplayed by his higher rated opponent.

16...♘d7 17 ♘e5

Since White now achieves nothing from opening the d-file the text seems a little premature.

17...♘xe5 18 dxe5 ♗f7 19 ♖ad1 ♖ad8 20 ♗f3 h6 21 b4 ♖xd1 22 ♖xd1 ♖d8 23 ♖d4 ♕h4

The problem for White is his vulnerable kingside. Note that White's bishop is busy defending the king, an inconvenience that Black does not experience with his superior kingside formation.

24 ♖xd8+ ♕xd8 25 ♕c3 ♕h4 26 ♕d2 ♗g6 27 a3 ♔h7 28 e4

The circumspect 28 ♕f2 holds together without further compromising White's pawns. Now both e4 and f4 are potentially weak, and the e5-pawn might also be undermined after ...g7-g5.

28...♗h5 29 ♗g2 ♕g4 30 ♕e3 ♕d1+ 31 ♔f2 ♕c2+ 32 ♔g3 ♗g6 33 ♗f3 b6 34 h4 h5 35 ♕e2 ♕b1 36 ♗xh5

Allowing the change of pace Black has been looking for. 36 ♕e3 looks sensible, while 36 f5!? is also possible.

36...♕g1+ 37 ♔h3 ♕h1+ 38 ♔g3 ♗xe4 39 ♗g4 ♕g1+ 40 ♔h3 ♕h1+ 41 ♔g3 ♕g1+ 42 ♔h3 ♗d5

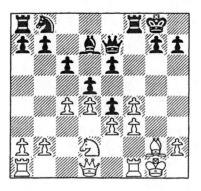

43 f5

Another committal move, but Black has this pawn covered. 43 ♗f3 is safer.

43...♕c1 44 fxe6 ♕xa3+ 45 ♔h2 ♕xb4 46 ♗f5+ ♔g8 47 ♗h7+ ♔h8

47...♔xh7 48 ♕h5+ ♔g8 49 ♕f7+ draws.

48 ♔g3 ♗xe6 49 ♗d3 ♔g8 50 h5 ♕d4 51 ♗g6 b5 52 ♗c2 a5 53 ♗g6 a4 54 ♕e1 b4 55 ♕e2 ♗c4 56 ♕e1 ♕c3+ 57 ♕xc3 bxc3 0-1

Game 28
Lobron-Hort
Munich 1991

---

1 d4 f5 2 g3 ♘f6 3 ♗g2 e6 4 ♘f3 d5 5 c4 c6 6 0-0 ♗d6 7 ♗f4 ♗xf4 8 gxf4 0-0 9 e3 ♗d7!?

Another natural looking try, intending to transfer the bishop to freedom on h5 as soon as possible. However with the b7-pawn now without protection White should waste no time highlighting the fact.

10 ♕b3!

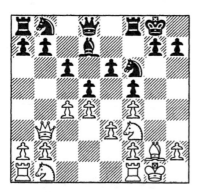

If there is a genuine test of 9...♗d7 then this is it, and it becomes more clear now why the previous game's 9...♕e7 deserves respect. Thanks to the vulnerable b7-pawn Black is unable to continue with normal development. Rather than follow a comfortable route to the early middlegame the next item on the agenda for Black is how to address the attack.

10...♕b6

The queen tends not to be well placed on b6, but Black wishes to reduce the pressure. 10...♕c8!? 11 ♘c3 ♗e8 12 ♖ac1 ♗h5 is the only decent alternative (for some reason Lobron mentions only 10...♕c7).

11 ♘c3 ♗e8

Trading queens does not damage White's pawn structure, rather presents White with a ready-made open a-file.

12 ♕c2!

Another example of this crafty retreat to a useful square to leave the black queen doing next to nothing on b6. In fact the queen is perhaps better placed on d8!

12...♘a6?!

And the knight must be poor here. Lobron suggests the more flexible 12...♔h8!? but I still prefer White.

13 a3 ♕d8 14 ♔h1 ♗h5 15 ♘g5!?

Tempting Black to nudge his h-pawn forward and thus weaken the g6-square. 15 ♘e5 also guarantees White an advantage.

15...♕e7 16 ♖g1 h6! 17 ♘f3 ♘b8 18 cxd5?

Presenting Black with an important equalising resource. Lobron's 18 ♘e5 maintains the tension and still favours White. Note that in these positions it would be unwise for Black to take on c4 as there is no sensible way to hold on to the pawn and Black's influence on the key square is drastically reduced.

18...cxd5?

Missing his chance. Instead Black should throw in 18...♗xf3! 19 ♗xf3 and only then 19...cxd5, when ...♘c6 should be enough for equality.

19 ♘e5

Now White continues to control. Sometimes when the bishop reaches h5 it is anyway dominated by White's knight, leading to a trade on e5. The problem for Black here is that this exchange will create further problems because the new e5-pawn restricts him considerably. Better to have removed the

---

horse when it was still on f3.

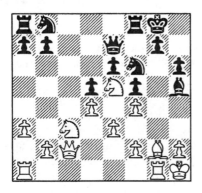

19...♘bd7 20 f3 ♘e8?!

Again 20...♔h8 improves, although White retains the advantage by switching plans with 21 ♕b3! ♖ab8 22 ♕b4 ♕xb4 23 axb4 a6 24 ♘a4.

Returning to the main game, from here the quality is not too high but what happens is another good illustration of the problems Black can experience if his opponent is able to exploit the g-file for his own ends. I have left in the annotations given by Lobron.

21 ♕f2 ♖c8 22 ♖ac1? ♘d6 23 ♗f1 a6 24 ♗d3 ♘f7 25 ♖g3 ♘dxe5 26 dxe5! ♖c7 27 ♖cg1 ♘d8 28 ♖h3 ♕e8! 29 ♕h4 ♗g6 30 ♖hg3 ♗h5! 31 e4 dxe4 32 fxe4 ♔h8 33 h3 ♖d7 34 exf5 exf5 35 ♗c4 ♖c7!? 36 ♗d5 ♖d7 37 ♔h2 g6? 38 ♗b3? ♘e6?? 39 ♗xe6 ♕xe6 40 ♖xg6 ♖d2+ 41 ♖6g2 ♖xg2+ 42 ♖xg2 ♗f3 43 ♖g3 ♗c6 44 ♘e2 ♔h7 45 ♘d4 ♕d7 46 ♕h5 ♕f7 47 ♕xf7+ ♖xf7 48 ♘xc6 bxc6 49 ♖c3 ♖c7 50 b4 ♔g6 51 ♔g3 ♔h5 52 ♔f3 ♔h4 53 ♖c1 ♖d7 54 ♖xc6 ♖d3+ 55 ♔e2 ♖d4 56 ♔e3 ♖e4+ 57 ♔f3 h5 58 ♖f6 ♖c4 59 ♖xf5 ♖c3+ 60 ♔e4 ♖xa3 61 e6 1-0

Game 29
Averkin-Ulibin
Elista 1997

---

1 d4 e6 2 ♘f3 f5 3 g3 ♘f6 4 ♗g2 d5 5 0-0 ♗d6 6 c4 c6 7 ♗f4 ♗xf4 8 gxf4 0-0 9 e3 ♘e4!

This is the main choice these days. Black occupies the usual outpost anyway before disturbing the queenside, being fully prepared to meet f2-f3. However, White's decision to evict the knight cannot be taken lightly because this removes protection from the e3-pawn and therefore leaves the dark squares on the kingside more susceptible to attack.
10 ♘e5

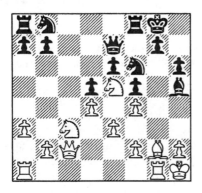

Not the most dangerous line. This game is a good illustration why.
10...♘d7

Black is prepared to eliminate the enemy knight when possible.
11 ♕c2 ♕e7 12 f3

White is trying to gain space and at the same time prevent Black from using the central squares. Black, for his part, is by no means unhappy with the course of the opening thus far, and the text leaves White surprisingly vulnerable in the event of a timely ...g7-g5 offensive.
12...♘d6 13 c5

Part of White's strategy to win territory. The wall of pawns looks impressive but a closer inspection reveals that it will require constant attention.
13...♘f7 14 ♘c3 ♘dxe5

Black keeps the busy king's knight in play – in fact the f7-square is a useful outpost indeed. Meanwhile the exit of the d7-knight frees the bishop and thus makes it easier to connect Black's rooks.

15 fxe5 f4!

A thematic challenge that gives Black a good compensation for White's extra space. As usual the c3-square is hardly an ideal home for the knight, White is certainly no better on the kingside and the text also undermines White's defence of the key d4-pawn. At the moment d4 is safe enough, but if it ever falls the c5- and e5-pawns will not be too healthy.

16 e4

After 16 exf4 Black's knight begins another journey: 16...♘h8!? 17 ♘e2 ♘g6 18 ♕d2 ♕h4 and the plan of ...b7-b6 and ...♗a6 offers Black at least an even game. However White deals with 15...f4 his d4-pawn is potentially weak.

16...♗d7 17 ♔h1 ♘g5 18 h4!?

Creating a virtually fatal weakness in front of his king, although it is understandable that White does not wish to give his opponent a free hand on the kingside. For example by clearing the e8-h5 diagonal Black introduces options of bringing the queen or bishop to g6 or h5. Nor does White have time to create his own play on the queenside.

18...♘f7 19 ♕f2 ♔h8

Note that Black has no interest in playing ...dxe4 because it is important to have a pawn on d5 if possible, denying White use of both c4 and e4.

20 ♗h3 g5 21 exd5 cxd5 22 ♖g1 ♖g8 23 hxg5 ♘xg5 24 ♕h4 ♖g6 25 ♖g4

25 ♘e2!? ♖f8 is also possible, with an unclear position. White prefers to make his own presence felt on the g-file.

25...♕g7 26 ♖ag1 ♖g8 27 ♘e2

It is fair to say the tension is mounting! With so many pieces concentrated on a couple of files something should give...

27...♘xf3!

Forcing the exit of all the major pieces. 27...♖h6 28 ♕xg5 ♖xh3+ 29 ♔g2 ♕xg5 30 ♖xg5 ♖xg5+ 31 ♔xh3 has a similar result,

favouring White slightly.

28 ♖xg6 ♘xh4 29 ♖xg7 ♖xg7 30 ♖xg7 ♔xg7 31 ♘xf4

The endgame is more or less equal. Black's passed h-pawn obviously has potential, but White's knight is good and e6 needs defending.

31...♔f7 32 ♗g4

Not 32 ♘xd5?? ♗c6.

32...♘g6 33 ♘h5 ♘e7 34 ♘f6

Winning the h-pawn but not the game since Black can regain the pawn shortly. White's big problem in trying to prove an advantage is the position of his king. In such endgames you should bring the king to the centre as soon as possible.

34...♗c8 35 ♘xh7 ♘c6 36 ♘g5+ ♔e7 37 ♘f3 ♘b4 38 a3?

The b-pawn will be easier to defend than its neighbour on the a-file. Unfortunately White has failed to see Black's main threat.

38...♘d3 39 b4?? ♘f2+ 40 ♔g1 ♘xg4 0-1

Game 30
Levitt-Porper
Badenweiler 1990

---

1 d4 e6 2 c4 f5 3 g3 ♘f6 4 ♗g2 c6 5 ♘f3 d5 6 0-0 ♗d6 7 ♗f4 ♗xf4 8 gxf4 0-0 9 e3 ♘e4!? 10 ♘bd2

Having seen that 10 ♘e5 can easily prove ineffective we turn to a different approach. This time White plans to exchange on e4 and follow up by further contesting the centre with f2-f3 to hit the new e4-pawn. Kramnik has written that this is a strategic error. If he is right then White is already without chances to obtain an advantage.

10...♘d7

The most relevant choice here, making sure that Black has at least one knight in the game. In Namgilov-Ulibin, Elista 1995, Black first played 10...♕e7, and after 11 ♕c2 ♘d7 12 ♖ac1 ♔h8 13 ♔h1 ♖f6 14 ♘g5 ♘xd2 15 ♕xd2 White had an edge. There is no need to commit the queen just yet.

11 ♘xe4

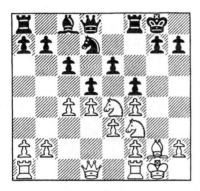

It appears that this exchange is not dangerous for Black, so White might have to find another plan here if he wants to fight for an advantage.

11...fxe4 12 ♘g5!?

For the more logical but not necessarily superior 12 ♘d2 see the next game.

12...♘f6 13 f3 h6 14 ♘h3

Believe it or not this knight is, ultimately, heading for e5! Levitt has suggested 14 ♘xe4!? dxe4 15 fxe4 but I am sure he rejected it in the game due to its probable unreliability.

14...exf3 15 ♕xf3 ♘e4 16 ♕e2 ♘d6!

This knight, too, is on a mission. From d6 both the e4- and f5-squares are available. Black has emerged from the opening with a perfectly reasonable game. Some commentators give White an edge while Levitt believes that the position is equal. I would say the truth lies somewhere in the middle.

17 b3

17 c5 ♘f5 and Black can strike with ...b7-b6.

17...♗d7 18 ♘f2

Here it comes.

18...♗e8 19 c5 ♘f5 20 ♘d3

Another knight finds a good square. Note there is no rush to jump into e5 just yet.

20...♕h4 21 ♖ae1

Bringing support to White's only weakness in anticipation of the coming offer to exchange queens.

21...♖c8 22 ♕f2

Prompting Black to lose ground or trade queens.

22...♖c7 23 ♕xh4 ♘xh4 24 ♗h3 ♖f6 25 ♘e5

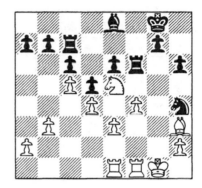

Both sides have their e-pawns covered and there is little else to attack, so the situation is level. Black should now play 25...♗h5 when it is difficult to see how White can progress.

25...♗g6?!

Offering White an advantageous exchange.

26 ♘xg6

At first it might seem strange to let the knight go, but if we look at what remains on the board we see that the bishop is stronger than the knight. Nevertheless this alone is not enough to make a difference.

26...♖xg6+ 27 ♔f2 ♖f7 28 ♔e2 ♔f8 29 ♖g1 ♖gf6 30 ♖ef1 ♘f5?!

Giving White the choice of removing the final pair of minor pieces. Instead 30...♔e7! followed soon by the tactical ...g7-g5 should lead to a draw.

31 b4 ♔e7 32 a4 a6 33 ♗xf5!

Good timing. White hopes that steering the game into a rook ending will enhance his winning chances, the plan being to double rooks on the g-file.

33...exf5

33...♖xf5 34 ♖g6 ♖5f6! is the most active defence, although White enjoys a slight pull.
34 h4 ♔f8 35 h5 g6?!

Helping White by opening the g-file for him. The route to a draw requires patience, putting the onus on White to make progress.
36 ♖f2! gxh5 37 ♖fg2 ♔e7 38 ♔f3 h4 39 ♖h1 ♔f8 40 ♖hg1 ♔e7 41 ♖g8! ♖f8 42 ♖1g7+ ♖6f7 43 ♖xf8 ♔xf8 44 ♖g6 ♖g7 45 ♖f6+ ♖f7 46 ♖xh6 ♔g8!

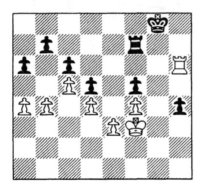

47 ♖h5!

Now Black is in zugzwang. The natural but unwise 47 ♖xh4? ♖h7 48 ♔g3 ♔g7! leads to a draw.
47...♖h7

After 47...h3 48 ♖xh3 ♖h7 White has 49 ♖g3+ ♖g7 50 ♖g5! etc. Notice that the quiet a4-a5 is being kept in reserve for the pawn ending.
48 ♖g5+! ♔h8 49 ♔g2!

Prevents Black's counterplay.
49...♖e7!

Black seeks alternative counterplay, trying to find the rook some action.
50 ♖xf5 ♖xe3 51 ♖f7 ♔g8!

This is the best try. Levitt gives the line 51...♖e4 52 ♖xb7 ♖xd4 53 b5 axb5 54 axb5 cxb5 55 c6 ♖c4 56 c7 and White wins.
52 ♖xb7 ♔f8 53 b5!!

So White is still winning – Levitt is playing this endgame very well.
53...axb5 54 axb5 cxb5 55 c6 ♖c3

55...♔e8? 56 ♖b8+ is standard fare.

56 c7 ♔e8 57 f5! ♔d7 58 f6 h3+ 59 ♔h2 ♔c8

59...♖f3 60 f7! ♖xf7 61 c8R+ also wins for White.
60 f7 ♔xb7 61 f8♕ ♔xc7 62 ♕e7+ ♔b6 63 ♕d6+ ♔a5 64 ♕xd5 ♔a4 65 ♕a8+ ♔b3 66 d5 b4 67 d6 ♖d3 68 ♕c6 ♔b2 69 d7 b3 70 ♕f6+ ♔c2 71 ♕f5 b2 72 d8♕ 1-0

Game 31
Astrom-Ulibin
Goteborg 1999

---

1 d4 e6 2 ♘f3 f5 3 g3 ♘f6 4 ♗g2 d5 5 0-0 ♗d6 6 c4 c6 7 ♗f4 ♗xf4 8 gxf4 0-0 9 e3 ♘e4 10 ♘bd2 ♘d7 11 ♘xe4 fxe4 12 ♘d2

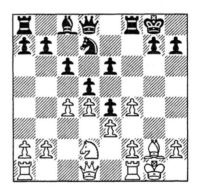

By dropping back to d2 White is able to recapture on f3 with his knight (not possible in the previous game after 13...h6). This must be a superior version of the line but even here Black has a straightforward means of equalising.
12...♘f6

Black should keep an open eye on the key squares. Similar to the game is Hertneck-Narciso Dublan, Berlin 1998, which went 12...♕e7 13 ♔h1 ♘f6 14 f3 exf3 15 ♘xf3 ♗d7 16 ♘e5 ♗e8 17 ♕b3. Now Black should play the careful 17...♔h8 but instead 17...♗h5?! 18 cxd5 exd5 19 e4 was better for White. Jonathan Levitt has suggested the

remarkable 12...g5!?, intending 13 ♕g4 ♖f5
14 ♗h3 ♔h8 15 ♕g2 gxf4 16 ♗xf5 exf5 and
Black has some compensation. I do not fully
trust this line but it will be of interest to the
adventurous player.

**13 f3 exf3 14 ♘xf3 ♕e7 15 ♕e2 ♗d7
16 ♘e5 ♗e8**

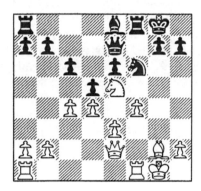

The amazing thing about the development
of the bishop around the back of the pawn
complex is not just that there is time to actually carry it out. What many players fail to
appreciate is that once it reaches its destina-
tion it the bishop is almost superior to the
one on g2.

**17 ♗f3 ♘d7 18 ♘xd7 ♕xd7 19 b4 ♗g6
20 a4 ♗f5 21 b5 a6 22 bxc6?!**

Voluntarily opening the b-file is an odd
plan when Black's bishop has the b1-square
in its sights. Now Black is on top.

**22...bxc6 23 a5 ♖fb8 24 ♔h1 ♖b3 25
♖fc1 h6 26 ♕e1 ♖ab8 27 ♖c3 ♖b2 28
♖ac1 ♖8b7 29 cxd5 cxd5 30 e4 dxe4 31**
♗xe4

31...♕xd4! 32 ♗xf5

32 ♗xb7 ♖xb7 33 ♕e3 ♕d5+ 34 ♔g1
♖b2 35 ♕f3 ♗e4 does not help White's
cause.

**32...exf5 33 ♕e6+ ♖f7! 34 ♖c7 ♕e4+
35 ♕xe4 fxe4 36 ♖xf7 ♔xf7**

The rook endgame is not difficult to win
for Black. He has extra material and his rook
is more active.

37 ♖c6?!

Not very active as the e-pawn is too
strong, but 37 ♖c5 loses, too, e.g. 37...♖f2!
38 f5 e3 39 ♔g1 ♔f6 40 ♖c3 ♖f3 41 ♔g2 e2!
etc.

**37...e3 38 ♖c1 ♔f6 39 ♖e1 e2 40 ♔g2
♔f5 41 ♔f3 ♖a2 42 ♖c1 ♖xa5 43 ♔xe2
♔xf4 44 ♖c4+ ♔f5 45 ♖c7 g5 46 h4
♔g4! 47 hxg5 hxg5 48 ♔f2 ♖a2+ 49
♔g1 a5 50 ♖c8 a4 51 ♖c4+ ♔g3 52
♖c3+ ♔h4 53 ♖c4+ g4 54 ♖c3 a3 55
♔h1 g3 0-1**

Summary

Black has no problems in the 7 ♗f4 variation. It makes sense to damage White's pawn structure with 7...♗xf4!. As for the light-squared bishop, in this line it is often best developed via d7 and e8 to h5 or g6, where it can become quite active, or even f7. Having said that, Games 24 and 26 see this so-called problem piece play important roles on the queenside. In general Black comes under no pressure after simple moves and, although White has had moderate success by trying to hinder Black's queenside development with ♕b3 at some point, this should not bring White any advantage with accurate play. For example Game 20 looks fine for Black in the opening, while 9...♕e7 in Game 21 takes the sting out of a future ♕b3. In any case the simple 9 e3 seems best, protecting the f4-pawn and generally solidifying the structure before deciding what to do with the queen and b1-knight. Again 9...♕e7 (Game 27) is okay for Black, but 9...♘e4 (Games 29-31) gets the vote over this and 9...♗d7. There is no reason to rush to activate the queenside as the position is closed, and this popular, provocative move threatens to interfere with White's development.

1 d4 f5 2 g3 ♘f6 3 ♗g2 e6 4 c4 c6 5 ♘f3 d5 6 0-0 ♗d6 7 ♗f4 ♗xf4
      7...0-0? – *Game 18*
8 gxf4 0-0 *(D)*
      8...♘bd7 – *Game 19*
9 e3
      9 ♕b3 – *Game 20*
      9 ♘bd2 *(D)*
            9...♕e7 – *Game 21*; 9...♗d7 – *Game 22*
      9 ♘e5
            9...♕e7 – *Game 23*; 9...♘bd7 – *Game 24*
      9 ♕c2 – *Game 25*
      9 ♘c3 – *Game 26*
9...♘e4
      9...♕e7 – *Game 27*; 9...♗d7 – *Game 28*
10 ♘bd2
      10 ♘e5 – *Game 29*
10...♘d7 11 ♘xe4 fxe4 *(D)*
      12 ♘g5 – *Game 30*; 12 ♘d2 – *Game 31*

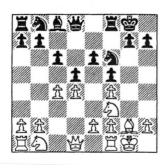
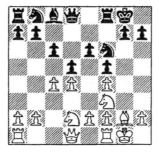
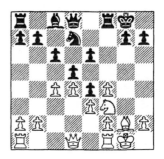

8...0-0   *9 ♘bd2*   *11...fxe4*

CHAPTER THREE

White's 7th Move Alternatives: 7 ♘bd2, 7 ♘e5, 7 ♕c2

1 d4 f5 2 g3 ♘f6 3 ♗g2 e6 4 c4 c6 5 ♘f3 d5 6 0-0 ♗d6 7 ♗f4

In this chapter we shall consider White's alternatives to 7 b3 and 7 ♗f4. The quiet 7 ♘bd2 can be met quite comfortably by either 7...b6 (Games 32-33) or 7...♘bd7 (Game 34), which leads us to the more active looking 7 ♘e5 0-0 8 ♗f4. Unable to bring a piece to d7 immediately due to the unprotected bishop on d6, Black can choose to challenge the new arrival on f4 with 8...♘h5 (Game 35) or the knight with 8...♘g4 (Game 36). 7 ♕c2 is the most popular move, no doubt because of its flexibility. After 7..0-0 White has several alternatives, including transpositions to Chapters One and Two. 8 ♗g5 announces an exchange on f6, and Black can play 8...h6 (Game 40) or ignore the bishop with 8...b6 (Game 41). Of the three available knight moves, 8 ♘bd2 gives Black time to decide between 8...b6 (Game 37) and 8...♗d7 (Game 38), and 8 ♘e5 (Game 39) is pretty harmless. The more consistent 8 ♘c3 (8...♘e4) is the subject of Games 42-44.

Game 32
Van Wely-Vaiser
Hyeres 1992

1 d4 f5 2 g3 ♘f6 3 ♗g2 e6 4 ♘f3 d5 5

0-0 ♗d6 6 c4 c6 7 ♘bd2

Nothing more than a normal developing move. Sensible enough, but I cannot recommend it purely because it is harmless. Under no pressure at all, Black has time and flexibility.

7...b6!?

As 7 ♘bd2 removes the immediate possibility of ♗f4 and is not linked with the advance b2-b4-b5 it is natural for Black to post his bishop on the queenside. It is also possible to deal with White's plan of a quick transfer of a knight to d3 in the following way: 7...0-0 8 ♘e5 ♘bd7 9 ♘d3 b6! 10 b4!? ♘e4 11 ♕b3 ♕f6! 12 b5! ♗b7 with a balanced game, I.Sokolov-Arkhipov, Pula 1988.

8 ♘e5 0-0

Black's game-plan in this game is effective. Vaiser intends to combine solidity with pressure against the white centre, and this policy does seem to nullify White's attempts to gain an advantage. Another option is the fianchetto 8...♗b7, as in Burmakin-Del Rio Angelis, Ubeda 1999. After 9 ♘d3 0-0 10 ♕c2 ♘bd7 11 ♘f3 ♖c8 12 ♗f4 ♘e4 White should have played 13 c5 with a slight advantage. The rest of the game can be found in the Introduction.

9 ♘d3

White rearranges the knights. It is worth

noting that the standard set-up with knights on d3 and f3 is not always appropriate, depending as it does on Black's development. Incidentally White gains nothing from 9 cxd5 cxd5! 10 ②dc4 ②e7. For 9 ②df3 see the next game.

9...②a6!

The point. Instead of the automatic development with ...②b7 Black monitors the c4-pawn and prepares to exert further pressure on c4 with ...②d7 and ...②c8. If White exchanges on d5 Black simply recaptures with the c-pawn, being more than happy to see the opening of the c-file.

10 ♕c2 ②e4 11 b3

This has been provoked by Black's aggressive play and is therefore not a sub-variation of 7 b3. Notice that White is already busy dealing with his opponent's action rather than concentrating fully on his own.

11...②d7 12 ②f3 ♖c8 13 ②f4 ♕e7 14 a4?!

Another feasible idea that is sometimes less relevant than others. In this particular case White judges that the time is right to advance the a-pawn now that Black's rook has left the a-file. Unfortunately for White his opponent's forces have their own agenda. Black's development is complete and his rook stands on the same file as the white queen, so Vaiser's next is hardly difficult to guess.

14...c5!

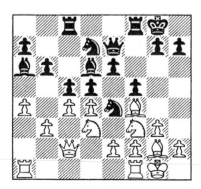

The logical culmination of Black's play thus far. Now White's centre is under fire, and the merit of his knight manoeuvres comes into question.

15 a5 b5

Ignoring the a-pawn and increasing the tension in the centre.

16 ②xd6 ♕xd6 17 b4

Introducing an interesting stand-off with the c4- and c5-squares coming under close scrutiny.

17...bxc4 18 ②xc5 ♖b8

Having established a protected passed pawn on c4 Black switches to the b-file to concentrate on a fresh target.

19 ♖ab1 ♖b5 20 ♖b2 ♖fb8 21 ♖fb1 ②c8

Of course White did not want to give up his c5-knight for this bishop, but as often happens the problem piece will have its day.

22 e3 ②df6 23 ②e5 ②xc5 24 bxc5

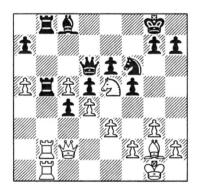

White's a-pawn is weak and the c4-pawn is potentially stronger than the c5-pawn (Black's bishop is already defending whereas White's is out of play on g2).

24...♕a6 25 ♕c3 ②d7 26 g4

White misjudges the coming structural alterations in the centre. Wholesale exchanges with 26 ♖xb5 ♖xb5 27 ♖xb5 ♕xb5 28 ②xd7 ♕b1+ 29 ②f1 ②xd7 leave Black more active.

26...②xe5 27 dxe5 fxg4 28 e4 ♖xb2 29 ♖xb2 ♖xb2 30 ♕xb2 ♕xa5 31 c6 ♕b6 32 ♕xb6 axb6 33 exd5 c3! 34 ②e4 exd5

35 ♗xd5+ ♔f8 36 ♗b3 ♔e7 37 ♔f1 ♗f5

The win for Black is merely a matter of time.

38 ♔e2 ♗e4 39 ♗a4 ♔e6 40 c7 ♗b7 41 ♔d3 c2 42 ♗xc2 ♔xe5 43 ♔c4 ♗a6+ 44 ♔b4 ♔d6 45 ♗xh7 ♔xc7 46 ♔c3 ♗c8 47 ♔d4 ♔d6 48 ♗d3 ♔e6 49 ♔e4 ♗d7 50 ♔f4 ♔f6 51 f3 gxf3 52 ♔xf3 ♔e5 53 h4 b5 0-1

Game 33
A.Petrosian-Vaiser
Belgrade 1988

---

1 d4 e6 2 c4 f5 3 ♘f3 ♘f6 4 g3 d5 5 ♗g2 c6 6 0-0 ♗d6 7 ♘bd2 0-0 8 ♘e5 b6 9 ♘df3

Better than 9 ♘d3 but still nothing to worry Black. This time Vaiser again finds a logical path to a level game, using simple, traditional Stonewall strategy. In fact it is no coincidence that the knights, though sitting pretty on d3 and f3, fail to make an impression. Other factors are important in the opening, one being development. It seems that in general White should address this before he starts shuffling his knights around.

9...♗b7 10 ♗f4 ♘e4 11 ♕c2 ♕e7 12 ♘d3 ♘d7

Remember that Black does not give White the satisfaction of lodging his knight on f4 with tempo.

13 ♗xd6 ♕xd6 14 b4

With the knight on d3 White at least maintains some influence on the c5-square, and the text adds more. As in the previous game Vaiser's key central break is actually quite a simple decision to make.

14...c5!

Freeing the bishop, denying White his planned offensive and challenging the centre on Black's terms. In fact this thematic break guarantees equality, as the rest of the game demonstrates.

15 bxc5 bxc5 16 dxc5 ♘dxc5 17 cxd5 ♗xd5 18 ♘xc5 ♘xc5 19 ♘g5 ♗xg2 20 ♔xg2 ♕e7 21 ♖fc1 ♖ac8 22 ♘f3 ♖c7 23 ♕c3 ♖fc8 24 ♕e5 ♕f6 25 ♖ab1 ½-½

Game 34
Kozul-L.B.Hansen,
Bled/Rogaska Slatina 1991

---

1 d4 e6 2 c4 f5 3 g3 ♘f6 4 ♗g2 c6 5 ♘f3 d5 6 0-0 ♗d6 7 ♘bd2 ♘bd7!?

Not entirely logical – castling is the flexible, popular choice – but at least keeping White's knight out of e5. By occupying d7 with his knight it seems that Black intends to play ...b7-b6, and White can try to exploit this with the aim of disturbing Black's development.

8 ♕c2

This prevents the immediate 8...b6 in view of the painful 9 cxd5! cxd5 10 ♕c6!.

8...0-0 9 ♘b3!?

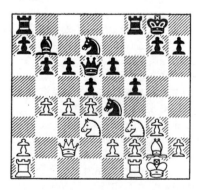

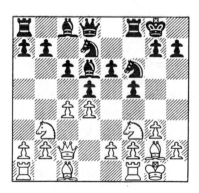

This is a highly original plan by Kozul, designed to counter ...b7-b6 and ...♗b7. However, it is made possible only because Black has already played ...♘bd7, which of course shuts in the bishop and therefore creates the problem in the first place.

9...♘e4

On 9...♕e7 L.B.Hansen recommends 10 ♗f4!?, as he was planning to meet 10 ♘e1 with 10...dxc4!? 11 ♕xc4 ♔h8 followed by ...e6-e5. I do not believe White is better here, so perhaps he should follow the same plan as in the game.

10 ♘e1

10 ♗f4!? with the idea of ♘c1-d3 is also possible, although it does not lead to anything particularly promising for White.

10...♕e7 11 ♘d3 b6 12 ♗e3!

Consistent with White's strategy in that the c5-square is crucial (note that Black, too, has been concentrating on this square). Black's next move is the natural, no-nonsense response.

12...♗a6!?

12...♗b7 is more careful but also rather passive. The nature of Black's piece placement in the Stonewall often means that there are ways to put White under pressure, or at least present him with opportunities to go wrong at little or no risk.

13 c5! ♗b8!

This retreat is forced. 13...♗c7?! allows 14 ♘b4 ♗b7 15 cxb6 ♘xb6 16 ♘d3! ♘c4 17 ♗f4 with a very good game for White and no fun for Black.

14 cxb6?!

The result of a misjudgement. White should maintain the tension with 14 ♖fc1, when White retains a small advantage according to Hansen. Perhaps he was being a little generous to his opponent and critical of himself, as I'm not sure that White is really better.

14...axb6 15 ♕xc6?

Did Kozul really think he was picking up a free pawn?

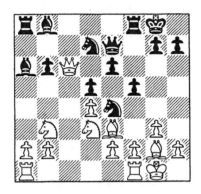

15...♗xg3!

16 hxg3 ♖fc8 17 ♕a4 ♗xd3 is the idea behind Black's play. Consequently White is in serious trouble. For example White finds no peace in 16 ♗xe4!? dxe4! 17 hxg3 exd3!? 18 exd3 (18 ♗g5 ♕xg5 19 ♕xd7 dxe2 20 ♕xe6+ ♔h8 21 ♖fe1 f4 and White is torn to pieces!) 18...♗xd3 19 ♖fc1 ♗e4 because his king is highly exposed. This leaves no choice but to retreat the queen.

16 ♕c2 ♗d6 17 f4

No real choice about that one!

17...♖ac8 18 ♕d1

An embarrassing end to White's queenside aggression.

18...♕h4 19 ♘e5

19 ♖f3 is better according to Hansen.

19...♘df6 20 ♘d2 ♘g4! 21 ♘xg4 ♕xg4 22 ♖f3 ♖c7!

Black is well ahead, the coming doubling on the c-file giving him a pull on both sides of the board.

23 ♔h1 ♖fc8 24 ♗f1 ♖c2 25 ♘xe4 dxe4! 26 ♖f2 ♗b7! 27 a4 ♗d5 28 a5 bxa5 29 ♖xa5 ♖xb2 30 ♕a4 ♗f8! 31 ♖g2 ♕h5 32 ♖a7 ♕e8 33 ♕a1 ♖cb8 34 ♔g1 ♖2b7 35 ♖a5 ♖b5 36 ♖a7 ♖5b7 37 ♖a5 ♖b3! 38 ♕c1 ♖c8 39 ♖c5

The only move that does not lose a piece, but by returning the exchange Black achieves an easily winning endgame.

39...♗xc5 40 dxc5 ♖xe3! 41 ♕xe3 ♕e7 42 ♕d4 ♖xc5 43 e3 h6 44 h3 ♖c1! 45

♕b2 ♕c7 46 ♖g3 ♔h7 47 h4 ♕c3?!

47...e5! 48 fxe5 ♗e6 followed by ...♕c5 leads to an easy win.

48 ♕xc3 ♖xc3 49 ♔f2 ♗c4 50 ♗xc4 ♖xc4 51 h5 ♖c2+ 52 ♔g1 ♔g8 53 ♔h1 ♔f7 54 ♔g1 ♖a2 55 ♔h1?! ♖f2 56 ♔g1 ♖f3 57 ♖xf3 exf3 58 ♔f2 g5 59 hxg6+ ♔xg6 60 ♔xf3 ♔f6 61 ♔g3 ♔e7 0-1

> ## Game 35
> ## A.Petrosian-Knaak
> *Erevan 1988*

1 d4 e6 2 c4 f5 3 ♘f3 ♘f6 4 g3 d5 5 ♗g2 c6 6 0-0 ♗d6 7 ♘e5!?

This is a very interesting idea, albeit one that cannot offer White any advantage. The idea is not simply to just lodge the knight on e5 but to bring the bishop to f4 with a crafty little trick in mind. After ♗f4 Black cannot play ...♗d7 because ♘f7! picks up the dark-squared bishop without White having to part with his own, while ...♘bd7 is even worse for Black thanks to ♘xc6. This puts the onus on Black to find alternative development or make an early strike.

7...0-0 8 ♗f4

8 ♕c2 transposes to Game 39.

8...♘h5

White would not invite this knee-jerk reaction if it favoured Black. Nevertheless, even though the coming exchange does seem to benefit White, I am not convinced it affords him much of an advantage. For the superior 8...♘g4! see the following game.

9 e3! ♘xf4 10 exf4

Given the choice White obviously wants to keep his king safe, the recapture with the e-pawn also providing access to the e-file. Less logical is 10 gxf4 ♘d7 11 ♘d2 ♘xe5 12 fxe5 ♗e7 13 f4 ♗d7 14 ♔h1 ♔h8 15 ♕e2 ♗e8 16 ♖g1 ♖g8 17 ♗f3 g5, when Black was fine in Izeta Txabarri-Panchenko, Linares 1995.

10...♘d7 11 ♘d2!

In his notes Petrosian suggested that White might keep a slight edge by exchanging knights. There have been several tests of this claim, e.g. 11 ♘xd7!? ♕xd7 12 ♘d2 b6 13 ♕b3 h6 14 ♖fe1 ♗b7 15 ♘f3 and Black was only a little worse in Fominyh-Sherbakov, Elista 1996. Perhaps it is more logical to recapture with the bishop instead. 11...♗xd7 12 ♘d2 gives White an edge, but White should not be tempted to push with 12 c5?, which gives Black something to attack and thus unnecessary counterplay. In Milov-Vaiser, Paris 1994, Black was already slightly better after 12...♗e7 13 ♘d2 b6 14 b4 bxc5 15 bxc5 ♕a5 16 ♘f3 ♗f6 17 ♕e1 ♕a4.

11...♘f6

11...♘xe5!? 12 fxe5 ♗e7 leaves White with a space advantage.

12 c5

This is possible now because Black cannot quickly arrange ...b7-b6.

12...♗c7

12...♗xe5!? is a possibility worth investigating, the key idea being 13 dxe5 ♘g4! 14 b4 ♘h6 followed by ...♘f7, ...h7-h6 and ...g7-g5 with counterplay on the kingside.

13 b4 ♗d7 14 ♕e2

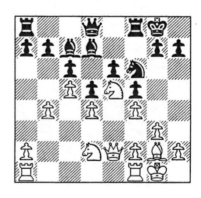

14...♗e8

Black's position is very difficult. The more cautious 14...♕e7 might be a lesser evil, but wrong is 14...a5, hoping for 15 a3?! b5! with a closed queenside and an unclear position. However, White should instead go for a plus with 15 bxa5! ♖xa5 16 ♖fb1 to pile up pressure on b7. Note that 14...b6? drops a pawn to 15 ♘xc6! (15...♗xc6 16 ♕xe6+).

15 ♘d3! ♗d7?!

The uncomfortable 15...♗f7 has to be played, when Black has no choice but to face the music and wait for b4-b5 and ♘b4 after 16 a4.

16 ♘f3 h6 17 ♘fe5 ♗e8 18 ♕e3 ♔h7 19 ♖ab1 ♖g8 20 a4 a6 21 f3 ♘d7 22 ♖fe1

White's absolute control of the e5-square is the key factor. Black now plays for ...g7-g5, but White is fine on the kingside and ready to take over the queenside.

22...♘f8 23 ♗f1 ♕f6 24 ♘f2 g5 25 ♘h3! ♗d8 26 b5 axb5 27 axb5 ♖g7 28 ♖a1! ♖c8 29 ♖a7

29 b6! is even stronger, intending an invasion down the a-file.

29...cxb5 30 ♖b1 b6 31 cxb6 ♗xb6 32 fxg5 hxg5 33 ♘xg5+ ♔g8 34 ♖xg7+ ♕xg7 35 f4 ♕a7 36 ♘ef3 ♕a2 37 ♖e1 ♗d7 38 ♕e5 ♗d8 39 ♕d6 ♕a7

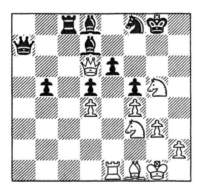

And finally a little firework...

40 ♘xe6! ♗xe6?

The least stubborn defence. White also wins after 40...♘xe6: 41 ♖xe6 ♖c6 42 ♖g6+ ♔h7 43 ♖h6+ ♔g7 44 ♕e5+!! ♗f6 (44...♔xh6 45 ♕h8+ ♔g6 46 ♘e5 is a pretty neat mate!) 45 ♖xf6 ♖xf6 46 ♘g5! ♗c6 (46...♔g6 47 ♕e7 ♕xd4+ 48 ♔g2) 47 ♘h7!

and White is a pawn up in a winning endgame after 47...♕f7 48 ♘xf6 ♕xf6 49 ♗d3.

41 ♖xe6 ♕b8 42 ♕xd5 1-0

1 d4 f5 2 ♘f3 ♘f6 3 g3 e6 4 ♗g2 d5 5 0-0 ♗d6 6 c4 c6 7 ♘e5 0-0 8 ♗f4 ♘g4!

This time Black challenges the knight instead of the bishop, although this in turn can also leave the bishop exposed. So far no one has been able to prove any disadvantage to this move.

9 ♘xg4

9 ♘d2 ♗xe5 10 ♗xe5 ♘xe5 11 dxe5 b6 12 ♖c1 ♗b7 13 cxd5 exd5 14 f4 ♘a6 15 ♕b3 ♔h8 16 ♕a3 ♘c7 was fine for Black in Romanishin-Grischuk, Bled 1999.

9...♗xf4 10 gxf4 fxg4 11 e3

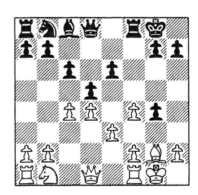

11...♕h4!

The kingside attack proves to give Black enough counterplay to later deal with the queenside. The simple threat is ...♖f6-h6.

12 ♘d2

12 ♕e1 ♖f6! has also been tried, with equality. In fact this is Gelfand-Nikolic, which featured in the Introduction (page 52).

12...♖f6 13 ♖e1 ♘d7 14 ♘f1

14 c5!? is the last attempt to try for an advantage.

14...dxc4!

This capture is justified here because White's pieces are too busy elsewhere to act, and creating a big centre with e3-e4 is not possible as this loses the f4-pawn. White gets some compensation, but not much.

15 ♕e2 ♘b6 16 f3 gxf3 17 ♕xf3 ♗d7 18 ♘d2 ♖af8 19 ♖ac1

The pawn is about to be rounded up and the players soon liquidate to a draw. Of course there is still much play left in the game.

19...♖g6 20 ♕f2 ♕h5 21 ♘f3 ♖h6 22 ♕g3 ♕b5 23 ♕f2 c5 24 dxc5 ♕xc5 25 ♘e5 ♗c6 26 ♗xc6 bxc6 27 ♕g2 ♖d8 28 ♔h1 ♖d5 29 ♖g1 ♕e7 30 ♘xc6 ♕b7 31 ♘a5 ♕d7 32 ♘xc4 ♘xc4 33 ♖xc4 ♖g6 34 ♕f3 ♖xg1+ 35 ♔xg1 ♖d1+ 36 ♔g2 ♖d2+ 37 ♔g3 ♕e8 38 ♕e4 ♖xb2 ½-½

Game 37
Kozul-Klinger
Sarajevo 1988

---

1 d4 e6 2 c4 f5 3 g3 ♘f6 4 ♗g2 d5 5 ♘f3 c6 6 0-0 ♗d6 7 ♕c2

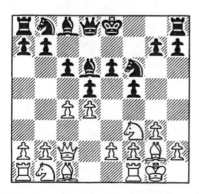

The attraction of 7 ♕c2 is its elasticity, this outpost fitting in with more than one plan. For example White could play 7 ♗g5 and later transpose, or 7 ♘bd2 or 7 ♘c3. Furthermore, if he so desires White can still select 8 ♗f4 or 8 b3 with transposition to the variations 7 ♗f4 and 7 b3.

7...0-0 8 ♘bd2

One of three knight moves available. 8 ♘e5 is Game 39 and 8 ♘c3 features in Games 42-44.

8...b6

As usual this is good development when it can be carried out without any annoying White tricks. The next game sees 8...♗d7.

9 ♘e5 ♗b7 10 ♘df3 ♕e7

Producing a fairly standard position. White's next deviates from normal procedure.

11 ♗g5!?

White wishes to disrupt his opponent's development with this pin, the bishop finding an alternative to the usual task of contesting the dark squares. Not surprisingly Black has ways of playing the position that take the sting out of the pin, and Klinger comes up with a plan according to the fundamental concept that when White weakens the dark squares in the centre Black should push his c-pawn. In fact with a knight on e5 the d4-pawn is kept busy, so Black should be ready to strike soon.

11...♖c8 12 ♖ac1 c5!

Black should be equal in this position.

13 ♕a4 ♘c6 14 cxd5

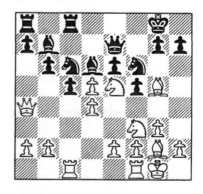

14...♘xd4?

A blunder. Black has nothing to fear after 14...exd5, with a definite presence in the centre and well placed pieces. Indeed after the sensible recapture he might even be on his way to achieving a slight pull.

15 ♘xd4 ♗xe5 16 ♘xe6 ♗xb2 17 ♖cd1

Material is level but White has a strong pawn on d5 and an elephant on e6 – significant factors for which Black has little to show. Consequently White also has the more comfortable game.

17...h6 18 ♕b3 hxg5 19 d6 ♕f7 20 ♗xb7 c4 21 ♕xb2 ♕xb7

21...c3 22 ♕b3 c2 23 ♖c1 ♕xb7 24 ♘c7+.

22 d7

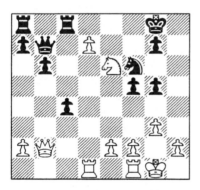

22...♖d8 23 ♘xd8 ♖xd8 24 ♕b5 ♕e4 25 e3 ♔h7 26 ♖d4 ♕f3 27 ♕xc4 ♖xd7 28 ♖xd7 ♘xd7 29 ♕d4 ♘f6 30 ♕d1 ♕e4 31 ♕e2 ♘g4 32 h3 ♘e5 33 f3 ♕c6 34 f4 gxf4 35 exf4 ♘f7 36 ♕h5+ ♘h6 37 ♕f3 ♕c5+ 38 ♕f2 ♕d5 39 ♕c2 ♘g8 40 ♖d1 ♕e6 41 g4 ♕e3+ 42 ♕f2 ♕c3 43 g5 ♘e7 44 ♔h2 ♘c6 45 h4 ♘b4 46 h5 ♕c7 47 ♕d4 ♘xa2 48 ♕d6 ♕c8 49 ♖d2 ♘c3 50 ♕g6+ ♔h8 51 h6 ♕c7 52 ♖d8+ 1-0

> ## Game 38
> ### Vladimirov-Liang Chong
> *Shenyang 1999*

1 d4 f5 2 g3 ♘f6 3 ♗g2 e6 4 ♘f3 d5 5 0-0 ♗d6 6 c4 c6 7 ♕c2 0-0 8 ♘bd2 ♗d7!?

A perfectly good means of bringing the bishop into play. Of course it is slower than 8...b6, but in this game White fails in his attempt to reduce the scope of the bishop on

h5.

9 ♘e5 ♘e4 10 ♘d3

There is no reason to hurry in bringing the knight back to d3. More consistent, and accurate, is 10 ♘df3, but White intends to kick the black knight away.

10...♗e8 11 f3 ♘g5!

Seeing that the knight will never be challenged here Black decides to keep it active. If the weakening h2-h4 should ever come the knight is well placed on f7.

12 ♘b3

Obstructing the queenside pawns, which White should be looking to advance in an effort to generate a queenside initiative. The knight lacks punch on b3.

12...♘d7 13 ♗f4 ♕e7 14 ♖ae1

White prepares for e2-e4, a plan he made quite clear with 12 ♘b3. Not surprisingly Black is ready.

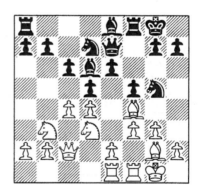

14...♗xf4! 15 ♘xf4 dxc4

Here we see another situation in which taking on c4 makes sense. Ironically it is Black's bishop that holds the key, patiently waiting in the wings until it is time to open the position.

16 ♕xc4 ♗f7 17 ♕c3 e5

In a short time White's pieces have become awkwardly placed. The stereotyped f2-f3 has compromised White's pawn formation and weakened the e3-square, and White must accept further damage with f3-f4 to free his bishop.

18 ♘d3 exd4 19 ♘xd4 ♕e3+ 20 ♔h1 g6
21 b3 ♘e6 22 ♘c2 ♕g5 23 ♕b4 ♖ab8
24 f4 ♕h5 25 ♕a5 a6 26 ♘e3 ♘g7 27
♕c3 ♖fe8 28 ♗f3 ♕h3 29 ♘f2 ♕h6

Black needs to return his queen to the game, which requires a little regrouping.

30 ♖d1 ♗e6 31 ♖d6 ♘h5 32 ♔g1 ♕g7
33 ♕d2 ♘hf6

Black is better due to the backward pawn on e2.

34 ♖d1 ♕e7 35 ♕a5 ♗f7

Finally tidying up his forces.

36 ♘c4?!

This does not improve White's chances.

36...♗xc4 37 bxc4 ♘f8

Black is aware of the solidity of his position and decides to play safe, not an ideal winning strategy. White, for his part, is unable to create anything.

38 a4 ♕f7 39 ♕c3 ♖e6 40 ♖6d3 ♖be8
41 a5 ♘8d7 42 ♕b4 ♘f8 43 ♖b3 ♖6e7
44 ♖d6 ♖c7 45 ♕b6 ♖ec8 46 ♕d4??

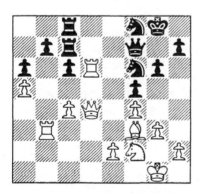

A blunder in a slightly worse position.

46...♘e8! 47 ♖d8 ♘e6 48 ♖xe8+ ♖xe8
49 ♕b6 ♕f6 50 ♖e3 ♖ee7 51 ♖e5 ♘f8
52 ♘d3 ♕d6 53 ♖d5 ♕e6 54 ♘e5 ♖c8
55 ♕d4 ♕f6 56 ♖d8 ♖xd8 57 ♕xd8 ♔g7
58 ♕d2 ♖e8 59 ♕b4 ♖e7 60 ♕d2 h6 61
h4 0-1.

White resigns rather than wait for Black to return the exchange on e5 and then, a pawn up, slowly make the remaining weaknesses tell.

Game 39
Hoffman-Vaiser
Mesa 1992

1 d4 e6 2 ♘f3 f5 3 g3 ♘f6 4 ♗g2 d5 5
0-0 ♗d6 6 c4 c6 7 ♕c2 0-0 8 ♘e5

Of course this is similar to other methods of development discussed earlier. Again Black is not exactly being challenged.

8...b6 9 ♘d2

Normal. Fooling around with the king's knight has already been exposed in this chapter as less ideal, but I believe that this point cannot be stressed too often, so here is another example of what can happen: 9 ♘d3
♗a6 10 c5? (10 b3 is more sensible, with a balanced position) 10...bxc5 11 ♘xc5 ♗xc5
12 ♕xc5 ♕b6! 13 ♕c3 ♘bd7 14 b4 ♘e4 15
♕b2 ♖ab8 with a definite advantage to Black. This is Douven-Vaiser from the Introduction (page 46).

9...♗b7 10 ♘df3 ♘e4 11 ♘d3 c5

By now this thematic push of the c-pawn should be a familiar tool.

12 ♖d1?

12 cxd5 exd5 13 ♗f4 is correct, with equality.

12...dxc4! 13 ♕xc4 ♗d5 14 ♕c2 c4

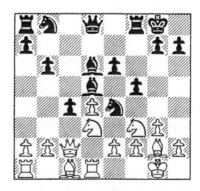

Black is already better, the all-seeing bishop on d5 helping the already threatening queenside pawn majority.

15 ♘de5 ♕c7 16 ♗f4 ♘c6 17 ♘xc6

♗xf4 18 ♘ce5 ♗h6 19 e3

White seems to have good control over the centre but this is illusionary. White has no active plans and Black has no weaknesses (at least none that can be attacked).

19...♕b7 20 ♘e1 b5 21 ♕e2 g6 22 f3 ♘d6 23 ♘c2 ♗g7 24 ♖e1 ♕c7 25 ♖ad1 ♗b7

Black's lot has improved since the diagram position. The text is directed against e3-e4, e.g. 26 e4 fxe4 27 fxe4 ♗xe5 28 dxe5 ♘f7. White shifts his rooks one file to the left, but Black's c-pawn will take some stopping.

26 ♖c1 ♖ac8 27 ♘a3?

The knight is doing nothing out here.

27...♖fd8 28 ♖ed1 ♕b6 29 h4 a5 30 ♔h2 ♘f7!

Removing White's only annoying piece.

31 ♘xf7 ♔xf7 32 f4 ♗d5

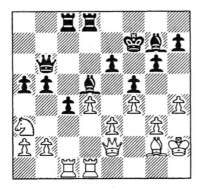

33 ♘b1

A most embarrassing retreat. White can only sit and wait.

33...b4 34 ♘d2 c3 35 bxc3 ♖xc3 36 ♗xd5 exd5 37 ♖xc3 bxc3 38 ♘b1 ♕b2!

A very precise assessment of the endgame.

39 ♕xb2 cxb2 40 ♔g2 a4 41 a3 ♗f8 42 ♖d2 ♖b8 43 ♖d3 ♖b3 44 ♖d2

44 ♖xb3 axb3 45 ♔f2 ♗e7 46 ♔e2 ♗d8 47 ♔d3 ♗a5 and it is impossible for the king to approach the pawns. Black then sends his king to a4, wins the a-pawn and infiltrates via c4 and d3, using the bishop to put White in zugzwang.

44...♖xa3! 0-1

45 ♖xb2 ♖b3! 46 ♖xb3 axb3 47 ♔f2 ♗b4 48 ♔e2 ♔g7 49 ♔d1 ♔f6 50 ♔c1 ♗e1! and Black creates a winning passed pawn on the h-file. 45 ♘xa3 does not work in view of 45...♗xa3 46 ♖d1 ♗b4 followed by the glorious march of the a-pawn.

Game 40
Cosma-Dumitrache
Romania 1996

---

1 d4 e6 2 g3 d5 3 ♗g2 c6 4 ♘f3 ♗d6 5 0-0 f5 6 c4 ♘f6 7 ♕c2

A similar idea to this game is 7 ♘c3 0-0 8 ♗g5 ♘bd7 (8...h6!? is probably best) 9 e3 h6 10 ♗xf6 (10 ♗f4, intending to recapture on f4 with the e-pawn, might give White something) 10...♘xf6 11 ♘d2 ♗d7 12 c5 ♗c7 13 f4, when 13...g5 14 ♘f3 ♖f7 15 ♘e5 ♖g7 16 ♕e2 h5 17 ♘f3 g4 18 ♘e5 h4 19 ♖fb1 ♖h7 gave Black sufficient counterplay in Wessman-Moskalenko, Moscow 1991. Instead of putting the question to the bishop with 9...h6, the interesting alternative 9...b6 has been played. Hoi-Knaak, Thessaloniki Ol 1988, continued 10 cxd5 exd5 11 ♘h4 ♗a6! (11...g6?! 12 ♘xd5! cxd5 13 ♗xd5+ ♘xd5 14 ♗xd8 ♖xd8 does not give Black enough for the queen) 12 ♖e1 g6 (now the rook on a8 is protected) 13 ♖c1 ♗b7?! (13...♕e7 is more logical as White is not threatening to immediately exploit the weakness on c6) 14 f3 ♕b8 and a draw was agreed. However White could have achieved an advantage with 15 e4!, e.g. 15...dxe4 (15...fxe4 16 fxe4 dxe4 17 ♕b3+ ♔g7 18 ♘xe4 ♘xe4 19 ♗xe4 is a little uncomfortable for Black) 16 fxe4 ♘g4?! (interesting tactics, although it might be wiser to transpose to 15...fxe4 with 16...fxe4) 17 e5 ♘dxe5 18 ♖xe5! ♘xe5 19 dxe5 ♗xe5 20 ♘f3 and White has the better of an unclear position.

7...0-0 8 ♗g5!?

An interesting approach that has one main drawback – White is practically forced to give

---

up his bishop for the knight. Overall I doubt the efficacy of this trade and I believe that it does not offer White a realistic chance to fight for an advantage.

8...h6

Simple chess. Ignoring the bishop with 8...b6 is dealt with in the next game. Good for White is 8...♘bd7 9 cxd5 cxd5 10 ♘c3 h6 11 ♗f4! ♗xf4 12 gxf4.

9 ♗xf6 ♕xf6 10 ♘bd2 ♘d7 11 e3

Black should be more or less equal here. In return for parting with a knight in an effectively closed position Black has the sole dark-squared bishop, the usual solid centre and enough space. A closed centre tends to be a condition of a flank attack, which is what prompts Black to embark on the following kingside offensive.

11...g5!?

Very double-edged and indicative of the ease with which Black can throw his pawns forward in the Stonewall. Equality results from the sober 11...♕e7 12 ♖fc1 b6 13 cxd5 cxd5 etc.

12 ♘e1 g4?!

I do not like this move at all. It hands over the f4-square and loses time, and the idea of immediately launching a mating attack down the h-file is naive. Better to maintain the tension with 12...♕e7 followed by ...b7-b6.

13 ♘d3 h5 14 b4 h4 15 ♖fc1 ♕e7 16 b5 ♔g7 17 bxc6 bxc6 18 c5 ♗c7 19 ♕a4

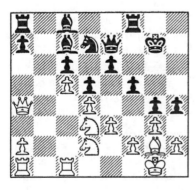

White has the advantage. Despite Black's

efforts to progress on the kingside he is simply tied down on the other wing, where White enjoys a nagging initiative. Nonetheless, making something of White's lead is another question.

19...♘b8 20 ♖ab1 ♖h8 21 ♘e5 hxg3 22 hxg3 ♔f6

Black cannot be faulted for his effort and his queenside is still intact. With so few black pieces actually on the kingside White decides to open up there before Black manages a genuine strike.

23 f4 gxf3 24 ♘dxf3 ♕g7 25 g4 fxg4 26 ♘h2 ♗xe5 27 dxe5+ ♔e7 28 ♘xg4 ♖h4 29 ♖b4 a5 30 ♖f4 ♗a6 31 ♘f6 ♖xf4 32 ♕xf4 ♘d7 33 e4 d4 34 ♖c2 ♖h8 35 ♖f2 ♗b5 36 ♖f3 ♘xc5?

After 36...d3! Black is very much in the game; now White enters via the queenside.

37 ♕c1 ♘b7 38 a4 ♗xa4 39 ♕a3+ ♔d8 40 ♕xa4 ♔c7 41 ♕xd4 ♖d8 42 ♕c4 ♕e7 43 ♖c3 ♖d1+ 44 ♗f1 ♘d8 45 ♕a4 ♖b1 46 ♕xa5+ ♔b8 47 ♕a3 1-0

Game 41
Gulko-Padevsky
Buenos Aires 1978

1 d4 f5 2 g3 ♘f6 3 ♗g2 e6 4 ♘f3 d5 5 0-0 ♗d6 6 c4 c6 7 ♕c2 0-0 8 ♗g5 b6

There is no reason why this should be less appropriate than 8...h6. By developing his queenside at once Black does not bother himself with the pin, hoping that the bishop will lack a significant role on g5.

9 ♘e5 ♗b7 10 cxd5 cxd5 11 ♘a3!

The idea is to fight for e5, winning a tempo with ♘ac4 thanks to another pin.

11...a6

Preventing ♘b5 is imperative.

12 ♖ac1 ♘bd7 13 ♘ac4 ♖c8 14 ♕d2 ♗e7

The knights fight for e5, but White has not been able to induce any weaknesses and a number of pieces are about to be exchanged. The position is now equal but

Gulko makes considerable effort to win against a weaker opponent. However, it becomes clear that Padevsky is far from weak!

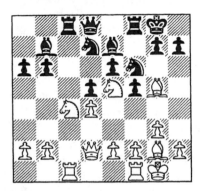

15 ♕e3 ♘xe5 16 ♘xe5 ♖xc1 17 ♖xc1 ♘e4 18 ♗xe7 ♕xe7 19 ♕b3 b5 20 ♕c2 ♘d6 21 ♕c7 ♖e8 22 b3 ♔f8 23 ♕xe7+ ♖xe7 24 e3 ♖e8 25 ♖c7 ♖e7 26 ♖c5 ♖e8 27 ♔f1 ♖c8 28 ♔e2 ♔e7 29 ♔d3 a5 30 a4 bxa4 31 bxa4?

Missing the last chance to play 31 ♖xc8! with a draw. Thus far Black has had to refrain from capturing on c5, but now the a4-pawn is potentially weak.

31...♖xc5 32 dxc5 ♘c4!

Is this what Gulko overlooked, or was it just the weakness of the a-pawn?

33 ♔d4 ♘xe5 34 ♔xe5 ♗c6 35 ♗f1!

Gulko finds his best chance but the a-pawn is very strong.

35...♗xa4 36 ♗a6 ♗c6 37 ♗c8 a4 38 ♔d4 e5+! 39 ♔c3 g6 40 f4 ♔f6 41 ♗a6 g5 42 ♗d3 gxf4 43 gxf4 d4+!

Here it is better to have two passed pawns far from each other than connected.

44 exd4 exf4 45 ♗c4 ♗g2 46 d5 ♔e5 47 d6 ♗c6 48 ♗e2 ♔e6 49 ♗c4+ ♔e5 50 ♗e2 ♔e4 51 ♔b4 f3 52 ♗c4 f2 53 ♗f1 f4 54 ♔c4 ♔e5 55 ♗h3 ♔e4 56 ♗f1 ♔e3 57 ♔c3 f3 58 ♗a6 a3 59 ♗f1 a2 60 ♔b2 ♔d2 0-1.

It is instructive to remember the contribution that can be made by Black's light-squared bishop!

Game 42
Gershon-Vaiser
New York 1998

1 d4 e6 2 c4 f5 3 ♘f3 ♘f6 4 g3 d5 5 ♗g2 c6 6 0-0 ♗d6 7 ♕c2 0-0 8 ♘c3

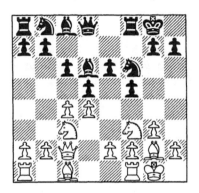

Here we have an example of White being content with the c3-square for his knight. Instead of using e5 White intends to concentrate on queenside play, the queen defending the knight in preparation for b2-b4 etc. Black does best to get on with it in the centre.

8...♘e4 9 e3

Solid enough but less taxing than the more aggressive approach 9 ♖b1, which is covered in the next two games. I do not like the manoeuvre ♘e1-d3 here since it gives Black too much time, as the present game demonstrates.

9 ♘d2?! makes little sense. Ardiansyah-Portisch, Thessaloniki Ol 1988, continued 9...♘d7 10 ♘dxe4 fxe4 11 ♗e3 ♘f6 12 f3 exf3 13 ♗xf3 ♗d7 14 ♗f2 b5! (Black takes over the initiative and is already better) 15 cxb5 cxb5 16 a3 ♖c8 17 ♕d3 ♕e8 18 e4 b4 19 axb4 ♗xb4 20 ♖fe1 (20 e5 ♗xc3 21 bxc3 ♗b5) 20...♗xc3 21 bxc3 ♗b5 22 ♕d2 dxe4 23 ♗xe4 ♘xe4 24 ♖xe4 ♗c6 and Black had a winning attack on the light squares.

Like the main game, 9 ♘e1?! sends the knight to d3, but this plan can only be recommended when there is a knight ready to go to f3. Here is what can happen to White against traditional development: 9...♕f6 10 e3 ♘d7 11 ♘e2 ♕e7! 12 ♘d3 b6 13 b3 ♗b7 14 ♗b2 ♖ac8 15 f3 ♘ef6 16 ♘f2 c5 17 e4? cxd4 18 ♘xd4 dxc4 19 bxc4? (19 exf5! is a better shot) 19...fxe4 20 f4 (20 fxe4 ♗a6) 20...♗a6 21 ♘xe4 ♖xc4 22 ♕f2 ♘xe4 23 ♗xe4 ♗c5 24 ♕e3 ♘f6 25 ♖fc1 ♘g4 26 ♕d2 ♖xc1+ 27 ♖xc1 ♖d8 28 ♖d1 e5 29 fxe5 ♕xe5 30 ♗f3 ♕e3+ 31 ♔g2 ♕xd2+ 32 ♖xd2 ♘e3+ 0-1, Lukacs-Tseshkovsky, Wijk aan Zee 1988.

9...♘d7 10 ♘e1 ♘xc3 11 ♕xc3 b5!?

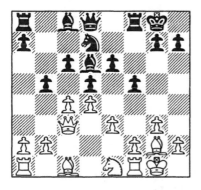

Black exploits his opponent's lagging development to nip any queenside play in the bud. With the knight still on e1 White has no firm grip on the centre, and he now has the choice of either closing or opening the position. The former seems to be the most logical since he is underdeveloped.

12 cxd5

12 c5!? ♗c7 13 ♘d3 a5 is okay for Black, while 12 b3? bxc4 13 bxc4 ♗a6 loses a pawn.

12...cxd5 13 ♕c6 ♕b6

Also possible is Hecht's 13...♘b6!? 14 ♕xb5 a5 15 ♕e2 ♗a6 with compensation for the pawn.

14 ♕xa8 ♗a6 15 ♕xf8+ ♔xf8

Hecht writes that White is certainly not worse, perhaps slightly better. I tend to agree, although the position is much easier to play for Black since he has the initiative.

16 ♘f3?!

Not a good square for the knight. Better is 16 ♘d3 b4 17 ♖d1 ♘f6 18 ♗f1.

16...b4 17 ♖e1 ♘f6 18 b3

Handing over c3 on a plate. The calm 18 ♗d2 and ♖ec1 is necessary.

18...♘e4 19 ♗b2 ♘c3 20 ♗f1 ♗xf1 21 ♔xf1?!

Another error, inviting the queen into the position with gain of tempo.

21...♕a6+ 22 ♔g2 ♕d3 23 ♖ec1 ♕e4 24 ♗xc3?

This makes the progress of the Black g-pawn impossible to stop. Hecht gives the following long drawing line: 24 h4 g6 25 ♗xc3 bxc3 26 ♖xc3 h6 27 ♖h1! ♔g7 28 ♖c6 ♗f8 29 ♖c7+ ♔g8 30 ♖xa7 g5 31 hxg5 hxg5 32 ♖h5 g4 33 ♖g5+ ♔h8 34 ♖h5+ and White makes a perpetual.

24...bxc3 25 h4 c2 26 a3 g6!

Of course not 26...h6? 27 h5 and the g-pawn is stopped in its tracks.

27 ♖a2 h6 28 ♖axc2 g5 29 ♖c8+ ♔e7 30 hxg5 hxg5 31 ♖h1 g4 32 ♖h7+ ♔f6 33 ♔g1 gxf3 34 ♖ch8

White has perpetual check in his sights...

34...♕b1+ 35 ♔h2

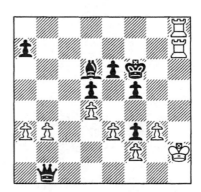

35...♗xg3+! 0-1

Game 43
Novikov-Gleizerov
Portoroz 1993

1 d4 e6 2 c4 f5 3 g3 ♘f6 4 ♗g2 c6 5

♘f3 d5 6 0-0 ♗d6 7 ♕c2 0-0 8 ♘c3 ♘e4 9 ♖b1

With the obvious intention of launching the b-pawn.

9...♕e7

9...♗d7 was seen in Chekhov-Yusupov in the Introduction. That game looks okay for Black.

9...a5 fails to halt the advance. Novikov-Moskalenko, Cap d'Agde 1994, continued 10 a3 ♕e7 11 b4! axb4 12 axb4 ♗xb4 13 ♘xe4 dxe4 14 ♗g5 ♕d7 15 ♖xb4 exf3 16 exf3 ♕xd4 17 ♖bb1 ♘d7 18 ♗e7 ♖e8 19 ♖fd1 ♕a7 20 ♗d6 ♕a5 21 f4 and White had more than enough compensation for the pawn, going on to win the game.

10 b4

10 ♗f4 will be investigated in the next game.

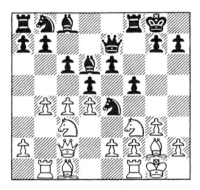

10...♗d7!

This move appears to be the best way to address White's ambition. Taking the pawn introduces complications that favour White, e.g. 10...♗xb4? 11 ♘xe4 dxe4 12 ♗g5 ♕d7 13 ♖xb4 exf3 14 exf3 ♕xd4 15 ♗e7 ♖e8 16 ♖d1 ♕e5 17 f4 ♕c7 18 ♗d6 with great pressure for a mere pawn. 10...a6 11 a4 ♘d7!? 12 b5 axb5 13 axb5 ♔h8?! 14 ♗f4! ♖a3!? is Gleizerov-Moroz, Lubniewice 1994. Now 15 ♘a4! secures White an edge.

11 b5 ♘xc3 12 ♕xc3 cxb5 13 cxb5 ♖c8 14 ♕b3 a6!

This liquidation of the queenside leads to

an equal endgame.

15 bxa6 ♖xa6 16 ♕xb7 ♖xa2 17 ♗f4 ♘c6

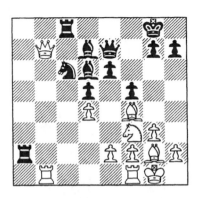

Black is slightly vulnerable structurally, but tidy enough to hold.

18 ♗xd6 ♕xd6 19 ♘e5 ♖a7 20 ♕b2 ♖b8 21 ♕c3 ♖xb1 22 ♖xb1 ♘xe5

Each exchange takes the game closer to a draw.

23 dxe5 ♕c7 24 ♕b2 ♖a4 25 ♕b8+ ♕xb8 26 ♖xb8+ ♔f7

Neither player has real winning chances in the ending, but Novikov decides to play on nonetheless.

27 f4 ♖a7 28 ♗f3 ♖c7 29 ♔f2 ♗a4 30 ♖h8 ♔g6 31 h4 ♗c2 32 h5+ ♔h6 33 ♖e8

White has made progress, albeit insufficient to win.

33...♖c6 34 ♖d8 g6 35 ♖d6 ♗a4 36

hxg6 hxg6 37 ♖xc6 ♗xc6 38 ♔e3 g5 39 fxg5+ ♔xg5 40 ♔d4 f4 41 gxf4+ ♔xf4 42 ♔c5

42...♔xe5!

Black decides to sacrifice a piece to remove every last pawn.

43 ♔xc6 ♔d4!

Cutting off the king.

44 ♔d6 ♔e3 45 ♔xe6 d4 46 ♔d5 d3 47 exd3 ♔xd3 ½-½

Game 44
Schandorff-Nielsen
Gistrup 1996

---

1 d4 e6 2 c4 f5 3 g3 ♘f6 4 ♗g2 d5 5 ♘f3 c6 6 0-0 ♗d6 7 ♘c3 0-0 8 ♕c2 ♘e4 9 ♖b1 ♕e7 10 ♗f4!?

Much in common with the 7 ♗f4 variation, here White wants b2-b4 and the exchange of Black's dark-squared bishop, too. This should not pose Black any problems, although in this game he reacts against the principles of the position.

10...♗xf4 11 gxf4 ♘d7?!

When White has weakened his structure on the kingside Black should normally transfer his bishop via d7 and e8 to h5 or g6.

12 b4 b6 13 b5 ♘xc3 14 ♕xc3 ♗b7

Having voluntarily weakened his queenside Black now has problems on the light squares

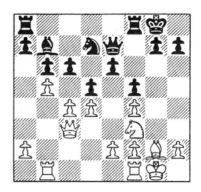

15 cxd5! exd5

15...cxd5 16 ♕c7 ♗c8 17 ♘e5 a6 18 bxa6 ♖xa6 19 ♖b2 is a little better for White.

16 bxc6 ♖ac8 17 ♘e5 ♘xe5 18 fxe5 ♗xc6 19 ♕b3

Black is worse due to the weakness on d5.

19...♕d7 20 ♖fc1 ♖fd8 21 ♖c3 h6 22 ♖bc1 ♔h7 23 ♕c2 ♗a4 24 ♕b1 ♖xc3 25 ♖xc3 ♕e6 26 ♗h3!

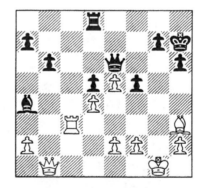

White's latest highlights Black's vulnerability on the light squares. The c-file, passed e-pawn and the d5- and f5-pawns give White an easy lead.

26...♗d7 27 ♖c7 ♕g6+ 28 ♔h1 ♗e6 29 ♖xa7 ♕h5 30 ♕d3 ♖d7 31 ♖xd7 ♗xd7 32 ♗g2 ♗e6 33 ♔g1 ♕e8 34 ♕c2 ♕d7 35 e3 ♗f7 36 ♗h3 ♗e6 37 ♗g2 ♗f7 38 ♗f1 ♗e6 39 ♗d3 ♕c8 40 ♕b1 h5 41 ♕xb6 1-0

Summary

These sidelines are not to be underestimated. 7 ♘bd2 is rather harmless and is only for the player who has no passion for opening advantages. Also lacking punch is ♗g5, against which Black should have no problems unless he gets too ambitious. 7 ♘e5 0-0 8 ♗f4 is more or less reduced to a draw after 8...♘g4! (Game 36). Against 8 ♘c3 Black concentrates on the centre with 8...♘e4, when the manoeuvre ♘e1-d3 appears too slow. However, there is plenty of play after 9 ♖b1 (Games 43-44). Note that in this system it is important that Black develops his bishop on d7 (not b7). In conclusion Black should not fear any of these lines, although they should not be considered inferior to 7 ♗f4 and 7 b3 just because they are less popular.

1 d4 e6 2 c4 f5 3 ♘f3 ♘f6 4 g3 c6 5 ♗g2 d5 6 0-0 ♗d6 7 ♕c2

       7 ♘bd2

              7...b6!? 8 ♘e5 0-0

                     9 ♘d3 – *Game 32*; 9 ♘df3 – *Game 33*

              7...♘bd7 – *Game 34*

       7 ♘e5!? 0-0 8 ♗f4 (D)

              8...♘h5 – *Game 35*; 8...♘g4! – *Game 36*

7...0-0 *(D)* 8 ♘c3

       8 ♘bd2

              8...b6 – *Game 37*; 8...♗d7!? – *Game 38*

       8 ♘e5 – *Game 39*

       8 ♗g5

              8...h6 – *Game 40*; 8...b6 – *Game 41*

8...♘e4 *(D)* 9 ♖b1

       9 e3 *Game 42*

9...♕e7 10 ♗f4 – *Game 44*

       10 b4 – *Game 43*

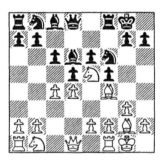

               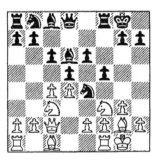

8 ♗f4   *7...0-0*   *8...♘e4*

CHAPTER FOUR

5 ♘h3

1 d4 f5 2 g3 ♘f6 3 ♗g2 e6 4 c4 d5 5 ♘h3

This is an intelligent alternative to the standard ♘f3. Remember that the knight can reach the desirable d3-square via either g1-f3-e5/e1-d3 or g1-h3-f4-d3. The important difference here is that from h3 the knight supports ♗f4 without the inconvenience of damaging the pawn structure in front of the king. In fact this is by far the most dangerous system for Black to face in the Stonewall.

In this chapter we shall investigate the different ways Black can handle the position. In Games 45-47 Black accepts that the bishop is exposed to a challenge if it goes to d6 and consequently settles for ...♗e7. Of course White is then under no obligation to obstruct the knight on h3 with ♗f4. The rest of the games see Black put his bishop on d6 anyway, Game 48 being slightly unusual in that White then switches plans with b2-b3 and ♗a3, confusing his knights after ...♗xa3. White sends his queen's knight to f3 before playing ♗f4 in Games 49-51, giving Black time to prepare for the challenge to his dark-squared bishop. The main line is 7 ♗f4, when Black's path to a decent game begins with 7...♗e7, rather than the accommodating 7...0-0 of Game 52. The point of waiting for ♗f4 and then dropping back to e7 (Games 53-59) is to demonstrate that White's bishop is misplaced, with ...g7-g5 (often assisted by ...h7-h6) a key feature of Black's strategy.

Game 45
Khenkin-Tukmakov
Metz 1991

---

1 d4 f5 2 g3

This is probably the most accurate order of moves. Unless you prefer funny lines with ♗g5 or ♘c3, White employs set-ups with the kingside fianchetto against all lines of the Dutch, and the knight is well placed on h3 in some of them.

2...e6 3 ♗g2 ♘f6 4 c4 d5 5 ♘h3! ♗e7

All in all I do not believe that this is a wise policy, and this game is just one illustration. However, 5 ♘h3 is not easy to deal with, anyway.

6 0-0 0-0

For the advantage of 6...c6 in this position see the next game.

7 b3

Since Black cannot support his bishop with his queen it is logical for White to seek an exchange of bishops here. Having said that I do not find that this tests Black. Another option is 7 ♘f4. Pinter-Agdestein, Haninge 1988, continued 7...c6 8 ♕c2 ♘e4 9

♘d2 ♗f6 10 e3 ♘d6 11 b3 g5 12 ♘d3 ♘f7 13 ♗b2 ♖e8 14 ♖ad1 ♘d7 15 ♔h1 ♘f8 16 ♘e5 ♘g6 with a complex game.

7 ♘d2!? looks strange and unconvincing, but after 7...♘c6!? 8 e3 e5? White played 9 dxe5 ♘xe5 10 cxd5! in Nogueiras-Nikolic, Zagreb 1987, and Black was already in trouble: 10...♔h8 11 ♘b3 ♘g6 12 ♘g5 ♘g4 13 ♘e6.

7...c6

7...♘c6 8 ♗b2 ♘e4 9 f3 ♘g5 10 ♘f2 ♗f6 11 e3 b6 12 ♘c3 ♗a6 13 ♖e1 ♘e7 was weird but probably okay for Black in Dorfman-Karlsson, Helsinki 1986.

7...♘e4!? is quite interesting. Now White cannot play as planned, as 8 ♗a3 dxc4! 9 e3!? (9 bxc4? ♗xa3 10 ♘xa3 ♘c3 11 ♕c2 ♕xd4 is not what White is hoping for, while 9 ♗xe7 ♕xe7 10 bxc4 e5 is equal) 9...♗xa3 10 ♘xa3 cxb3 11 axb3 ♗d7 12 ♕c2 ♗c6 13 ♘f4 ♕e7 14 ♖fd1 ♖d8 15 ♘c4 ♘f6 16 ♘a5 gave White pressure for his pawn in Ftacnik-Agdestein, Lyon 1998, but apparently no advantage.

8 ♗b2

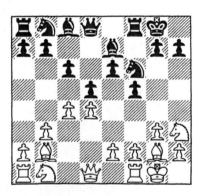

8 ♗a3 appears most natural, but after 8...♗xa3 9 ♘xa3 both knights are on their way to d3 and not one to f3!

8...♘e4 9 ♘d2 ♗f6 10 ♘xe4!

White has no advantage after 10 f3? ♘xd2 11 ♕xd2 dxc4! 12 bxc4 c5 13 e3 ♘c6 14 ♖ad1 e5! 15 d5 ♘a5.

10...dxe4!?

An interesting decision. Perhaps 10...fxe4 is better, with the idea of 11 f3 exf3 12 exf3 dxc4! 13 bxc4 ♕b6 14 ♖b1 ♖d8!. After 15 c5 ♕b4 16 ♘f2! ♗xd4 17 ♗xd4 ♕xd4 18 ♕xd4 ♖xd4 19 ♖fd1 ♖xd1+ 20 ♖xd1 ♘d7 21 ♘e4 White has compensation but probably no advantage. Khenkin writes in his annotations to the game in Chess Informator that he had intended 11 ♕c2!, intending to delay the break in the centre.

11 ♕c2 ♕e7?!

This puts Black in trouble. Instead Black can settle for a slightly inferior position with 11...♕c7 12 f3 exf3 13 exf3 e5! 14 dxe5 ♗xe5 15 ♗xe5 ♕xe5 16 ♖fe1, when he has some problems with his development but no real weaknesses.

12 f3 c5

Black has to do something before the centre is opened to his disadvantage.

13 fxe4!

Accurate play. On 13 d5 Black can keep the position closed and later finish his development with 13...e3!.

13...♗xd4+ 14 ♗xd4 cxd4 15 exf5 exf5 16 ♘f4 ♘c6 17 ♖ad1 ♗d7 18 c5! ♔h8!

Preventing 19 b4 by denying White an assisting check.

19 ♘d5 ♕e5

20 e3!

White opens up the position to exploit his better placed pieces and slightly better development.

20...dxe3

Khenkin gives the following line: 20...♗e6 21 ♖fe1! ♗xd5 22 exd4 ♕f6 23 ♗xd5 ♘xd4 24 ♕f2! ♘c6 25 ♖e6 and White wins.

21 ♖fe1 f4?!

This pawn sacrifice does not work. 21...♖ae8 22 ♖xe3 ♕b8 23 ♖de1! ♖xe3 24 ♖xe3 ♖e8 25 ♕c3! is also good for White, but not as strong as the game.

22 gxf4 ♕h5 23 ♖xe3 ♖ad8 24 ♖de1! ♗g4 25 ♕c4 ♕f5 26 b4 ♗h5

White is also winning after 26...a6 with the idea of 27 a4 ♗h5 28 b5 axb5 29 axb5 ♘a5, as suggested by Khenkin, followed by 30 ♕c3! ♖xd5 31 ♗xd5 ♕xd5 32 ♖e7! ♖g8 33 ♕xa5 ♕xc5+ 34 ♖1e3.

27 b5 ♘a5

27...♗f7 is not much of an alternative: 28 bxc6 bxc6 29 ♘e7! ♗xc4 30 ♘xf5 ♖xf5 31 ♖e8+ ♖f8 32 ♗xc6 ♗xa2 33 ♖xf8+! ♖xf8 34 ♗d7 and the powerful c-pawn will decide the game.

28 ♕c3 ♖xd5 29 ♗xd5 ♕xd5 30 ♕xa5 ♕xc5 31 ♕c3! ♕xb5 32 ♕e5 a6 33 ♖b3!

The game is effectively over.

33...♕xe5 34 fxe5 ♖f7 35 ♖eb1! ♖e7 36 ♖xb7 ♖xe5 37 ♖b8+ ♗e8 38 ♖a8 ♔g8 39 ♖bb8 ♔f7 40 ♖b7+! ♔f6 41 ♖xa6+ ♔f5 42 ♖xg7 ♗g6 43 ♔f2 ♔g4 44 ♖a3 ♖f5+ 45 ♔e2 ♖h5 46 h3+! 1-0

Game 46
Dokhoian-Vaiser
Sochi 1988

---

1 d4 e6 2 c4 f5 3 g3 ♘f6 4 ♗g2 d5 5 ♘h3 c6 6 0-0 ♗e7 7 b3

7 ♕c2 0-0 8 ♘d2 ♗d7 9 ♘f3 ♘e4 10 ♘e5 ♗f6 11 b3 was Nikolic-Short, Belgrade 1987, and now Black could have achieved a fine position with 11...c5! 12 e3 ♘c6.

7...b5!?

This move is interesting and attempts to justify an early 6...c6. However, a possible improvement is 7...♘a6!. Then 8 ♗b2 0-0 9 ♘d2 ♗d7 10 ♘f3 ♗c8 11 ♘f4 ♘c7 12 ♕c1

♘e4 13 ♘d3 ♗h5 was fine for Black in Dlugy-Tukmakov, New York 1990. 8 ♗a3 is met by 8...♘b4 with an interesting position. Black might soon play ...c6-c5 and then drop his knight back to c6.

8 ♗a3 0-0 9 ♘f4 b4?!

Not a wise decision since Black's a-pawn proves to be weak for a long time in the game. White has only a slight edge after 9...a5!? 10 ♗xe7 ♕xe7 11 ♘d2 ♘bd7.

10 ♗b2 a5 11 a3 ♘a6 12 axb4 ♘xb4 13 ♘c3 ♗d6 14 ♘a4

Black is weak on the central squares a5, c5 and e5.

14...g5?

This is just too optimistic. Black should patiently finishing developing. Now White obtains a very promising position.

15 ♘d3 ♘xd3 16 exd3! f4 17 ♖e1 ♖a7

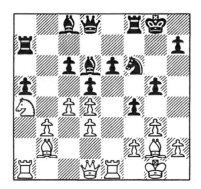

18 ♖e5!?

A tempting but unnecessary sacrifice. However, for players of this strength it is more important how the pieces play than what they are. The point is to gain full control over the dark squares and reduce Black to passivity.

18...♗xe5 19 dxe5 ♘e8 20 ♗d4 ♖b7

The only way to defend against ♗b6.

21 ♘c5 ♖b8?

Black is under pressure and does not find the best defence. Better is 21...♖bf7! 22 cxd5 cxd5 23 ♕d2 ♘g7 24 ♕xa5 ♕xa5 25 ♖xa5 ♘f5 26 ♗c3 ♘e7 27 ♖a2 with an advantage to White in the endgame despite the missing exchange. The b-pawn is potentially very strong.

22 ♗c3 fxg3 23 hxg3 ♖a8 24 ♕d2 ♕e7 25 d4 ♘g7 26 b4!

Securing White a strong outside passed pawn; Black continues to defend, but has a difficult position.

26...♗d7 27 bxa5 ♖fb8 28 ♘xd7 ♕xd7 29 cxd5 cxd5 30 ♕xg5

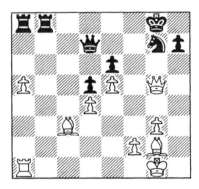

Black is worse on both sides of the board and has no prospects of counterplay, so now he seeks to relieve the pressure.

30...♖b3 31 ♗d2 ♖d3 32 ♗e3 ♕d8! 33 ♕g4! ♖xe3 34 fxe3 ♖xa5 35 ♖f1 ♖a7 36 ♖f6 ♕e8 37 e4 dxe4 38 ♗xe4 ♖a1+ 39 ♔g2 ♕b5 40 ♕f3 ♕b4 41 ♖f8+! ♕xf8 42 ♗xh7+ ♔xh7 43 ♕xf8 ♖d1 44 ♕d8 ♘f5 45 ♕d7+ ♘g7 46 g4 ♖d2+ 47 ♔g3 ♖d1 48 ♕d8 ♖f1 49 ♕f6! ♖d1

The tactical justification of White's queen offer is 49...♖xf6 50 exf6 e5 51 d5! and the pawn ending is winning in view of 51...♘e8 52 f7.

50 ♕f2 ♖c1 51 ♔h4 ♖c7 52 ♕f3! ♔g8 53 ♕a8+ ♔f7 54 ♕d8 ♖e7 55 ♔g5 1-0

Game 47
Dautov-Hort
Bad Homburg 1998

---

1 d4 f5 2 g3 ♘f6 3 ♗g2 d5 4 c4 e6 5 ♘h3 c6 6 ♕c2 ♗e7 7 0-0 0-0 8 ♘d2

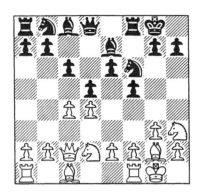

White develops his pieces normally. The problem for Black in lines with ...♗e7 is that his queen has no natural square available, as h5 is covered by ♘f4 and e7 is already occupied. Incidentally playing 8 b3 here can meet with several moves. 8...dxc4? 9 ♕xc4 b5 10 ♕d3 ♘d5 11 ♘f4, as in Khenkin-Karapanos, Corfu 1991, is excellent for White, while 8...b5 9 ♗a3! a5 10 ♗xe7 ♕xe7 11 ♘d2 ♖a7 12 ♘f4 g5 13 ♘d3 g4 14 ♖ac1 ♘a6 15 ♘e5 ♖c7 16 ♕c3 b4 17 ♕e3, Jukic-Kiroski, Pula 1991, and 8...♘a6 9 ♗b2 h6 10 ♘f4 ♕e8 11 a3 g5 12 ♘d3 ♕g6 13 ♘e5, Hoffman-Ginzburg, Villa Martelli 1997, give White an edge. Instead Black should try either 8...a5, e.g. 9 ♗a3 ♗xa3 10 ♘xa3 ♕e7 11 ♕b2 ♘bd7 12 ♘f4 ♔h8 13 ♘d3, Gual-Campos Moreno, Terrassa 1994, which was close to equal, or 8...♗d7 9 ♘f4 ♘a6!? 10 ♘d3 ♘b4 11 ♘xb4 ♗xb4 12 c5 ♗a5, when Korpics-Kiss, Hungary 1993 saw Black gain counterplay after 13 ♘d2 ♗e8 14 ♘f3 ♗c7 15 b4 a6 16 ♗d2 ♕e7 17 ♖ad1 ♘e4 18 ♗c1 ♗h5.

8...♘a6?!

This is not as good here as in other positions. The knight will (eventually) go a long way before reaching d6 and, as it plays no part on a6, I would recommend the traditional route, even though it is temporarily closed due to 8...♘bd7 9 ♘f4! with pressure against e6. The dubious alternative 8...♕e8?! was good for White in Piket-Timman, Wijk aan Zee 1995: 9 ♘f3 ♘e4 10 b3! ♘d7 11 ♘f4 ♗d6?! 12 ♘d3 ♕h5 13 ♘fe5!. Chekhov-Paehtz, Halle 1987, saw both sides throw their pawns forward, White emerging with a minute lead after 8...h6 9 ♘f4 ♕e8 10 ♘f3 g5 11 ♘d3 ♘bd7 12 b4 ♖f7 13 a4 ♖g7 14 b5 cxb5 15 axb5 dxc4 16 ♕xc4 ♘b6 17 ♕b3 which was only slightly better for White. Again Black has superior moves. Nikolic-Short, Belgrade 1987 went 8...♗d7! 9 ♘f3 ♘e4 10 ♘e5 ♗f6 11 b3, and now Black could have played 11...c5! 12 e3 ♘c6 with equality. The standard 8...b6 9 ♘f3 ♘e4 10 ♘f4 ♗d6 11 ♘d3 ♗b7 12 ♗e3 ♘d7 was played in Farago-Klinger, Texta 1988. White tried 13 b4 ♕e7 14 c5 ♗c7 15 ♘fe5, but 15...♘xe5 16 dxe5 bxc5 17 bxc5 a5 was unclear.

9 a3

9 ♘f3 seems more natural as White should not fear ...♘b4.

9...♘c7 10 ♘f3 ♘g4?!

Strange. Black wants to fight for e5 but White will play ♘f4 and h2-h3 with hardly any weakening of his kingside, and the knight will then drop back to f7 via h6. The problem is that Black's other knight is also on its way there (...♘e8-d6-f7)! Eingorn-Schubert, Vienna 1994 favoured White after 10...♗d7 11 ♘e5 ♗e8 12 ♘f4 ♘d7 13 ♘xd7 ♕xd7 14 ♘d3 ♗h5 15 ♗f4 ♘e8 16 b4.

11 ♘f4 ♘e8 12 h3 ♘h6

A lesser evil is 12...♘gf6 13 ♘e5 ♘d6.

13 ♘e5 ♘f7?!

This is the wrong knight!

14 ♘fd3

14 ♘xf7!? is playable, trying to make it harder for Black to bring the other knight to f7.

14...♘xe5

This does not help and leads to a strategically poor game for Black, who can now only hope for chances in any ensuing complications.

15 dxe5!

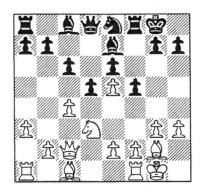

The knight on e8 is out of play, the f6- and d6-squares unavailable to anything, and White even plans to rid Black of his dark-squared bishop. White has a clear advantage.

15...♘c7 16 ♗d2 ♗d7

Black cannot avoid the coming bishop trade as after 16...a5? 17 ♗e3 d4? 18 ♗d2 White will simply open the position with e2-e3 and come to the d-file.

17 ♗b4 ♗e8 18 ♗xe7 ♕xe7 19 b4 ♖d8 20 a4 g5 21 cxd5?!

21 f4!? – as suggested by Tyomkin – looks like a better way for White to consolidate.

21...♘xd5!?

Understandably Black wishes to give his knight some breathing space, but this recapture reduces Black's influence in the centre and increases the scope of the g2-bishop. Of course Black is also seeking some sort of activity. After 21...exd5 22 e3 ♘e6 23 f4 h5 Black has chances to create a distraction with ...h7-h5-h4 etc.

22 ♕c5!

Disturbing Black's queenside.

22...b6 23 ♕xe7 ♘xe7 24 f4

Black still has some problems with his structure but at least his forces are enjoying a little more freedom.

24...h6

24...gxf4 25 gxf4 ♗h5 26 ♔f2 ♖d4! 27 ♖fc1 ♖fd8 28 ♗f3 ♗xf3 29 ♔xf3 ♔f7 is fine for Black according to Dautov.

25 a5

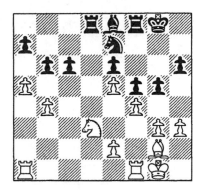

25...♘d5?

Perhaps an automatic centralisation of the knight, but with this move Black forgets his other pieces. Instead 25...♗h5! 26 ♔f2 ♖d4 is much better and puts White under a little pressure at last.

26 axb6 axb6 27 ♖fc1

Forcing Black to defend once more.

27...♖f7 28 ♔f2 ♖b7 29 ♖a3 ♔f8 30 ♖ca1 ♔e7 31 ♗f3 ♗d7 32 fxg5!

Altering the pawn structure in order to gain control of f4.

32...hxg5 33 h4 gxh4?

Opening yet another file is too accommodating and makes it easier for White to support his h-pawn. 33...g4 is necessary, although Black is still struggling. White should then reply 34 ♗g2! and reserve the option of exchanging bishop for knight for later.

34 gxh4 ♗e8 35 h5 ♘c7 36 ♖a7 ♖db8 37 h6 ♔f8

37...♖xa7 38 ♖xa7 ♔d7 39 ♖b7!! is nice.

38 ♖g1! 1-0

The h-pawn queens.

> ## Game 48
> ## Flear-Knaak
> ### *Wijk aan Zee 1988*

1 d4 e6 2 c4 f5 3 g3 ♘f6 4 ♗g2 d5 5 ♘h3!? c6

The immediate 5...♗d6 6 0-0 0-0 7 c5 ♗e7 8 b4 b6 9 ♗b2 a5 10 a3 ♘c6 11 ♕a4

♗d7 12 b5 ♘a7 13 c6 was much better for White in Chandler-Arizmendi Martinez, Bermuda 1999.

6 0-0 ♗d6

Unlike the previous games Black refuses to deviate from the standard set-up with the bishop on d6, waiting to see how White will justify ♘h3.

7 b3

Usually a popular approach, this does not really fit in well with ♘h3 because here White's knights might get in each other's way, as the game demonstrates. The rest of the games in this chapter are devoted to posting the bishop on f4.

7...0-0

7...♕e7 fails to prevent the exchange of bishops as White can play 8 ♗f4. An idea that deserves more tests is 7...dxc4!? 8 bxc4 e5. In Karasev-Moskalenko, Moscow 1992, Black was even slightly better after 9 e3 ♕e7 10 ♕b3 ♘a6 11 ♗a3 ♗xa3 12 ♘xa3 0-0 13 ♘g5 ♘g4 14 f4 e4 15 ♖ab1 c5.

8 ♗a3 ♗xa3!

Accurate play. The point is that both white knights cannot occupy d3! Black can also play 8...b6!? 9 ♘f4 ♗xa3! 10 ♘xa3 ♕d6 11 ♕c1 ♗b7 12 b4 ♘bd7, e.g. 13 ♕b2 (13 c5! is better) 13...♖fe8 14 ♖ac1 a6 15 e3 b5 16 cxd5 cxd5 17 ♘d3 ♘b6 18 ♘c5 ♗c6 19 ♖fd1 ♘c4 20 ♕b3 a5 and Black had an initiative in Reinderman-Vaiser, Andorra 1998.

9 ♘xa3

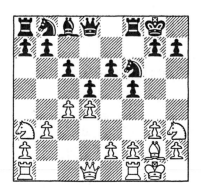

9...♗d7

Black also has a good game with 9...♕e7 10 ♕c1 b6 11 ♘f4 ♗b7 12 b4 ♘bd7 13 ♕b2 a6 14 ♖fc1 b5 15 c5 ♘e4 16 ♘c2 g5 17 ♘d3 f4, when Black had fine play in Hansen-Yrjola, Espoo 1989.

10 ♕c1 ♗e8 11 ♘f4 ♕e7 12 b4!? ♘bd7 13 ♕e3?!

13 ♖b1 a6 is preferable, with chances for an edge for White.

13...♗f7 14 cxd5 ♘g4 15 d6?

15 ♕d3 cxd5 is equal.

15...♕xd6 16 ♕c3 e5!

Black is already better, but after the next move White is in trouble.

17 ♘c4?

17 dxe5 ♘dxe5 18 ♖fd1 ♕f6! 19 ♕c5 ♖fd8 favours Black, although this is still the best White can hope for.

17...♕h6 18 ♘h3 ♖ae8 19 ♘a5 ♗d5! 20 ♘xb7 ♘b6 21 ♖fe1 ♗xg2 22 ♔xg2 ♘d5 23 ♕b3 exd4 24 ♖ad1

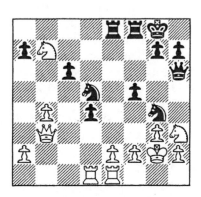

Nothing else saves White: 24 ♘a5 ♔h8 25 ♖ac1 ♖e3! 26 fxe3 (26 ♖xc6 ♘f4+!!) 26...♘dxe3+ 27 ♔f3 ♕xh3 with a winning attack.

24...♖f7! 25 ♖xd4

25 ♘c5 ♖e3! is similar to the previous note.

25...♖xb7 26 e4 fxe4 27 ♖exe4 ♖xe4 28 ♖xe4 ♘gf6 29 ♖e6 ♕g6 30 ♕c4 ♖xb4 31 ♕xc6 ♖b8 32 ♖e5 ♖e8! 33 ♖xe8+ ♕xe8 34 ♕b7 a5 35 ♕a6 a4 36 ♘g5 h6

37 ♘e6 a3! 38 ♘c5 ♕f8 39 ♘e6 ♕e7 40 ♕a8+ ♔f7 41 ♘d8+ ♔g6 42 ♕b8 ♕e4+ 43 ♔g1 ♘c3 44 ♕c7 ♘e2+ 45 ♔f1 ♘d4 46 ♕f7+ ♔h7 0-1

Game 49
Akesson-Niesen
Munkebo 1998

1 d4 e6 2 c4 f5 3 g3 ♘f6 4 ♗g2 d5 5 ♘d2 c6 6 ♘h3 ♗d6 7 0-0 0-0 8 ♘f3

By shutting in the queen's bishop with an early ♘d2 White first transfers the knight to f3 before playing ♗f4. This gives Black more time to decide what to about the challenge to his bishop.

8...b6

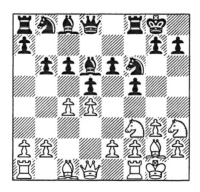

8...♘e4 9 ♕c2 b6 leads to the following game, while in Game 51 Black tries ...♗d7-e8. Karpov-Kolosowski, Koszalin Simul 1997, went 8...♕e8 9 ♗f4 ♗xf4 10 ♘xf4 b6 11 ♖c1 ♗b7 12 ♕c2 ♘e4 13 b4 ♘d7 14 b5 c5 15 e3 ♕e7 16 h4 with a good game for White.

9 ♗f4 ♗a6?

This seems to lose almost by force. After the sensible 9...♗b7 White might have an edge, but interesting is 9...♗e7.

10 cxd5 cxd5

10...exd5 11 ♖c1 makes Black's development very difficult.

11 ♖c1 ♘e4 12 ♗xd6 ♕xd6 13 ♘e5 ♘f6 14 ♘f4 ♗b7 15 ♕a4 ♘bd7 16

♘xd7 ♘xd7 17 ♕a3!

Leaving Black with a simple choice: allow ♖c7 or lose the e-pawn.

17...♕xa3 18 bxa3 ♘f6 19 ♘xe6 ♖fc8 20 ♘c7

20 ♘f4 is safe and easily winning.

20...♖ab8 21 ♘b5 ♗a6 22 ♘d6?!

An illogical pawn exchange. White should play 22 a4.

22...♖xc1 23 ♖xc1 ♗xe2 24 ♘xf5 ♗c4 25 a4 g6 26 ♘e7+?

26 ♘e3 ♗xa2 27 ♖c6 ♘e4 28 f3 ♘d2 29 ♖c7 is still winning.

26...♔f8 27 ♘c6 ♖e8 28 ♘xa7 ♖a8 29 ♘b5 ♖xa4 30 ♘c3 ♖a3 31 ♗f1 ♗xa2 32 ♘xa2?

And even here White can stay well ahead with 32 ♘b5!.

32...♖xa2 33 ♖c6 ♔g7 34 ♖xb6 ♖a4 35 ♖b7+ ♔h6 36 f3 ½-½

Game 50
Golod-Ulibin
Vienna 1998

---

1 d4 e6 2 c4 f5 3 g3 ♘f6 4 ♗g2 c6 5 ♘d2 d5 6 ♕c2!? ♗d6 7 ♘h3 0-0 8 ♘f3!? ♘e4!?

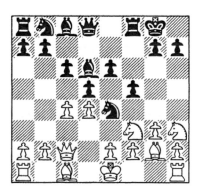

9 0-0 b6!?

White obtains a small advantage after 9...♗d7 10 ♘e5 ♗e8 11 ♘d3 ♘d7 12 f3 ♘ef6 13 ♗f4, Efimov-Kovacevic, Formia 1995. Lautier-Schmittdiel, Berlin 1997 was

also better for White after 9...♘d7 10 ♘f4 ♕e7 11 ♘d3 b6 12 b4 ♗a6?! 13 c5 ♗c7 14 a4, but Black could have improved with 12...♗b7.

10 ♗f4

10 ♘f4 should be harmless if Black plays 10...♕e7 instead of 10...♘a6?!, when 11 ♘e5 ♕c7 12 cxd5 cxd5 13 ♕xc7 ♘xc7 14 ♗e3 ♗xe5 15 dxe5 ♘a6 16 ♖fc1 ♗d7 17 f3 ♘ec5 18 ♗d2 gave some advantage to White in Speelman-Relange, London 1991.

10...♗b7

10...♗a6 11 cxd5! cxd5? (Black must recapture with the e-pawn to keep the c-file closed) 12 ♖fc1 ♕e7 13 ♗xd6 ♘xd6 14 ♘f4 ♖c8 15 ♕a4 ♖xc1+ 16 ♖xc1 gave White a large plus in Chernin-Ulibin, Stockholm 1997.

11 ♖fd1

It seems as if White has no other way to guarantee an advantage. 11 ♖ac1!? ♘d7!? 12 ♗xd6 ♘xd6 13 cxd5 exd5 14 ♘f4 ♕e7 was fine for Black in Madebrink-Wiedenkeller, Norrköping 1988, 11 ♖ad1 ♗e7!? 12 ♕c1 ♕e8 13 ♘hg5 ♗f6 14 ♘e5 c5 was unclear in Georges-Klinger, Zurich 1992 and Kandba-Iljushin, Briansk 1995 was equal after 11 ♗xd6 ♕xd6 12 ♘f4 ♘d7 13 ♖fd1 ♖ac8 14 b3 ♖fd8 15 ♕b2.

11...♘d7 12 ♗xd6 ♘xd6 13 ♘f4 ♕e7 14 cxd5 exd5 15 ♖ac1

15 e3!? is more logical.

15...♘e4 16 ♘d3 c5

Now that Black has the centre covered this desired, aggressive advance is possible.

17 dxc5 bxc5 18 ♘d2!? c4 19 ♘xe4! fxe4 20 ♘f4 ♘f6 21 b3 g5 22 ♘h3 cxb3 23 ♕xb3 h6 24 f3! ♗a6 25 ♕e3 ♖ab8 26 fxe4 ♖b2 27 ♖d2 ♖xd2 28 ♕xd2 dxe4 29 ♕e3 ♖b8?!

Better is 29...♘g4!? 30 ♕xe4 ♕xe4 31 ♗xe4 ♗xe2 with a draw.

30 ♘f2 ♖b2 31 ♘xe4 ♘xe4 32 ♕xe4

32 ♗xe4!? ♖xe2 33 ♕b3+ ♔h8 offers White some chances in the endgame due to Black's exposed king.

32...♕xe4 33 ♗xe4 ♗xe2!

Forcing a draw.

34 ♖c8+ ♔f7 35 ♖c7+ ♔e6 36 ♖xa7 ♔e5! 37 ♖e7+ ♔d6 38 ♖a7 ♔e5 39 ♖e7+ ♔d6 40 ♖h7 ♔e5 41 ♗g2 ♗c4! 42 ♖xh6 ♖b1+ 43 ♔f2 ♖b2+ 44 ♔g1 ½-½

Game 51
Anand-P.Nikolic
Wijk aan Zee 2000

---

1 d4 f5 2 g3 ᐃf6 3 ♗g2 e6 4 c4 d5 5 ᐃh3 c6 6 0-0 ♗d6 7 ♕c2 0-0 8 ᐃd2 ♗d7

I do not recommend this form of development in the ᐃh3 variation, and this game is a good illustration why. Perhaps Black might throw in an early ...ᐃe4, as in the note to Black's 9th move in Game 50, but this also favours White.

8...ᐃh5!? 9 ᐃf3 ᐃd7 is interesting. Then Brenninkmeijer-Winants, Lyon 1990, ended in a draw after 10 ᐃf4 ᐃxf4 11 ♗xf4 ♗xf4 12 gxf4 ᐃf6 13 e3 ♗d7 14 ♔h1 ♗e8 15 ᐃe5 ᐃg4 16 ♗f3 ᐃxe5 17 dxe5. ♕h4 18 ♕e2. Dreev-Borges Mateos, Linares 1999, went 10 ᐃe1 h6 11 ᐃd3 g5 12 ♗d2 ᐃhf6 13 f3 ♕e7 14 ♖ae1 c5 15 e3 b6, with good counter-chances for Black.

8...b6 9 ᐃf3 ♗a6!? is playable here as White has spent a move on ♕c2 compared with Game 49. Lautier-Nikolic, Monte Carlo 1997 continued 10 cxd5 cxd5 11 ♗f4 h6 12 ♗xd6 ♕xd6 13 ᐃf4 ♖c8 14 ♕a4 g5 15 ᐃd3 ♗xd3 16 exd3 ᐃc6 17 ♖fe1 b5 18 ♕xb5 g4 with a complicated game that is no worse for Black. Normal is 9...♗b7.

9 ᐃf3 ♗e8 10 ♗f4! h6 11 ♕b3!

This appears to be a virtual refutation of the ...♗d7-e8 idea. 11 ♗xd6 ♕xd6 12 ᐃf4 ᐃbd7 13 ᐃd3 dxc4 14 ♕xc4 ᐃh5 15 b4 ᐃe4 16 ♖fd1 ᐃb6 17 ♕b3 was only slightly better for White in Kasparov-Nikolic, New York 1994. Nikolic probably had an improvement for the present game, but the text is strong and therefore makes this irrelevant.

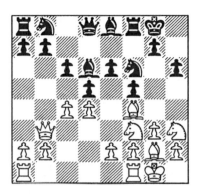

11...b6

11...g5 12 ♗xd6 ♕xd6 13 ♕xb7! g4 14 ♕xa8 gxh3 15 ♕xa7 hxg2 16 ♖fc1 gives White a significant advantage.

12 ♖fc1! ♗e7 13 cxd5 ᐃxd5

Sadly forced as 13...exd5 14 ᐃe5 is very good for White.

14 ♗d2 g5 15 ᐃe5 a5! 16 e4 fxe4 17 ♗xe4 ♖a7 18 f4!

Highlighting the risk involved in ...g7-g5. The advanced g-pawn can become an easy target, allowing White a well timed and advantageous opening of the kingside.

18...gxf4 19 ♔h1 ♗f6 20 ᐃxf4 ♕d6 21 ᐃfg6 ♗xg6 22 ᐃxg6 ♖ff7 23 ♗f4! ᐃxf4 24 gxf4 ♗g7

24...♗xd4 25 ♕h3 ♗xb2 26 ♖d1 ♗d4 27 ♕xh6 is also excellent for White.

25 ♕h3 ♖f6 26 ♖c3! ♕xd4 27 ♕g2 ♖d7 28 ♖g1 b5 29 ♖g3

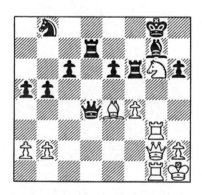

Three major pieces on the same (open) file as Black's king, a powerful knight and strong bishop clearly put White firmly in the driving seat!

29...♕a7 30 ♘e5 ♖e7 31 ♕d2 ♕c7 32 ♖d3 ♖e8 33 ♖d6 c5 34 ♘g4 ♖ff8 35 ♘xh6+ ♔h8 36 ♘g4 ♖d8 37 ♕g2 ♖xd6 38 ♕h3+ ♔g8 39 ♕h7+ ♔f7 40 ♗g6+ 1-0

Game 52
Goldin-L.B.Hansen
Warsaw 1990

---

1 d4 e6 2 c4 f5 3 g3 ♘f6 4 ♗g2 d5 5 ♘h3 c6 6 0-0 ♗d6 7 ♗f4

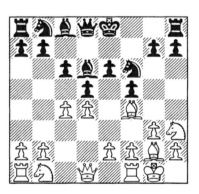

This is the usual way for White to play, quickly justifying ♘h3 with a challenge to the d6-bishop. Now Black must choose between allowing the exchange, as here, or avoiding it with ...♗e7, which is covered in the rest of the games in this chapter.

7...0-0 8 ♘d2 b6 9 ♖c1 ♗b7 10 cxd5 cxd5?

Allowing a familiar idea. Instead 10...exd5 11 ♘f3 ♘e4 is only a shade worse for Black, with play along the lines of Game 50.

11 ♘c4! ♗xf4 12 ♘xf4 ♕e7 13 ♘e5 ♘a6 14 ♕a4

White has a very strong position. He has control of the centre, and Black has no active counterplay.

14...♖fc8 15 h4 ♘c7 16 ♖c2 a5 17 ♖fc1

Black's problem is not just the c-file – often this is no more than a route to a draw through mass exchanges – but White's overall superiority. A look at the relative strengths of the knights, for example, highlights Black's plight.

17...♘a6 18 a3 ♖xc2 19 ♕xc2 ♕d6 20 e3 ♘e8 21 ♗f1

Preparing to bring his final piece into the game.

21...♘ac7 22 g4!

The beginning of the final attack. Once again an advantage in one sector presents aggressive possibilities in another.

22...fxg4 23 ♗d3

Black has no defence.

23...g6 24 ♗xg6! ♕e7

24...hxg6 25 ♕xg6+ ♘g7 26 ♕f7+ ♔h8 27 ♖xc7 and White wins.

25 ♗f7+ ♔g7

25...♔h8 drops the queen to 26 ♘fg6+.

26 ♘h5+ ♔h8

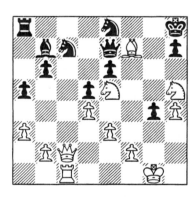

27 ♘g6+!! hxg6 28 ♕xg6 ♕f8 29 ♖xc7! ♘xc7 30 ♘f6 1-0

Black cannot prevent mate.

Game 53
Gulko-Short
Reykjavik 1990

---

1 d4 e6 2 c4 f5 3 g3 ♘f6 4 ♗g2 d5 5 ♘h3 c6 6 ♕c2

6 0-0 ♗d6 7 ♘c3 0-0 8 ♕c2 leads to simi-

lar positions. J.Horvath-Moskalenko, Budapest 1991, went 8...♘a6 9 ♗f4 dxc4 10 e3 ♘b4 11 ♕e2 ♘d3 12 ♗xd6 ♕xd6 13 ♘f4 e5 14 ♘xd3 cxd3 15 ♕xd3 ♗e6 with a balanced game. 9 ♖b1 dxc4 10 e4 e5 11 ♕e2 exd4 12 ♕xc4+ ♔h8 13 ♕xd4 ♕e7 14 ♗g5 ♗e5 15 ♕e3 ♘c5 16 exf5 ♗xf5 17 ♖bd1 ♖ae8 favoured Black in Pinter-Rechlis, Beersheba 1988.

6...♗d6 7 ♗f4 ♗e7!?

Black hopes to profit from the potentially awkward situation of White's minor pieces on the kingside, either by leaving White to untangle or attacking with the g-pawn. In this and the next game White forgoes the thematic ♘d2-f3.

8 0-0 0-0 9 ♘c3!? h6?!

Automatically setting about an understandable kingside expansion, but in this particular case it is not a good idea. Gulko suggests the improvement 9...dxc4!? 10 e4 ♕xd4 11 exf5 e5! 12 ♖ad1 ♕c5, which he assesses as unclear.

10 ♖ad1 g5 11 ♗c1 ♗d7 12 f3!

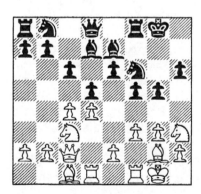

It is true that with 9 ♘c3 White has taken his eye off the e5-square, but he still has considerable influence in the centre in general and the d-file holds more potential after ♖ad1.

12...dxc4 13 e4 ♘a6 14 a3! b5 15 ♘f2?!

15 f4! g4 16 ♘f2 favours White.

15...♘c7?

Black returns the favour. 15...fxe4! 16 fxe4 ♔g7 is unclear.

16 f4! g4 17 b3! cxb3 18 ♕xb3 fxe4 19 ♘cxe4 ♘xe4 20 ♗xe4 h5 21 ♘d3?

Razuvaev's 21 h3! gxh3 22 g4! creates a terrible attack.

21...♘d5 22 ♘e5?!

22 ♘c5! with some advantage was better.

22...♗f6 23 f5 ♗xe5 24 dxe5 ♕b6+ 25 ♖f2 exf5 26 ♖xd5 ♗e6 27 ♗e3

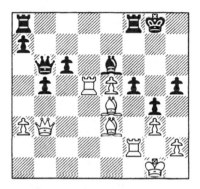

27...♕a6?

Black should keep control of the seventh rank. 27...♕b7!? 28 ♖xb5 ♕f7! is unclear.

28 ♗h6

White is running short of time. 28 ♖xf5! ♖xf5 29 ♖d8+ ♖xd8 30 ♕xe6+ ♖f7 31 ♗h7+! ♔h8 32 ♕xf7 ♖d1+ 33 ♔g2 ♕xa3 34 ♗c2 wins easily.

28...cxd5 29 ♗xd5 ♗xd5

Or 29...♖fe8 30 ♕e3! ♔h7 31 ♕g5 ♖g8 32 ♕xh5.

30 ♕xd5+ ♔h7 31 ♗xf8 ♖xf8 32 e6 ♕c8 33 e7 ♖f6 34 ♕e5 1-0

Game 54
Bareev-Vaiser
Pula 1988

---

1 d4 e6 2 c4 f5 3 g3 ♘f6 4 ♗g2 d5 5 ♘h3 c6 6 0-0 ♗d6 7 ♗f4 0-0

Of course if Black intends to play the ...♗e7 system he should do so immediately.

8 ♕b3

By no means inconsistent with the ♘h3 set-up is 8 ♗xd6 ♕xd6 9 ♕b3. After 9...b5!? 10 cxb5 cxb5 the natural 11 ♘f4 or 11 ♘d2 might offer White something, but 11 ♕xb5?! ♘c6 12 ♕d3 ♖b8 13 ♘c3 ♖xb2 14 ♖fb1 ♖b4 15 e3 ♘e4 was good for Black in Flear-Moskalenko, Fuerteventura 1992.

8...♗e7! 9 ♘a3!?

9 ♘d2 h6 10 ♗xb8 ♖xb8 11 ♘f4 ♗d6 12 ♘g6 ♖f7 13 ♘e5 ♖c7 14 ♘df3 b6 15 ♖fd1 ♘d7 led to equality in Guliev-Keitlinghaus, Ostrava 1993.

9...h6!? 10 ♖ad1 g5 11 ♗d2 a5!

Preventing ♗b4.

12 f3

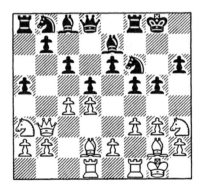

12...b5!

A logical pawn sacrifice with which Black generates a healthy initiative.

13 cxb5 cxb5 14 ♘xb5

14 ♕xb5 ♗a6.

14...a4 15 ♕e3 ♕b6 16 ♘c3 ♘c6 17 ♔h1!

Maintaining the balance. 17 ♗e1 ♕xb2 favours Black.

17...♘xd4 18 ♕g1 ♗c5 19 ♗e3 ♘b3 20 ♗f2! ♗xf2 21 ♘xf2 ♘c5 22 ♘d3 ♘cd7

In a level situation White now takes too many liberties, soon ending up in a worse position.

23 e4?! d4 24 e5?

24 ♘e2 e5!? 25 exf5 ♘d5 is also uncomfortable but not losing.

24...dxc3 25 exf6 cxb2 26 ♕xb6 ♘xb6

27 f4?

27 ♘xb2 f4! limits White to a deficit of a pawn.

27...a3! 28 ♗xa8 ♘xa8 29 ♘c5 ♘c7! 30 ♖d6 ♘d5 31 ♔g1 ♔f7 32 ♖e1 gxf4 33 gxf4 ♘c3 34 ♖d3 ♘xa2

A quicker finish is 34...♘e2+! 35 ♔f2 ♘c1.

35 ♖b1 ♘c3 36 ♖xc3 a2 37 ♖cc1 bxc1♕+ 38 ♖xc1 ♖d8 39 ♔f2 ♖d2+ 40 ♔e3 ♖c2! 0-1

Game 55
Shipov-Moskalenko
Moscow 1996

1 d4 e6 2 c4 f5 3 g3 ♘f6 4 ♗g2 d5 5 ♘h3 c6 6 ♕c2 ♗d6 7 0-0 0-0 8 ♗f4 ♗e7

8...b6 9 ♘d2 ♗b7 10 a3 ♕e7 11 ♖ac1 ♗xf4 12 ♘xf4 ♘bd7 13 cxd5 cxd5 14 ♕a4 was a little bit better for White in Farago-Keitlinghaus, Dortmund 1988. However 9...♗a6? 10 cxd5 cxd5 11 ♘f3 ♘e4 12 ♖fc1 ♖e8 13 ♗xd6 ♘xd6 14 ♘f4, Yrjola-Agdestein, Gausdal 1987, is unpleasant for Black.

8...♘a6?! worked out poorly for Black in Gulko-Moskalenko, Helsinki 1992. After 9 ♘d2 ♘e4 10 ♖ad1 ♕e7 11 ♘f3 ♘b4 12 ♕b3 ♗xf4 13 ♘xf4 g5 14 ♘d3 ♘xd3 White found 15 exd3! ♘d6 16 ♕b4 a5 17 ♕c5 ♖d8 18 ♖de1 ♕f6 19 ♘e5 with an excellent position.

9 ♘d2

Heading for f3. Black now turns his attention to the bishop on f4.

9...♘h5 10 ♗e3

White is not obliged to retreat. In fact 10 ♘f3 ♘d7 11 ♗g5! h6 12 ♗xe7 ♕xe7 13 e3 has been played. In Karpov-Vaiser, Baden-Baden 1995, Black saw White's knights as a juicy target, prompting him to try 13...g5. The game continued 14 ♘e1 ♘df6 15 ♘d3 ♗d7 16 f4 ♘g4 17 ♖fe1 ♕g7 18 ♘hf2 gxf4 19 ♘xg4 fxg4 20 gxf4 ♗e8 21 ♘e5 ♘f6 22

♕f2 ♗g6 23 ♕h4 ♗f5 with approximate equality, although there is a lot of play left in the position. Jacimovic-Djurhuus, Yerevan 1996, went instead 11 ♗d2 ♗d6 12 ♘f4, and now Black could have equalized with 12...♘xf4! 13 ♗xf4 ♗xf4 14 gxf4 ♘f6.

It is possible that 10 ♗xb8!? might prove strong. White seemed to have a small edge after 10...♖xb8 11 e3 g5 12 f3 ♗d7 13 ♘f2 in Cramling-Vaiser, Cap d'Agde 1996. However, after 13...f4 14 exf4 gxf4 15 g4 ♘g7 16 ♘d3 ♗f6 17 ♘e5 ♗xe5 18 dxe5 ♗e8 19 ♘b3 Black was not without counterplay.

10...♗d6 11 ♘f3 ♘d7

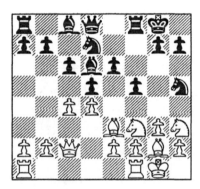

12 ♖ad1?!

Shipov recommends the following line as an improvement on the game: 12 ♕c1! (with the idea of 13 ♘f4) 12...♕c7 13 c5 (13 ♘f4!? ♘xf4 14 ♗xf4 ♗xf4 15 ♕xf4 ♕xf4 16 gxf4 ♘f6 is a traditional position that Black should not fear) 13...♗e7 14 ♘f4 ♘xf4 (14...♘df6 15 ♘e5 favours White) 15 ♗xf4 ♕d8 16 b4 and White has an initiative on the queenside.

12...♘df6

12...h6! 13 ♘f4 ♘xf4 14 ♗xf4 ♗xf4 15 gxf4 g5! offers Black promising play according to Shipov.

13 ♘e5 ♘g4?!

Despite Shipov's mistrust of 13...h6! 14 ♘g6 ♖f7 15 f3 it seems to me that Black might be okay after the unusual 15...dxc4! 16 ♕xc4 ♘d5.

14 ♗g5

14 ♘xg4?! fxg4 15 ♘g5 ♘f6 16 ♗c1 h6 17 e4 hxg5 18 e5 ♗e7 19 exf6 ♗xf6 nets a pawn for Black, and the tripled g-pawns are not so bad.

14...♕e8 15 ♘d3 ♕g6 16 ♘df4 ♘xf4 17 ♗xf4 ♗xf4

17...♗e7 18 f3 ♘f6 19 ♘f2!? followed by e2-e4 gives White the initiative.

18 ♘xf4

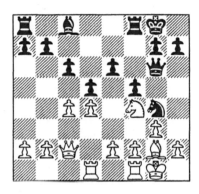

White has won the opening battle and is slightly better.

18...♕h6 19 h3 ♘f6 20 ♘d3

Here or on the next move White should get going with b2-b4!.

20...g5 21 e3 a5 22 a3 a4?!

This pawn is weak here.

23 ♖c1 ♘e4 24 ♘e5 ♘d6 25 ♕d2 ♘f7!

26 ♘d3 ♘d6! 27 ♘e5 ♘f7 28 f4!

White is playing for the full point.

28...♘xe5 29 dxe5 ♕g7 30 ♔h2 ♔h8 31 ♖g1 ♖g8 32 ♗f3 ♗d7 33 ♕c3 g4 34 ♗e2 gxh3

An oversight in time-trouble. Black should play 34...h5 and accept a slightly worse position.

35 g4 fxg4 36 ♖xg4 ♕f7 37 ♖cg1 ♖xg4 38 ♖xg4 ♖g8 39 cxd5 cxd5 40 ♕b4 ♗c6 41 ♖xg8+ ♕xg8 42 ♗f1! d4?

Too optimistic, although 42...♔g7! 43 ♕e7+ ♕f7 44 ♕d8! leaves White well ahead.

43 ♕xd4 ♗g2 44 ♗c4 ♗c6 45 ♕d2 ♗e4 46 ♗f1 ♗f5 47 ♕d7 ♕g4 48 ♕c8+ ♔g7

49 ♕xb7+ ♔g6 50 ♕b5 ♕h4 51 ♕e8+ ♔g7 52 ♕d7+ ♔h8 53 ♕d2 h5 54 ♗b5 ♔g7 55 ♗xa4 ♗e4 56 ♗d1 ♔h6 57 b4 ♕e7 58 ♕d6 ♕f7 59 ♕d8 ♕b7 60 ♕h8+ ♗h7 61 ♕f8+ 1-0

Game 56
Aleksandrov-Gleizerov
Voskresensk 1993

1 d4 e6 2 c4 f5 3 g3 ♘f6 4 ♗g2 c6 5 ♘h3 d5 6 0-0 ♗d6 7 ♗f4 0-0 8 ♘d2 ♗e7 9 ♕c2

9 e3 ♘e4 10 ♘xe4 fxe4 11 f3 exf3 12 ♖xf3 ♘d7 was agreed drawn in Volkov-Gleizerov, Kstovo 1997.

9...♘a6!?

The knight is occasionally okay on a6, with b4, c5 and c7 in its sights.

10 ♖fd1

White brought the other rook to d1 in Rogozenko-Nielsen, Yerevan 1996: 10 ♖ad1 h6 11 ♗e5 g5 12 ♗xf6 ♗xf6 13 e3 ♗d7 14 a3 ♘c7 15 f4 g4 16 ♘f2 h5 17 ♘d3 a5 18 c5 ♕e7 19 ♖a1 ♖a7 20 b4 ♖fa8 21 ♘b3 axb4 22 axb4 ♘b5 with chances for both sides.

10...h6! 11 a3 g5 12 ♗e5 ♘g4!

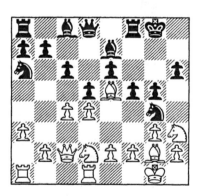

Black has equalized.

13 b4 ♗d7 14 b5?!

This is too optimistic. An even game results from 14 ♕b3 ♗e8 15 f4 ♗h5.

14...♘c5!

The knight jumps into action.

15 bxc6 bxc6 16 ♘f3 ♘e4

Black's position is preferable. The knight on h3 is terribly misplaced.

17 ♖db1 ♘d6 18 ♗xd6

Black threatened ...♘xe5 followed by ...♘f7.

18...♗xd6 19 ♘e1 ♕a5 20 ♘d3 ♖ab8 21 c5 ♗e7 22 ♖xb8 ♖xb8 23 ♖b1 ♕c7 24 f4 gxf4 25 gxf4 ♗h4! 26 ♕c1 ♗e8 27 ♗f3 ♖xb1 28 ♕xb1 ♕g7 29 ♕b8!

White has defended well, earning equality.

29...♔h7?!

29...♕xd4+ 30 ♔g2 ♘f6 31 ♗h5 ♕e4+ 32 ♗f3 ♕e3 33 ♗h5 draws.

30 ♕xe8! ♘f6+

31 ♘g5+!

Black must have underestimated this.

31...♕xg5+! 32 fxg5 ♘xe8 33 gxh6 ♘c7?!

33...♗f6!? 34 e3 a5 is the best defence, although White has some chances to win.

34 ♘e5 ♗g5 35 ♔f2 ♗h4+ 36 ♔f1 ♗g5 37 ♔f2 ♗h4+ 38 ♔e3 ♗g5+ 39 ♔d3 ♗f4 40 ♘xc6 ♗xh2 41 ♘xa7 ♔xh6 42 a4 ♔g5 43 ♘c6 ♔f6 44 ♔c3 ♗g3 45 ♔b4 ♗e1+ 46 ♔b3 ♗f2 47 a5 f4?!

47...♔f7!? is better.

48 ♔a4 ♔f5 49 ♘a7! ♔f6 50 ♘b5 ♘a6 51 c6 ♔e7 52 ♗g4 ♔d8 53 ♗xe6 ♘c7 54 ♘xc7 ♔xc7 55 ♗xd5 ♗xd4 56 ♔b4 ♗e3 57 ♔c3 ♔d6 58 ♔d3 ♗c1 59 ♔e4 ♗d2 60 a6 ♗e3 61 ♔f5 ♘c7 62 ♔e5!

Black is now without moves.

62...♗g1 63 ♔xf4 ♔b6 64 ♔f5 ♗h2 65
♗c4 ♔xc6 66 e4 ♗g1 67 ♔f6 ♗d4+ 68
e5 ♔c7 69 ♔e6 ♗c3 70 ♔d5 ♗b4 71
♗b5 ♔b6 72 ♔e6! ♗c5 73 ♗d3 ♗d4 74
♔d6 ♗c5+ 75 ♔d7 1-0

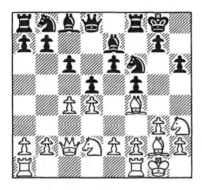

Game 57
Gleizerov-Moskalenko
Balatonbereny 1994

1 d4 e6 2 c4 f5 3 g3 ♘f6 4 ♗g2 d5 5
♘h3 c6 6 0-0 ♗d6 7 ♗f4 0-0 8 ♕c2
♗e7 9 ♘d2 h6

The most direct and popular continuation,
intending to harass White with the g-pawn.
Consequently White has little choice but to
part with his bishop, a part of the strategy
that White is happy with anyway, since the
h3-knight will soon need the f4-square.
10 ♗xb8 ♖xb8 11 ♘f4
This is the main line of the ♘h3 variation
these days. Black has a variety of choices
which will be investigated in this and the
following two games. I believe that White
should be slightly better but his edge is no
more here than in other defences. There are
many positions where Black defends slightly
inferior positions in the King's Indian,
Nimzo-Indian, QGD and all other openings.
At least in the Stonewall Black has his fair
share of space.
11...♕e8
The next two games deal with 11...g5 and

11...♗d6 respectively.
12 e3
12 ♘d3!? might be preferable.
12...♗d6 13 ♘d3 ♕e7
Opting for the alternative development of
the bishop with 13...b6 deserves attention.
After 14 ♖fe1 ♗d7?! 15 b4 g5 16 ♘f3 ♕h5
17 c5 ♗c7 18 cxb6 ♖xb6 19 ♖ab1 ♖fb8 20
♘fe5 White was in control in Vanheste-
Kern, Groningen 1990. However, 14...♘e4!
15 ♘f3 ♗a6! 16 ♘fe5 c5! was Black's improvement in Roeder-Vaiser, Bern 1992,
giving Black promising counterplay.
**14 ♖ab1! ♗d7 15 b4 ♗e8 16 a4 ♘e4 17
c5?!**
17 ♘f3! is enough for a modest advantage.
17...♗c7 18 b5?!
18 ♘f3 is still better.
18...♘xd2 19 ♕xd2 b6
Black is no longer worse.
**20 ♖fc1 cxb5 21 axb5 bxc5 22 ♘xc5
♗xb5! 23 ♘xe6 ♕xe6 24 ♖xc7 ♗c4! 25
♖bb7!? ♖xb7 26 ♖xb7**

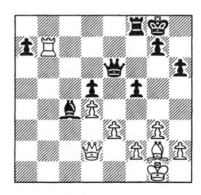

26...♖f7?
Missing the draw which, according to
Moskalenko, is 26...♕a6! 27 ♕b2 ♖f6!, e.g.
28 h4 ♖b6 29 ♖xb6 ♕xb6 and Black is okay.
27 ♖b8+! ♔h7?
Another mistake after which White has a
winning attack. 27...♖f8 28 ♕b4 ♕f7 keeps
Black in the game, although 29 ♖b7 leaves
White well ahead.

28 ♕a5 ♖d7 29 ♕c5 ♖d6 30 h4!

White secures his king before the final attack.

30...♖b6 31 ♖d8! f4!?

One last try to muddy the waters.

32 exf4!

32 gxf4?? ♕f6 followed by ...♖b1 and ...♕xh4 wins for Black.

32...♕e1+ 33 ♔h2 ♕xf2 34 ♕c8! ♗f1 35 ♖h8+ ♔g6 36 h5+ 1-0

36...♔f6 37 ♖f8+ ♔e7 38 ♕d8+ ♔e6 39 ♕xd5+ mates.

Game 58
Dragomarezkij-Moskalenko
Alushta 1993

---

1 d4 e6 2 c4 f5 3 g3 ♘f6 4 ♗g2 c6 5 ♘h3 d5 6 ♕c2 ♗d6 7 0-0 0-0 8 ♗f4 ♗e7 9 ♘d2 h6 10 ♗xb8 ♖xb8 11 ♘f4 g5!?

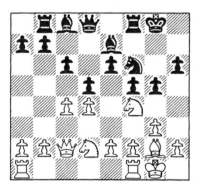

A very aggressive reaction. Black decides that he can afford to part with his dark-squared bishop as White has already done so. The natural 11...♗d6, granting the bishop a longer life, is considered in the next game.

12 ♘g6

In general White should accept the invitation, but 12 ♘d3!?, intending ♘f3-e5, also makes sense.

12...♖f7 13 ♘xe7+ ♕xe7 14 ♖ae1!?

14 ♖ac1 is a logical possibility.

14...♗d7 15 ♘f3 ♖g7

Lining up against White's king.

16 ♘e5 ♖f8 17 e3?!

Restricting White to operating only on the queenside after Black's excellent response. Danish GM Lars Bo Hansen's suggestion of 17 f3!? g4! 18 ♗h1!, with the idea of breaking in the centre with e2-e4, deserves attention.

17...g4!

Effectively fixing the structure so that any push by White does not reduce Black's control of key squares.

18 cxd5 cxd5 19 ♖c1 ♗b5! 20 ♖fe1 ♘d7!

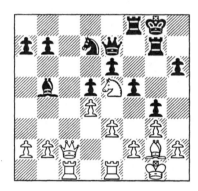

Black has equalized. His structure is not worse, nor his bishop. Indeed it is worth taking time to consider the bishops and pawn formations here. Despite having nearly all his pawns fixed on the same colour squares as his bishop, Black is not worse – in fact the g2-bishop is doing nothing.

21 ♕c7 ♘xe5 22 ♕xe5 ♕f6! 23 ♕xf6 ♖xf6 24 ♖c5 a6 25 ♖ec1 h5

Highlighting the solidity of Black's set-up.

26 b3! ♖e7 27 a4 ♗e2 28 ♖5c2 ♗d3 29 ♖d2 ♗e4 30 ♗xe4

Black cannot be allowed to plant his bishop on e4.

30...fxe4 31 b4 ♖ff7 32 ♖dc2 ♔g7 33 b5 axb5 34 axb5 ♔f6 35 ♖c8

White has created some chances, but Black defends well.

35...e5!

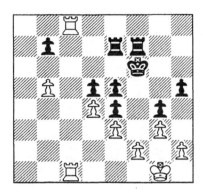

Even at this late stage of the game the Stonewall pawn mass plays a part.

36 dxe5+ ♔xe5 37 ♖h8 ♖f5 38 ♖d8 ♖e6 39 ♖d7 ♖b6 40 ♖c5 ♔e6 41 ♖d8 ♖d6 42 ♖h8 b6 43 ♖c7 d4! 44 exd4 ♔d5 45 ♖ch7 ♔xd4 46 ♖xh5 ♖c5?

Black can draw with 46...♖xh5 47 ♖xh5 e3! 48 fxe3+ ♔xe3 49 ♖e5+ ♔f3 50 ♖f5+ ♔e3 etc. After the text Black's rooks become rather passive.

47 ♖h4 ♖g6 48 ♖d8+ ♔c3 49 ♖e8 ♔d4 50 h3! ♖xb5 51 hxg4 ♖bg5 52 ♖b8 b5 53 ♔g2 e3!?

Trying to gain counterplay.

54 fxe3+?

L.B.Hansen offers the improvement 54 f4! e2 55 ♖e8 ♖xg4 56 ♖xg4 ♖xg4 57 ♔f3 ♖g7 58 f5 with good winning chances. Now we have a draw.

54...♔xe3 55 ♔h2 ♔d4 56 ♔h3 ♔c3 57 ♖c8+ ♔d4 58 ♖d8+ ♔e3 59 ♖e8+ ♔f3 ½-½

Game 59
Kozul-Bareev
Biel 1991

1 d4 e6 2 c4 f5 3 g3 ♘f6 4 ♗g2 c6 5 ♘h3 d5 6 0-0 ♗d6 7 ♗f4 ♗e7 8 ♘d2 0-0 9 ♕c2 h6 10 ♗xb8 ♖xb8 11 ♘f4 ♗d6

Allowing the removal of this bishop is not a problem for Black, but keeping it, for the

moment at least, might well be preferable.

12 ♘d3

Sensibly monitoring the e5-square. This can also be done with 12 ♘g6 ♖e8 13 ♘f3 ♘e4 14 ♘fe5, when Andruet-Dolmatov, Marseille 1988, continued 14...♕f6 15 ♗xe4 dxe4 16 c5 ♗xe5 17 ♘xe5 ♖d8 18 e3 ♗d7 19 f3, which has been evaluated as giving an edge to White. However, I am not sure that this is true. White has some weak squares on the kingside and Black has good chances of generating counterplay on the b-file. In fact Black went on to win the game.

12...♗d7

Black is attracted to the e8-square for his bishop, affording easy access to both sides of the board. The alternative 12...b6 seems equally playable, e.g. 13 ♘f3 ♖f7 14 b4 ♗a6 15 ♘fe5 ♖c7, Sturua-Vaiser, Biel 1995. After 16 ♖ac1 ♘d7 17 ♘f4 ♕e8 18 ♕a4 ♗xe5 19 ♕xa6 ♗xf4 20 gxf4 ♘f6 21 ♖c2 ♕e7 Black was okay. Black's use of the king's rook along his second rank is worth noting.

13 ♘f3 ♗e8 14 b4!?

14 ♘fe5 ♘d7 15 b4!? is another option. After 15...♘xe5 16 dxe5 White seems to be a little better.

14...g5

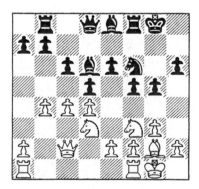

It is nice to be able to make such aggressive moves in the opening in relative safety. The g5-pawn introduces possibilities of both ...g5-g4 and ...f5-f4, creates space behind which Black can better organise an attack and

---

even denies White use of the f4-square. Of course moving pawns creates weaknesses, so this should also be borne in mind.

15 a4

White is not distracted from his queenside offensive.

15...a6 16 ᐁfe5 ♕e7?!

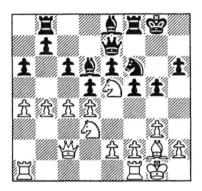

Too passive. Consistent is 16...ᐁd7 17 ᐁxd7 ♕xd7 18 e3 f4! (Black has no counterplay after 18...♗g6 19 c5 ♗c7 20 f4) 19 exf4 gxf4, when White has no advantage.

17 c5 ♗c7 18 b5!

A little tactic that gives White the edge.

18...cxb5 19 axb5 ♗xb5?

A dubious exchange sacrifice. After 19...axb5 20 ♖a7 ♕d8 21 ♖fa1 ᐁd7 22 ᐁxd7 ♗xd7 23 e3 White will win back the pawn with interest.

20 ᐁg6 ♕g7 21 ᐁxf8 ♖xf8 22 ♖fb1

Black has insufficient compensation for the exchange.

22...f4

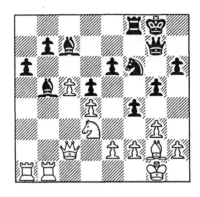

23 c6!?

The beginning of a great combination – I am just not so sure that it is correct. See the note to Black's 24th move.

23...bxc6

23...fxg3 24 hxg3 ᐁg4 25 ♖xb5! axb5 26 cxb7 ♗b8 27 ♕c8! is a line given by Kozul.

24 ♖xb5! axb5

24...cxb5 25 ♖xa6 ♖e8 26 ♖a7 ♖e7 27 ♕c6 clearly favours White according to Kozul. I feel less sure about this assessment. It seems to me that White's initiative is too slight to be significant.

25 ♖a7 ᐁe8

25...♖c8 26 ♕xc6 ♕d7 27 ♕b7 and ᐁc5-a6 wins.

26 ♕xc6 ♕xd4

Or 26...♕f7 27 ♗h3.

27 ♕xe6+ ♔g7 28 ♗xd5! 1-0

White wins a piece after 28...♕f6 29 ♕d7+ ♔h8 30 ♗e4 ♕g7 31 ♕xg7+ ♔xg7 32 ♗c6 fxg3 33 hxg3 ♔f6 34 ♗xe8.

Summary

The line with 5 ♘h3! is definitely the one that asks the most questions of the Stonewall. Nevertheless it must be said that Black has good chances to equalize and to generate interesting play. However, to succeed in this variation requires more accuracy from Black than in any of the other main lines, so I suggest that you play through all the games in this chapter in detail. Although avoiding ...♗d6 is not necessary Black should not be too uncomfortable when settling for ...♗e7. In fact Black is not without ideas, Tukmakov's 7...♘a6!? (mentioned in Game 46) being a good example. If Black does play ...♗d6 White does best to waste no time in playing ♗f4, and after the tactical retreat to e7 at least Black has a target in the shape of the bishop on f4. Notice that in Game 55 White is not forced to answer 9...♘h5 with 10 ♗e3, but 9...♘a6!? (Game 56) is an interesting alternative to the more common 9...h6 of Games 57-59, when expanding with 11...g5 (Game 58) is fine and 11...♗d6 (Game 59) is sensible.

1 d4 f5 2 g3 ♘f6 3 ♗g2 e6 4 c4 d5 5 ♘h3
>   5 ♘d2 c6
>>   6 ♘h3 – *Game 49*; 6 ♕c2 – *Game 50*

5...c6
>   5...♗e7 – *Game 45*

6 0-0
>   6 ♕c2 ♗e7 – *Game 47*

6...♗d6
>   6...♗e7 – *Game 46*

7 ♗f4 *(D)*
>   7 b3 – *Game 48*; 7 ♕c2 – *Game 51*

7...♗e7!
>   7...0-0 *(D)*
>>   8 ♘d2 b6 – *Game 52*
>>   8 ♕b3 – *Game 54*

8 ♕c2 0-0 9 ♘d2
>   9 ♘c3 – *Game 53*

9...h6
>   9...♘h5 – *Game 55*; 9...♘a6 – *Game 56*

10 ♗xb8! ♖xb8 11 ♘f4 *(D)* **♗d6** – *Game 59*
>   11...♕e8 – *Game 57*; 11...g5 – *Game 58*

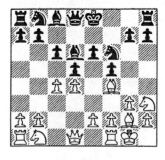

7 ♗f4

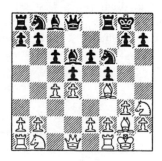

7...0-0

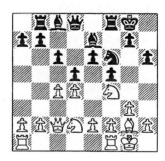

11 ♘f4

CHAPTER FIVE

Other Stonewalls

1 d4 e6 2 c4 f5 3 g3 ♘f6 4 ♗g2

In this chapter we turn to a brief investigation of other ways of playing the Stonewall with Black. In Games 60-61 Black dispenses with ...c7-c6 with the simple aim of stealing a tempo (and not unduly weakening the dark squares). Without the c7-square available Black's options are reduced, which is why White forces the bishop back to e7 in Game 60. Black combines ....♗e7 with ...♘c6 in Games 62-64, leaving White to decide whether to trade bishops (Games 62-63) or fianchetto (Game 64). Black plays ...♗e7 and ...c7-c6 in Games 65-67. In a bid to steer the game to a standard Stonewall (avoiding ♘h3, for example) Black even delays ...d7-d5 in Game 65, only to lose a tempo when promoting the bishop to d6. Nigel Short is in experimental mode in Game 66 and, finally, tries to justify ...♗e7 in Game 67 with a later ....♗f6. It is important to note with these lines that delaying ...c7-c6 can allow Black to modify his play according to White's development.

Game 60
Lautier-Karlsson
Malmö 1999

1 d4 f5 2 g3 ♘f6 3 ♗g2 e6 4 ♘f3 d5 5

0-0 ♗d6 6 c4 0-0!?

A Scandinavian speciality. As the selection in this chapter demonstrates, Karlsson is fond of sidelines in the Stonewall, most notably ...♘c6. The reasoning behind the text is to play ...b7-b6, continue as if ...c7-c6 were not necessary and later play ...c7-c5 in one go. Of course White knows that in this variation Black must recapture on d5 with the e6-pawn, but this should not be too restrictive for the second player as this is often the desired option in any case. However, White can seek to exploit the d6-bishop's lack of flexibility in the case of c4-c5, the unavailability of the c7-square introducing more than one possibility. In this game Lautier immediately gains space on the queenside.

7 c5!?

Less logical when the bishop can continue to reside on the b8-h2 diagonal, here this simple advance gives White extra control of the e5-square as well as the makings of queenside expansion. Note that with the pawn still on c7 White can play b2-b4 in the knowledge that ...a7-a5 can be safely met with b4-b5. The next game deals with 7 b3.

7...♗e7 8 b4 b6 9 ♗b2 a5 10 a3

White wishes to combine his territorial superiority with a grip on the centre to severely restrict his opponent. The thematic response to a flank offensive is a vigorous reaction in the centre, but breaking with ...e6-e5 is by no means easy to engineer.

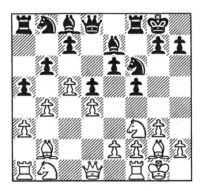

10...c6

Tempting the pawns further forward with 10...♘c6 11 cxb6 cxb6 12 b5 ♘a7 13 a4 does not help Black according to Lautier, who gives 13...♗d7 14 ♘bd2 ♘c8 15 ♘e5 ♘d6 16 ♖c1 ♖c8 17 ♕b3 with an advantage to White.

11 ♘e5 ♘fd7 12 ♘d3 axb4?!

Tidying up the queenside, but Black's plan is faulty. After 12...♗a6! 13 ♘f4 ♖f6 the position is far from clear.

13 axb4 ♖xa1 14 ♗xa1 bxc5?!

Consistent with the plan. 14...♗f6 limits White to a modest edge.

15 bxc5 e5?!

Unfortunately for Black his entire strategy – undermining White's ambitious c5-pawn in order to fight it out in the centre – serves only to grant White control over the now vacant squares on the queenside. Again 15...♗f6 is preferable.

16 dxe5 ♘xc5 17 ♘xc5 ♗xc5 18 ♘d2 ♔h8 19 ♕c2 ♗b6 20 ♘b3 f4 21 ♗d4 ♗xd4

21...♗f5 22 ♕c3! underlines Black's problems by strengthening White's hold on the dark squares on the queenside. By taking on d4 Black reduces pressure on the c5-square in the hope of freeing the self-inflicted backward pawn on c6.

22 ♘xd4 ♕b6 23 ♕c3 ♗g4!

Black is not falling for 23...c5? 24 ♖c1! cxd4 25 ♕xc8 here, but this theme soon returns!

24 h3?!

24 gxf4! ♖xf4 25 e3 ♖f8 26 ♖c1 ♖e8 27 f4 ♗d7 is more testing, although Black is still in the game.

24...♗c8?

24...♗d7! is much better; the bishop has nothing to do on c8.

25 g4 c5? 26 ♖c1! ♘d7 27 ♗xd5 ♘xe5 28 ♕xc5 ♕xc5 29 ♖xc5 ♘d7?!

The stubborn 29...♖d8 creates more of an inconvenience. Now White is winning.

30 ♖c7 ♘f6 31 ♗e6 ♗xe6 32 ♘xe6 ♖e8 33 ♘xg7 ♖xe2 34 ♘f5?

Time-trouble. 34 ♖f7! ♘d5 35 ♘h5 ♔g8 36 ♖f5 wins.

34...h5! 35 ♔f1 ♖e5?

35...♖a2 is less accommodating, although White is close to winning after 36 f3.

36 ♖f7 ♘d5 37 g5 ♖e6 38 h4 ♖a6 39 ♔g2 ♖b6 40 ♖d7 ♖b5 41 ♖d8+ ♔h7

42 ♖xd5! 1-0

Black resigned due to 42...♖xd5 43 g6+ ♔h8 44 g7+ ♔h7 45 g8♗+.

Game 61
Schussler-Agdestein
Espoo 1989

---

1 d4 e6 2 c4 f5 3 ♘f3 ♘f6 4 g3 d5 5

♗g2 ♗d6 6 0-0 0-0 7 b3

Schussler's is another way to try and profit from the omission of ...c7-c6. White threatens to trade dark-squared bishops with ♗a3 and Black can do nothing to prevent it as the usual ...♕e7 simply loses a piece to c4-c5, trapping the bishop. However, White's plan takes time, a luxury that Black has already gained by leaving his c-pawn untouched – at least for the moment. Furthermore, Black's experiment has left him less vulnerable on the dark squares than after ...c7-c6. These factors take the sting out of 7 b3.

7...b6 8 ♗a3 ♗b7 9 ♗xd6 ♕xd6

During the execution of White's plan Black has sensibly continued his development, even getting to develop his queen free of charge in the process! The diagram position illustrates how well Black is able to address matters in the centre without the help of the dark-squared bishop. In fact Black, thanks to his accelerated development, is the first to stake a claim in the centre.

10 ♕c2 ♘e4

With this and his next Black steps up the pace, concentrating on the c5-square in readiness for an advance of the c-pawn.

11 ♘c3 ♘a6 12 cxd5 exd5 13 ♖ac1 c5

A typical Stonewall position that is similar to the kind seen in the g3-system of the Queen's Indian Defence. Black has a pleasant game.

14 ♖fd1 ♕e6 15 e3 ♖ae8

Now every one of Black's pieces has a role to play. Note that Black a presence across the board.

16 a3 h6 17 h4?

An attempt to hold Black at bay that instead acts to accelerate Agdestein's creation of an attack. 17 ♘e5! cxd4 18 exd4 ♖c8 19 ♕b2 f4 20 ♘e2!? fxg3 21 fxg3 is a more aggressive continuation that keeps Black sufficiently occupied to leave the game balanced.

17...♖e7 18 ♕b2 g5!?

A rather complicated sacrifice that is diffi-

cult to resist playing. Black has a comfortable game and prospects of generating pressure on the kingside without having to take risks, and it seems that White can find a path to an advantage after 18...g5, but I would be careful with any final judgements here, as the line is very sharp.

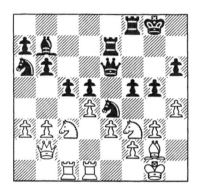

19 hxg5 hxg5 20 ♘xe4?

Opening the d-file makes a big difference: 20 dxc5! bxc5 21 ♘xe4 fxe4 22 ♘xg5! ♕h6 23 ♘h3 ♗c8 24 ♘f4 ♖h7 25 ♖xd5 ♗g4 26 ♗xe4 and White strikes back, although this is too complex for a concrete assessment.

20...fxe4 21 ♘xg5 ♕h6 22 ♘h3 ♗c8 23 ♘f4 ♗g4 24 ♔f1

24 ♘xd5 ♖h7 25 ♗xe4 ♕h2+ 26 ♔f1 ♕h1+! 27 ♗xh1 ♖xh1+ 28 ♔g2 ♗f3 mate!

24...♕h2 25 dxc5 ♖h7! 26 ♔e1

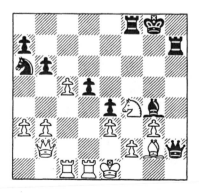

26...♖xf4 27 gxf4 ♕g1+ 28 ♔d2 ♕xf2+ 29 ♔c3 ♕xe3+ 30 ♔c2 ♗xd1+ 31 ♖xd1

🜚h2 32 🜚d2 ♘xc5?

32...♛xd2+ wins immediately.

33 ♛c3 ♛xf4?! 34 b4 ♘d3 35 ♛c8+ ♚g7 36 ♛d7+ ♚f6 37 ♛xd5?

37 ♛d8+ puts up more resistance.

37...🜚xg2 38 ♛d4+ ♚e7 39 🜚xg2 ♘e1+ 40 ♚b3 ♘xg2 41 ♛g7+ ♛f7+ 42 ♛xf7+ ♚xf7 43 ♚c3 e3 44 ♚d3 ♚e6 0-1

Game 62
Beliavsky-Short
Linares 1989

1 d4 e6 2 c4 f5 3 g3 ♘f6 4 ♗g2 d5 5 ♘f3 ♗e7

This move is no longer popular. Short played it for some time but not with truly satisfactory positions from the opening. Black delays ...c7-c6 but denies White the tempo-gaining c4-c5 seen in Game 60. The attraction for Black is flexibility, as he can decide later whether to play ...♘c6 or ...c7-c6.

6 0-0 0-0 7 b3! ♘c6 8 ♗a3

Now Black can choose where he prefers to see his opponent's knight. For 8 ♗b2 see Game 64.

8...♗xa3

Ignoring the bishop with 8...♗d7 transposes to Game 63.

9 ♘xa3 ♗d7 10 ♘c2

It is true that the knight does little on c2. Black continues with his bishop manoeuvre.

10...♗e8 11 ♘e5 a5

Standard fare, eyeing b4 and forcing White to consider the implications of a future ...a5-a4.

12 ♛d3

12 ♛c1 ♗h5 13 f3!? with the idea of 🜚d1 might offer White something according to Beliavsky, but even if this is true it cannot be much (White's bishop is no better than its counterpart).

12...🜚a6?!

This seems strange as the rook has no real path to activity. 12...♛d6 looks better, challenging White's hold on the centre.

13 🜚fd1 ♗g6 14 f4?!

14 ♘e1!? has been suggested by Beliavsky, with the following line in mind: 14...♘xe5 15 dxe5 f4 16 ♛c3 ♘e4 17 ♗xe4 ♗xe4 18 f3 ♗g6 19 ♘g2 and White has a clear advantage.

14...♘e4 15 a3 ♗h5 16 ♘e3 ♘xe5 17 dxe5 c6 18 g4!?

This seems to give White an excellent game but Short has a strong piece sacrifice that makes his position tenable.

18...♗xg4! 19 ♘xg4

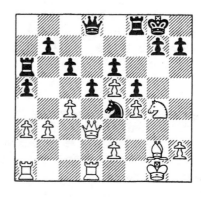

19...♛h4!!

Putting an end to White's positional plan. Now White has no choice but to take the piece and allow Black's queen to infiltrate the kingside.

20 ♘e3 ♛xf4 21 ♗xe4 fxe4 22 ♛c3 ♛f2+ 23 ♚h1 ♛xe2 24 🜚d2 ♛h5 25 🜚g1 🜚aa8 26 🜚dg2 ♛f3 27 cxd5 cxd5

It is a testament to the Stonewall that the pawn mass in the centre affords Black such confidence if an opportunity such as Short's should present itself.

28 ♕c7 ♖f7 29 ♕b6 ♖e8 30 ♘c2 ♕f4 31 ♕d6 ♖fe7! 32 ♘d4 h5! 33 ♘b5 h4 34 h3 ♕f3 35 ♔h2 ♕f4+ ½-½

Game 63
Timman-Short
Tilburg 1990

---

1 d4 e6 2 c4 f5 3 g3 ♘f6 4 ♗g2 ♗e7 5 ♘f3

I think this is the main reason why Short played the Stonewall with ...♗e7, as White has no better move than the text. On 5 ♘h3?! Black has 5...d6!, switching plans.

5...d5 6 0-0 0-0 7 b3 ♗d7 8 ♗a3 ♘c6

This position could have been reached in the previous game, but 7...♗d7 can be an independent line. Short, for example, has had some success with 8...♗e8!?. Then 9 ♕c1 a5 10 ♗xe7 ♕xe7 11 ♕a3?! is not a good plan (as seen in the Introduction). In Lautier-Short, Paris 1990, Black already had a good game after 11...♕b4 12 ♖c1 ♘c6 13 e3 ♘e4, going on to outplay his opponent: 14 ♘e1 dxc4 15 bxc4 e5 16 ♕xb4 axb4 17 ♘c2 exd4 18 exd4 b3! 19 axb3 ♖xa1 20 ♘xa1 ♘xd4 21 ♖e1 ♗h5 22 ♘a3 ♘e2+ and Black is winning. 9 ♕c2 c6 10 ♕b2!? has also been played, Tukmakov-Short, Germany 1991, continued 10...♘bd7 11 ♘bd2 ♗h5 12 ♖ac1 a5! 13 ♘g5!? ♖e8! 14 ♗xe7 ♕xe7 15 ♖fe1 h6 16 ♘h3 g5 17 f4 ♕g7 18 ♕c3 ♔h8 with a complicated game ahead.

9 ♕c1

The queen is not heading for a3. Another decent path for White is 9 ♗xe7 ♕xe7 10 ♘c3 ♗e8 11 cxd5 exd5 12 ♖c1 (12 ♕d3 ♖d8! 13 ♖ac1 is equal according to Illescas), e.g. 12...♖d8 13 ♘a4 ♘e4 14 ♘c5 ♘xc5 15 ♖xc5 f4 16 ♕d2 fxg3 17 hxg3 and White had a pull in Illescas Cordoba-Bareev, Linares 1992.

9...a5 10 ♗xe7 ♕xe7 11 ♘c3 ♗e8 12 ♕e3!

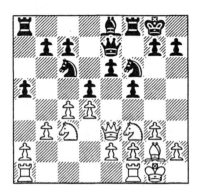

Previously 12 e3 had been played. However, with this move, monitoring the centre, Timman practically sealed the fate of this variation. Timman believes White is already better.

12...dxc4?!

Black should not open the b-file for his opponent. Sensible is 12...♖d8, supporting the centre and leaving White to weigh up ...dxc4.

13 bxc4 ♖d8 14 ♖fd1 ♘g4 15 ♕f4 ♗f7 16 ♖ab1 e5!?

16...b6 17 ♘g5 is very difficult for Black.

17 dxe5 ♖xd1+ 18 ♖xd1 ♕c5?

This loses by force, but Timman has little faith in Black's prospects anyway after 18...♘cxe5 19 ♘d5 ♕d6 20 ♘d4! and 18...♘gxe5 19 ♘d5 ♕d6 20 ♘g5.

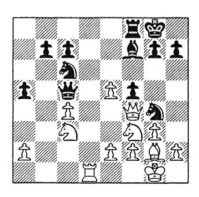

Now White sends in his knights.

19 ♘g5! ♗xc4 20 ♘d5 ♘d8 21 e6 ♗xd5 22 ♖xd5 ♕a3 23 ♖d7 ♘c6 24 ♗xc6 bxc6 25 e7 ♖e8 26 ♕c4+ ♔h8 27 ♘f7+ ♔g8 28 ♘h6+ ♔h8 29 ♕g8+ ♖xg8 30 ♘f7 mate

---

Game 64
Yrjola-Karlsson
Gausdal 1987

---

1 d4 e6 2 c4 f5 3 g3 ♘f6 4 ♗g2 ♗e7 5 ♘f3 d5 6 0-0 0-0 7 b3 ♘c6 8 ♗b2!?

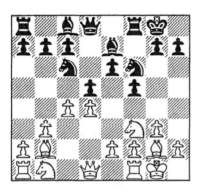

Avoiding the exchange of bishops, White decides that his own will have some influence on the long diagonal.

8...♘e4

Later Karlsson deviated from this with 8...a5 but had no success after 9 ♘c3 ♘e4 10 ♘a4 b6 11 ♖c1 ♗b7 12 ♘e1 ♘b4?! 13 a3 ♘c6 14 e3 ♖f6 15 ♘d3 ♕f8, Polugaevsky-Karlsson, Haninge 1990. Then 16 f3 ♘g5 17 cxd5 exd5 18 ♘c3 ♘a7 19 ♘e5 was excellent for White. Perhaps the immediate 8...♗d7 is worth a try. Polugaevsky-Spassky, Tilburg 1983, continued 9 ♘c3 ♗e8 10 ♘g5 ♗f7 11 e3 ♕d7 12 ♘xf7 ♖xf7, when 13 ♘a4 b6 14 ♖c1 ♘d8 15 ♘c3 ♖f8 16 f3 ♘f7 17 e4 left White only slightly better after his opponent's manoeuvres to f7. White went for manoeuvres of his own in Schmidt-Spassky, Buenos Aires 1978, but 9 ♘e5 ♗e8 10 ♘d3 ♗f7 11 ♘d2 a5 12 ♘f3 ♘e4 13 c5

♗f6 was fine for Black, who successfully handled White's queenside expansion after 14 a3 b6 15 ♖c1 ♗e8 16 ♕c2 bxc5 17 ♘xc5 ♘xc5 18 ♕xc5 ♕b8 19 ♘d2 ♖a6 20 e3 ♖b6.

9 e3 a5!? 10 a3 ♗d7 11 ♕c2 ♗e8 12 ♘e1 a4!?

Seeking to make progress on the light squares on the queenside. 12...♗f6, preparing ...♘e7, is a more patient treatment of the position.

13 b4

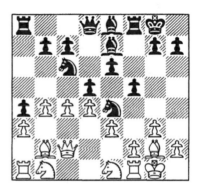

13...b5!?

Notice how Black's light-squared bishop makes a valid contribution on e8, from where it can also transfer to the kingside.

14 cxd5!

The main idea behind Black's plan is to meet 14 cxb5? with 14...♘a7, when Black has good control of the light squares. Closing the queenside with 14 c5 is roughly level and shifts the play over to the other flank. The text, on the other hand, denies Black use of the b5-square while keeping the play open.

14...exd5 15 ♘d3 ♘b8!?

A decent alternative is 15...♘a7 to quickly send the knight to c4.

16 ♘e5 ♖a6 17 f3 ♘d6 18 ♘d2 ♘c4 19 ♘dxc4 dxc4 20 f4!

Clamping down on the centre.

20...♖d6 21 ♖ad1 ♗h5 22 ♖d2 ♘d7 23 h3 ♗g6 24 d5?

24 ♗f3! ♘f6 25 ♖g2 ♘d5 26 ♕d2! gives

White an advantage. Now it is Black's turn to play.

24...♗f6! 25 ♖e1 ♖e8 26 ♘c6 ♕c8 27 ♘d4 ♕a6 28 ♘e6 ♕b6 29 ♔h2 ♗xb2 30 ♕xb2 ♘f6 31 g4!? fxg4 32 e4

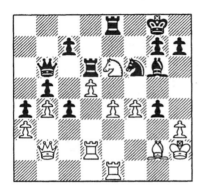

32...gxh3?

The advantage swings once more – 32...♖dxe6 33 dxe6 ♕xe6 34 e5 ♕f5! demonstrates the type of position Black is looking for – a healthy pawn structure and a powerful light-squared bishop!

33 ♗xh3 ♖dxe6 34 ♗xe6+ ♔h8?

Despite the material deficit the best chance lies in another exchange sacrifice: 34...♖xe6! 35 dxe6 ♕xe6, when Black can generate threats around White's exposed king.

35 f5 ♗h5 36 ♖g1??

Throwing the win away. Correct is 36 ♕d4, e.g. 36...♕xd4 37 ♖xd4 ♘g4+ 38 ♔g3 ♘e5 39 d6! ♘f3 40 d7 ♖d8 41 ♖ed1.

36...♕e3! 37 ♖dg2 c3 38 ♕f2??

And this throws the draw away. 38 ♕c1 ♕xc1 39 ♖xc1 ♘xe4 40 ♖gg1 leads to equality.

38...♘g4+ 39 ♖xg4 ♕xf2+ 40 ♖1g2 ♕d4 0-1

Game 65
I.Sokolov-Yusupov
Nussloch 1996

---

1 d4 e6 2 c4 f5 3 g3 ♘f6 4 ♗g2 ♗e7 5 ♘f3 0-0 6 0-0 c6

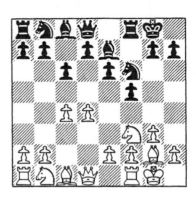

Preparing a more traditional Stonewall setup while intending to counter the threat to exchange bishops after 7 b3 with, for example, 7...a5!?, so that 8 ♗a3 can be answered with 8...d6 or even 8...♗xa3 9 ♘xa3 d6.

7 ♘bd2 d5 8 ♕c2 ♗d7 9 ♘e5 ♗e8 10 ♘df3 ♘e4 11 b3 ♔h8 12 ♗b2 ♗d6

In order to avoid lines such as ♘h3 on the way to the standard Stonewall Black pays the price in the loss of a tempo.

13 ♘e1 ♘d7 14 ♘1d3 ♕e7 15 ♘xd7?!

Sokolov believes that White has an advantage after 15 f3! ♘ef6 16 c5 ♗c7 17 b4, with opportunities on the queenside. The text reduces Black's defensive burden.

15...♗xd7 16 c5 ♗c7 17 b4 ♗e8 18 f3

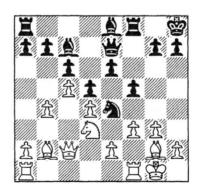

In reply to the automatic 18 ♘e5 Black has a promising pawn sacrifice in 18...♗xe5 19 dxe5 f4!, when 20 ♗xe4 dxe4 21 ♕xe4

♗g6 brings our old friend the light-squared bishop to life with sufficient compensation.

With his knight attacked Black should now refuse to retreat and instead try to exploit the voluntary weakening of White's kingside pawn complex with 18...♘xg3! 19 hxg3 ♗xg3. Then 20 f4 ♗h5! sees the other bishop take a piece of the action, and after 21 ♘e5 ♕h4 22 ♘f3 ♕xf4 the situation is complicated indeed.

18...♘f6 19 ♕d2

White has an edge.

19...♖g8?!

The thematic 19...♘d7 is preferable, aiming to address the traditional positional matter of the e5-square by pushing the e-pawn at the appropriate time.

20 ♖ae1 a5 21 a3 axb4 22 axb4 ♖a2

Handing over the a-file to White. 22....♗g6 connects the rooks.

23 ♖a1 ♖xa1 24 ♖xa1 g5 25 e4!

With no worries on the queenside White is free to turn his attention to the centre, and in so doing to Black's king.

25...fxe4 26 fxe4 dxe4 27 ♘f2 ♘d5

This has to be played sooner or later.

28 ♘xe4 h6 29 ♖e1 ♗g6 30 b5 ♗f5 31 ♕e2

Black is much worse.

31...♕g7 32 ♘d6 ♗a5

32...♗xd6 33 cxd6 ♖d8 34 bxc6 bxc6 35 ♕e5 is winning for White.

33 ♗xd5 cxd5 34 ♖f1 ♖f8 35 g4

Slightly stronger is 35 ♘xf5 exf5 36 ♕e6.

35...♗g6 36 ♕xe6 ♖xf1+ 37 ♔xf1 ♗d3+ 38 ♔f2 ♕f8+ 39 ♘f5

An easier win is 39 ♕f7! ♕xf7+ 40 ♘xf7+ ♔g7 41 ♘d6 etc.

39...♗c7 40 b6 ♗xh2 41 ♕e7!

White is still on the way to the full point.

41...♕xe7 42 ♘xe7 ♗c4 43 ♗a3! ♔h7 44 c6! bxc6 45 ♘f5! ♗d3 46 ♔e3! ♗e4 47 ♘d6 ♗g1+ 48 ♔d2 ♗xd4 49 b7 ♗a7 50 ♘c8 ♗b8 51 ♗d6 d4 52 ♗xb8 c5 53 ♘d6 1-0

Game 66
Speelman-Short
London 1991

1 d4 e6 2 c4 f5 3 g3 ♘f6 4 ♗g2 ♗e7 5 ♘f3 d5 6 0-0 0-0 7 ♕c2 ♗d7!? 8 b3 a5

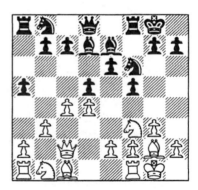

Short really experiments in this game, testing the limits of the Stonewall.

9 ♗a3 c6

Speelman has always been an imaginative player. In his annotations he suggests 9....♗b4!? with the idea of 10 ♗b2 a4! 11 a3 axb3 12 ♕xb3 ♗a5, when Black does not lose the b-pawn but must face a strong knight after 13 ♘e5!, with a complicated position.

10 ♗xe7 ♕xe7 11 ♘e5 ♗e8 12 ♘d3 ♗h5 13 ♘f4 g5?!

Exposing the king without gaining anything. The circumspect 13...♗f7 maintains a normal Stonewall position that should be slightly favourable for White.

14 ♘xh5 ♘xh5 15 ♘d2 ♘d7 16 a3 ♘hf6 17 ♕c3 ♘b6 18 ♖ab1! ♖f7

Not 18...♕xa3?! 19 ♕e3.

19 b4 axb4 20 axb4

White seems to be making progress on the queenside, suggesting that Black should perhaps prepare for b4-b5 with 20...♖c8. Also possible is 20...dxc4 21 ♘xc4 ♘fd5, e.g. 22 ♕b3 ♘xc4 23 ♕xc4 ♖a4. What is clear is that Black should refrain from the following move.

20...♘e4? 21 ♗xe4! fxe4 22 b5

Thanks to 20...♘e4 White's attack has just gained another tempo and will soon be impossible to stop.

22...♖a3?!

Speelman proposes 22...♘d7.

23 ♖b3 ♖xb3 24 ♕xb3 c5 25 ♕e3!

Concentrating on key dark squares in the centre.

25...♘d7

25...cxd4 26 ♕xd4 ♘xc4 27 ♘xc4 dxc4 28 ♕xc4 e3 29 f3 gives White a clear lead in the ending.

26 dxc5 ♘xc5 27 ♕d4! ♖f5 28 ♖a1 ♔f7?!

The losing move. Black can still hang on after 28...♕f8 29 g4!? ♖f4 30 cxd5 ♖xg4+ 31 ♔h1 exd5 32 ♕xd5+ ♔h8 33 ♖g1!?, although White is much better. Now the game is almost over.

29 ♖a8 ♘d7 30 ♖a7! ♘f6 31 ♕b6 ♔g6 32 ♕xb7 ♕c5 33 ♕f7+ ♔h6 34 e3 ♕b4

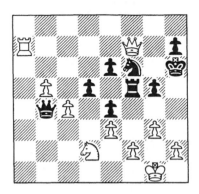

35 g4! 1-0

Game 67
Kasparov-Short
Brussels 1987

---

1 d4 e6 2 g3 f5 3 ♗g2 ♘f6 4 ♘f3 ♗e7 5 c4 d5 6 0-0 0-0 7 ♘bd2

For the moment Kasparov refrains from b2-b3 and avoids the ...♘c6 lines, developing normally like Sokolov.

7...c6

Black decides to play a normal Stonewall with the bishop on e7.

8 ♘e5 ♘bd7 9 ♘d3 ♘e4 10 ♕c2!

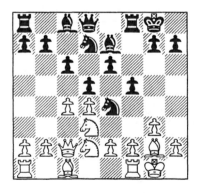

Kasparov believes that White is already better. It is possible, of course, that this is true. In Game 65 Black accepted the loss of a

tempo with ...♗d6 to be slightly worse, so
here we investigate the move that gives
...♗e7 independent significance.

**10...♗f6 11 ♘f3 ♔h8 12 b3 ♕e8 13
♗a3**

13 a4! is stronger, as Black has no choice
but to play 13...a5 to prevent the march of
White's a-pawn, as illustrated in the
Introduction.

**13...♖g8 14 ♖ac1 a5 15 ♗b2 ♕h5 16 a4
♖d8 17 ♗a3 ♖g8 18 ♖b1**

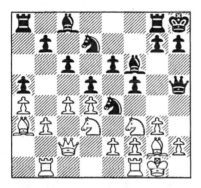

Latching on to the thematic plan of b3-b4.
Black opts to trade knights.

**18...♘g5 19 ♖fe1 ♕f7 20 ♘xg5 ♗xg5
21 ♗d6**

The freedom of White's bishop does highlight the drawback of posting Black's on f6.

**21...♗f6 22 e3 g5 23 b4! axb4 24 ♖xb4
♘f8 25 ♖eb1**

25 ♘e5! Gives White a clear advantage.

25...♘g6 26 ♘c5 ♖a7 27 ♕b3?

White is playing too slowly. Now is the
time to strike: 27 a5! ♖d8 28 ♗b8 ♖a8 29
♘xb7 and White has a commanding position.

27...♖g7 28 ♕c2 ♕g8! 29 h3?

29 ♘d3 leaves White on top.

**29...♕d8! 30 ♗b8 ♖a8 31 cxd5 cxd5 32
♗e5 ♘xe5 33 dxe5 ♗xe5 34 ♘xb7
♗xb7 35 ♖xb7 ♖xb7 36 ♖xb7 ♖b8! 37
♕c6 ♖xb7 38 ♕xb7 ♕c7 39 ♕b5 ♔g7**

Black should in no way lose this endgame,
but Kasparov finds a way to set Black new

problems.

40 a5 d4

40...♗d6 is the simplest, leading to a draw.

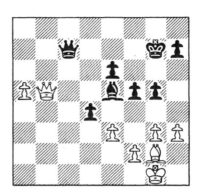

41 a6!

Winning a piece.

**41...dxe3 42 a7 exf2+ 43 ♔h1 ♕xa7 44
♕xe5+ ♔f7 45 ♗f1 h5?**

Black should make the draw with
45...♕a8+ 46 ♔h2 ♕d5. If the queens come
off Black has no problems in making a draw,
as White needs his g-pawn to win the game
since the h-pawn + light-squared bishop is a
theoretical draw.

46 ♗c4!

Forcing Black to give up his f-pawn to
keep his centre together.

**46...f1♕+ 47 ♗xf1 ♕a8+ 48 ♔h2 ♕d8
49 ♗e2 ♕d2 50 ♔g1 ♕e1+ 51 ♔g2 ♕d2
52 ♔f2 g4 53 h4 ♕d8 54 ♔e3 ♕f6 55
♕a5 e5?**

It is difficult to see how White can make
any progress without this help. Now White's
bishop teams up with the queen.

**56 ♗c4+ ♔g6 57 ♕c7 ♕g7 58 ♕d6+
♕f6 59 ♕d7 ♕b6+**

Another winning line for White is
59...♕g7 60 ♕e8+ ♔h7! 61 ♗e2! ♔h6 62
♕e6+ ♕g6 63 ♕xe5 etc.

60 ♔d3 ♕b1+ 61 ♔c3 1-0

Kasparov gives the following: 61...♕c1+
62 ♔b4 ♕e1+ 63 ♔b5 ♕b1+ 64 ♔c5 ♕g1+
65 ♔c6 ♕g2+ 66 ♔c7 ♕c2 67 ♕e6+ ♔h7 68
♔d8 ♕d2+ 69 ♔e8 and White wins.

Summary

Of the plans put forward in this chapter I prefer delaying ...c7-c6 (Games 60-61), an idea that seems perfectly reasonable. Moreover, stereotype play from White saves Black a tempo! The only problem for Black might be ♘h3. The Short/Spassky/Karlsson treatment of ...♘c6 (or delaying any move involving the c6-square) avoids ♘h3 but introduces other inconveniences for Black. Games 63, 65 and 67 are good examples of how these lines should be handled by White, who can count on a slight advantage.

1 d4 e6 2 c4 f5 3 g3 ♘f6 4 ♗g2 d5

    4...♗e7 5 ♘f3 0-0 6 0-0 c6 – *Game 65*

5 ♘f3 ♗e7

    5...♗d6 6 0-0 0-0!? (D)

        7 c5!? – *Game 60*

        7 b3 – *Game 61*

6 0-0 0-0 *(D)* **7 b3**

    7 ♕c2 – *Game 66*

    7 ♘bd2 c6 8 ♘e5 – *Game 67*

7...♘c6 (D)

    7...♗d7 – *Game 63*

8 ♗a3 – *Game 62*

    8 ♗b2!? – *Game 64*

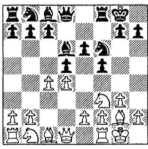

6...0-0

6...0-0

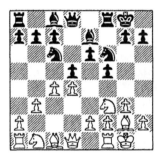

7...♘c6

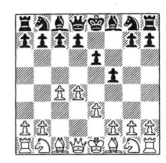

CHAPTER SIX

White Plays an early e2-e3

In this final chapter we shall investigate the different positions arising in the Stonewall when White plays e2-e3 and develops his bishop to e2 or d3. These variations occur most often from the Meran (Queen's Gambit), but it is also possible to reach them in the Dutch proper after 1 d4 f5 2 c4 e6 3 ♘c3 ♘f6 4 e3!?. In Game 68 Black pays too big a price to play the Stonewall, allowing White to actively post his dark-squared bishop and then launch an attack with g2-g4. Games 69-70 feature less threatening versions of g2-g4. In Game 71 White monitors the e4-square with ♗d3, ♘ge2 and f2-f3; the unavailability of e4 is not a problem for Black here. Black delays ...♘f6 in Game 72 in order to leave the square free for the queen – a rather ambitious approach. White tries for an initiative of his own in Game 73, throwing his queenside pawns forward, whereas Games 74-76 see White play b2-b3 and ♗b2. Finally, Karpov's answer to ...f7-f5 is f2-f4 in Game 77, locking the centre pawns!

Game 68
Serper-Sequera
San Felipe 1998

---

1 c4 e6 2 ♘c3 d5 3 d4 f5

This version of the Stonewall cannot be recommended. White's fluid development soon leads to a dangerous initiative.

4 ♘f3 c6 5 ♗f4

White should not be allowed the luxury of bringing out both bishops.

5...♘f6 6 e3 ♗e7 7 ♗d3 0-0 8 ♕c2 ♘e4 9 g4!

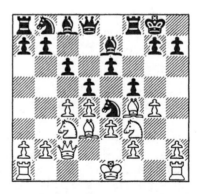

This is the key position. Black's play thus far has concentrated on the traditional grip on the centre, but the text highlights how fragile this can be when White has been allowed to deploy his forces as in the diagram position. Black needs to protect e4 as well as keep the b1-h7 diagonal closed, leaving White free to push his g-pawn with the simple plan of opening the g-file.

9...♕a5

After 9...fxg4 10 ♘e5 Black is already under pressure. Note that only by postponing castling could White play 9 g4, while his next is testament to his own centre's solidity.

10 ♔e2!

By now it is clear that White intends to attack and must connect his rooks. The king is safer in the centre than on the queenside.

10...♔h8 11 ♖hg1!

Clearly the strongest continuation, although White also had a good game with the more optimistic 11 h4!? ♘d7 12 h5 in Aagaard-Williams, Hampstead 1998. After 12...♘df6? (Black should not relinquish control of e5) 13 ♘e5 ♘xc3+ 14 bxc3 ♘e4? 15 ♗xe4 fxe4 Black was already losing.

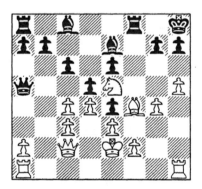

The game continued 16 ♘g6+!! hxg6 17 hxg6+ ♔g8 18 ♕c1 ♕d8 19 ♗c7!!, when the best defence 19...♗h4! leads to a win for White after 20 ♗xd8 ♖xf2+ 21 ♔d1 ♗xd8 22 ♔e1 ♖f3 23 ♔e2 ♖g3 24 ♕a3! with the idea of 25 ♖h8+! etc. Instead Black tried 19...♖xf2+ 20 ♔xf2 ♗h4+ 21 ♔e2 ♕g5, but after 22 ♕g1 e5 23 ♕h2 ♗xg4+ 24 ♔d2 exd4 25 cxd4 dxc4 he resigned.

11...♘d7 12 ♖g2! ♘df6 13 ♖ag1 ♘e8

13...♘xg4 14 h3 ♘gxf2 15 ♖xf2 ♘xf2 16 ♔xf2 does nothing to diminish White's initiative.

14 ♘e5 ♘4d6?!

14...♗b4 15 gxf5 exf5 16 ♗h6! is worth remembering.

15 c5

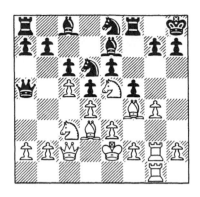

15...♘e4

Serper offers the following line: 15...♘f7 16 gxf5 exf5 17 ♗xf5 ♘xe5 18 ♗xe5! ♖xf5 19 ♖xg7 ♘xg7 20 ♖xg7 ♗f8 21 ♖d7+! ♔g8 22 ♕xf5 ♗xd7 23 ♕xd7 followed by ♕e6.

16 f3 ♘xc3+ 17 bxc3 ♗f6 18 h4 ♕d8 19 h5 ♗e7 20 gxf5 exf5 21 h6 ♗f6

Black loses after 21...g6 22 ♖xg6 hxg6 23 ♘xg6+ ♔g8 24 ♘xf8+ ♔xf8 25 h7 ♗f6 26 ♖g8+ ♔f7 27 ♗xf5 etc.

22 hxg7+ ♘xg7 23 ♗h6 ♕e7 24 ♗xg7+ ♗xg7 25 ♖xg7 ♕xg7 26 ♖xg7 ♔xg7 27 ♕b1 ♔h8 28 ♕h1 ♔g7 29 ♕h4 ♗e6 30 ♕e7+ ♗f7 31 ♗xf5 1-0

Game 69
Agrest-Lautier
Harplinge 1998

---

1 c4 e6 2 ♘c3 d5 3 d4 c6 4 e3

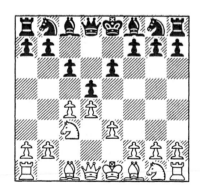

Only with the bishop on c1 should Black head for the Stonewall set-up.

4...♗d6

Waiting for White to show his hand. The immediate 4...f5 is also possible, when 5 g4 should be taken very seriously. Taking on g4 involves some risk, e.g. 5...fxg4?! 6 ♕xg4 ♘f6 7 ♕g2. Then 7...b6 8 ♘f3 ♘bd7 9 ♗d2 ♗d6 10 ♕xg7 ♖g8 11 ♕h6 ♕e7 12 0-0-0 ♗b7 13 cxd5 exd5 14 ♗h3 was better for White in Gomez Esteban-Antunes, Mesa 1992, while in Neidhardt-Novak, Germany 1997, White should have followed 7...♕c7 8 ♘f3 ♗b4 9 ♗d2 0-0 with 10 0-0-0 and a promising attack. The active 7...c5! is better, e.g. 8 ♘f3 ♘c6 9 ♗d2, when Ftacnik recommends 9...cxd4 10 exd4 ♗d7 11 0-0-0 ♖c8. Instead of 9...cxd4, Seirawan-Yermolinsky, USA 1994, continued 9...a6?! 10 0-0-0 ♕c7 11 dxc5! ♗xc5 12 ♖g1 0-0 13 ♘g5! ♔h8 14 ♔b1 ♘e5? 15 ♘a4 ♗a7 16 ♗b4 ♖g8 17 ♕g3 and Black resigned.

More circumspect is 5...♘f6, which is similar to our main game. Typical is Nadanian-Lputian, Yerevan 1999, which continued 6 gxf5 exf5 7 ♘f3 ♗d6 8 ♕b3 dxc4 9 ♗xc4 ♕e7 (also possible is 9...b5 10 ♗f7+ ♔f8 11 ♗e6 ♗xe6 12 ♕xe6 ♕d7 with equality) 10 ♘g5! ♖f8 11 ♗d2 h6. Now 12 ♗e6 ♘bd7 13 ♘f3 ♘b6 14 ♗xc8 ♖xc8 is equal, but instead there came an interesting piece sacrifice after 12 ♘e6!? b5! 13 ♘xb5 cxb5 14 ♗xb5+ ♘bd7 15 ♖c1 ♖b8 16 ♖g1 g5 17 ♘c7+, when Black could have maintained the balance with 17...♔d8 18 ♘e6+ ♔e8 19 ♘xf8 ♔xf8. It is important to note that White's bishop went straight to c4 here, whereas Lautier's 4...♗d6 denies White this luxury.

7 ♘h3!? has been suggested by Ftacnik, but 7 ♕b3! is dangerous, when Black's best is probably 7...dxc4 8 ♗xc4 ♗d6! 9 ♗f7+ ♔e7 10 ♗c4 b5 11 ♗e2 ♗e6 with a complicated position, rather than the automatic 8...♕e7?! 9 ♘h3! b5 10 ♗d3 g6 11 ♘f4 ♗h6 12 ♘ce2! which was very good for White in Portisch-

Haba, Yerevan Ol 1996.

5 ♗d3 f5 6 g4!? ♘f6

Sensibly continuing with development.

**7 gxf5 exf5 8 ♕b3 dxc4 9 ♗xc4 ♕e7!
10 a4**

White does not wish to be pushed back after ...b7-b5.

10...♘bd7!

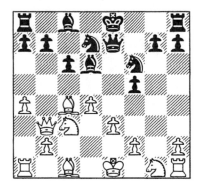

The knight prepares to go to f6 to support its partner, rather than a6 and b4. Comparing the diagram position with Nadanian-Lputian in the note to Black's 4th move, above, we see the key difference is the location of White's king's knight. Here it remains at home on g1, while Nadanian's knight soon jumped into e6.

11 a5

Without this Black would obtain a better position with ...♘b6 and (after the c4-bishop retreats) ...♗e6.

11...♘e4 12 ♘f3 ♘df6

Petursson believes that Black already has the advantage. Castling kingside is not an option due to White's command of the a2-g8 diagonal, but White's king has been equally inconvenienced by g2-g4. In fact by concentrating on action in the centre Black hopes to exploit this.

13 h3 ♖b8 14 ♖g1 g6 15 ♘xe4 ♘xe4 16 h4 f4!?

Lautier elects to attack the white king. Another possibility is 16...b5 17 axb6 axb6, when Black plans to fight for the a2-g8 diagonal, thus prompting White to play the rather awkward 18 ♕a2 b5 19 ♗b3. Then the displacement of White's pieces favours Black (the a-file offers White nothing). The direct text, however, also looks promising for Black.

17 ♘g5

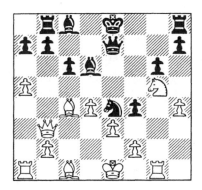

17...♖f8

Defending f7 is not really necessary, so Black should try 17...♗f5. There is no reason to fear 18 ♘f7 ♖f8 19 ♘xd6 ♘xd6 as now the c4-bishop is under fire, and White needs to keep this piece on the board. Alternatively, after (17...♗f5) 18 ♘xe4 Black can recapture with the bishop.

18 ♘xe4 ♕xe4 19 ♗d3

Preventing ...♗f5 but relinquishing the e6-square.

19...♕e7 20 e4?!

Consistent, and it is natural to try to close the centre with the enemy queen and rook posted so menacingly. Unfortunately for White the d4-pawn is left without protection and the e3-square is not available to the bishop. Consequently the d-file now becomes the focus of Black's attention.

20...♗e6!

Suddenly Black's forces jump to action.

21 ♕c2 ♗b4+ 22 ♗d2 ♖d8!

The d-pawn is doomed and White is in serious trouble.

23 a6 ♖xd4 24 axb7 ♕xb7 25 ♗c3!

A good defensive move, hoping to make

it more difficult for Black to infiltrate.

25...♖f7!

It is preferable to bring the rook into play on this rank in order to provide the a-pawn with extra protection.

26 h5 ♖fd7 27 hxg6 hxg6

Not 27...♖xd3?? 28 gxh7 ♖h3 29 ♖g8+.

28 ♗a6 ♕b6 29 ♖xg6 ♗f7 30 ♖h6

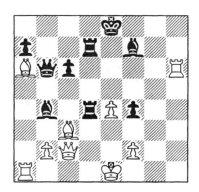

30...♖d2!

Winning a piece and the game.

31 ♗xd2 ♖xd2 32 ♕xc6+ ♕xc6 33 ♖xc6 ♖c2+ 34 ♔d1 ♖xc6 35 ♗b5 ♗b3+?

35...♗h5+ 36 ♗e2 ♖d6+!

36 ♔e2 ♗c4+ 37 ♗xc4 ♖xc4 38 ♖xa7 ♖xe4+ 39 ♔f3 ♖d4 40 ♖a4 ♔e7 41 ♔g4 ♔e6 42 f3 ♔e5 43 ♖a8 ♗d2 44 ♖e8+ ♔d5 45 ♖c8 ♗e3 46 ♖b8 ♔c5 47 ♖c8+ ♔b4 48 ♖b8+ ♔a4 49 b3+ ♔a3 0-1

Game 70
Gelfand-Short
Tilburg 1990

---

1 d4 e6 2 c4 f5 3 ♘c3 ♘f6 4 e3 d5

4...♗b4 is also a good move here, giving Black a comfortable version of the Nimzo-Indian.

5 ♗d3 c6 6 h3!?

Insisting on the g2-g4 thrust, this idea is too slow to trouble Black. In the next game White concentrates on e4 with f2-f3.

6...♗d6 7 g4?! 0-0

Black has responded calmly to White's

show of kingside aggression with sensible development. In the previous game the odd 7 h3?! 0-0 would have led to the diagram position, above, which suggests that Gelfand's treatment lacks punch.

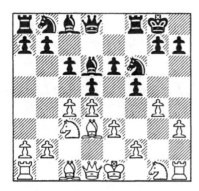

8 ♕c2?!

Presenting Black with a chance to develop an early initiative. 8 ♘f3 is better, with a complex game ahead.

8...♘a6! 9 a3 dxc4 10 ♗xc4 b5 11 ♗e2

11 ♗a2 b4 12 ♘a4 ♚h8 illustrates how misplaced White's pieces can become.

11...b4 12 ♘a4 bxa3 13 bxa3 ♘e4

Black has the advantage thanks to his superior development. His knight has found the usual influential outpost on e4, giving him a commanding presence in the centre, and White is in no position to use the g-file. The f2-pawn, meanwhile, is particularly susceptible to attack.

14 ♘f3

14 ♕xc6 ♕a5+ 15 ♚f1 ♖b8 cannot be recommended to White.

14...♕a5+ 15 ♚f1 ♘c7!

15...c5 16 gxf5 exf5 17 dxc5 ♘axc5 18 ♘xc5 ♗xc5 19 ♗b2 is less clear according to Short. 15...♘c7 keeps the tension and prepares to bring the light-squared bishop into play.

16 ♘b2 ♗a6 17 ♘c4?

Another natural choice as White does not wish to part with a potentially useful defender (and the text also returns the knight to

the struggle). However White should in fact exchange bishops and decentralise Black's queen with 17 ♗xa6 ♕xa6+ 18 ♚g2, although Black is still ahead.

17...♕d5!

A wonderful posting for the queen, defending the advanced knight, relieving the f5-pawn of its duty and in turn preparing to launch an attack on the f-file.

18 ♖g1 fxg4 19 ♖xg4

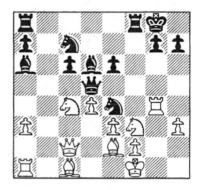

White has finally given his rook the g-file, but the result is to see Black with an open file of his own. Ironically White's problems are his own making, having inaccurately followed up his rather slow kingside build-up. In the diagram position Black has the opportunity to win the game with a nice combination.

19...♘g3+?!

Not the strongest move. Instead 19...♘xf2! 20 ♚xf2 ♗xc4 21 e4 ♕xd4+ 22 ♗e3 ♕xa1 23 ♕xc4 ♕xa3 gives Black a completely winning position.

20 ♖xg3!

Black wins easily after 20 fxg3? ♖xf3+ 21 ♗xf3 ♕xf3+ 22 ♚g1 ♖f8

20...♗xg3 21 ♚g2! ♗h4 22 e4 ♕h5 23 ♘xh4

23 ♘ce5! ♗xe2 24 ♕xe2 offers more chances to survive, although White is still struggling.

23...♕xh4 24 ♗e3 ♖f6 25 ♖h1 ♖af8 26 ♖h2?

A mistake in a hopeless position.

**26...Ξxf2+ 27 ♗xf2 ♕xf2+ 28 ♔h1
♕e1+ 0-1**

Game 71
Korchnoi-P.Nikolic
Sarajevo 1998

**1 d4 f5 2 c4 ♘f6 3 ♘c3 e6 4 e3 d5 5
♗d3 c6 6 ♕c2 ♗d6 7 f3 0-0 8 ♘ge2**

White's set-up is, of course, designed to
deprive Black of the e4-square. The drawback is that the knight is less actively placed
on e2, with the reduced control of the e5-
square being a key difference. Furthermore,
f2-f3 voluntarily weakens White's dark
squares. These factors give Black a comfortable game.

8...♕c7

This is probably not the best from the options available. 8...dxc4?! was seen in Lobron-
Sveshnikov, Budapest 1996. After 9 ♗xc4 b5
10 ♗b3 ♔h8 11 e4 b4 12 e5 bxc3 13 bxc3
♗c7 14 exf6 ♕xf6 15 0-0 e5 16 dxe5 ♗xe5
17 f4 ♗c7 18 ♗b2 ♘d7 19 c4 White stood
better. The following are improvements on
this and the game continuation: 8...♘bd7 9
♗d2 ♕e7 10 cxd5 ♘xd5 11 a3 ♘7f6 12 h3?!
e5 13 ♘xd5 ♘xd5 14 e4 fxe4 15 fxe4 ♘b6
was already better for Black in Bykhovsky-
Vekshenkov, Pavlodar 1991, while 8...♔h8 9
♗d2 ♕e7 10 0-0 dxc4 11 ♗xc4 b5 12 ♗d3
♘a6 13 a3 b4 14 ♘a4 bxa3 15 bxa3 ♗xa3 16
Ξfb1 Ξb8 17 ♕xc6 Ξxb1+ 18 Ξxb1 ♘b4 19

♕c3 ♘bd5 20 ♕a5 ♗d6, Yasinsky-
Sveshnikov, Novgorod 1995, also favoured
Black. Golod-Dgebuadze, Antwerp 1999,
featured a third, slower mode of development, with 8...♘a6 9 a3 ♘c7 10 0-0 b6 11 h3
♗a6 12 b3 Ξc8 13 e4 fxe4 14 fxe4 e5 leading
to complications.

9 cxd5 ♘xd5

9...cxd5 seems like a justification of putting the queen on the c-file, but obliging with
10 ♘b5 leaves White slightly better after
10...♕xc2 11 ♗xc2 ♗b4+ 12 ♗d2 ♗xd2+ 13
♔xd2.

10 ♕b3

Also possible is 10 a3!? ♘d7 11 ♘xd5
cxd5 12 ♕xc7 ♗xc7 13 ♗d2 ♗d6 14 ♔f2
♘f6 15 ♗b4! with an edge for White.
Korchnoi is happy to trade pieces eventually
but first he turns to development, putting the
onus on Black to unravel and to find decent
squares for his pieces.

10...♔h8

Stepping off the a2-g8 diagonal.

11 ♗d2 ♘d7 12 Ξc1

Threatening to eliminate Black's dark-
squared bishop with ♘b5.

12...♕b6 13 ♗c4 ♘7f6 14 0-0 ♗d7

In return for losing the knight outpost on
e4 Black has been given the d5-square, although it is in the nature of White's pawn
structure that e3-e4 might well come (White
must be careful that this advance does not
leave his pawns vulnerable on e4 and d4).

15 ♘a4

Practically forcing Black to exchange
queens as otherwise White's will be superior.

15...♕xb3 16 ♗xb3 b6

Keeping the knight out of c5.

17 ♘ac3 Ξfe8 18 ♘g3

18 e4?! ♘xc3 19 ♘xc3 e5! is fine for
Black.

18...♘xc3

Instigating a series of exchanges that Black
judges (correctly) to bring about a level ending.

19 ♗xc3 c5

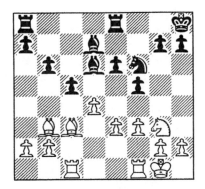

Notice how Black has sufficient control of key squares to enable him to challenge the centre in this fashion. The backward e6-pawn is certainly not a problem.

20 ☖fd1 ☖ac8 21 d5

21 dxc5 ♗xc5 22 ♗xf6 ♗xe3+ illustrates how f2-f3 can have a direct impact on White's dark squares.

21...♗xg3 22 hxg3 ♘xd5 23 ♗xd5 exd5 24 ☖xd5 ♗e6 25 ☖d6 ☖cd8 26 ☖cd1 ☖xd6 27 ☖xd6

This ending is indeed drawn, but Korchnoi's fifty years of international experience afford him the ability to pose Nikolic problems – even in this position.

27...♔g8 28 a4 ♔f7 29 a5 b5

29...bxa5 30 ☖a6 ☖e7 31 ☖xa5 c4 32 ♗d4 ☖b7 is the simplest route to a draw.

30 ☖a6 ☖e7 31 ☖c6 b4?

Necessary is 31...c4, e.g. 32 ♗d4 ☖b7 33 a6 ☖d7 34 ☖c5 b4 35 ☖b5 c3! with a draw.

32 ♗e1 ☖d7 33 ☖xc5 ☖d1 34 ♔f2 ☖b1??

The losing move. There is another draw here: Tyomkin gives 34...☖d5 35 ☖c6 b3 36 ♗c3 ☖d7 37 ♗d4 ♗d5 38 ☖a6 ♗c4 39 ☖xa7 ☖xa7 40 ♗xa7 ♔e6 41 ♔e1 ♔d5 42 ♔d2 ♗f1.

35 ☖c2!

Black is now going to pay for leaving pawns on dark squares.

35...♗b3 36 ☖c7+ ♔g8 37 ♗xb4 ☖xb2+ 38 ♔g1 a6 39 ♗c3 ☖c2 40 ☖xg7+ ♔f8

41 ♗d4 ☖a2 42 ☖xh7 ☖xa5 43 ☖h4 ♗e6 44 e4 fxe4 45 ☖xe4 ♔f7 46 g4 ☖a2 47 ☖f4+ ♔g8 48 g5 ♗f7 49 ☖f6 1-0

Game 72
Golod-Delemarre
Dieren 1999

---

1 d4 d5 2 c4 c6 3 ♘f3 e6 4 e3 f5 5 ♗d3 ♗d6 6 0-0 ♕f6!?

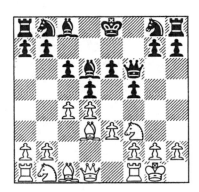

This is an interesting departure from the traditional deployment of ...♘f6. However, with accurate play White should succeed in achieving a modest advantage out of the opening, although it must be said that ...♕f6 does have surprise value.

7 b3

With Black's queen already committed this is a good time to aim for ♗a3.

7...♘e7 8 ♗a3! ♗c7!?

Sensibly avoiding the exchange. Without both a knight on e5 and a pawn on g3 the bishop has a good home on the h2-b8 diagonal, and the queen is well within striking distance on f6.

9 ♘c3 a5

Gaining some ground on the queenside.

10 ♕c2!

Straight to the point and highlighting a problem Black can experience in this line. The queen takes up residence on the c-file to monitor the unprotected c7-bishop from afar, thus introducing possibilities on b5 and d5 – hence Black's next, which defends the bishop and eyes the b4-square.

10...♘a6 11 cxd5 exd5!

Black offers the f-pawn, which is a consistent and wise decision considering the complexities that follow.

12 ♗xe7 ♕xe7 13 ♗xf5 ♘b4 14 ♕b1 0-0!

Again Black is not afraid to invest for the cause of development.

15 ♗xh7+ ♔h8

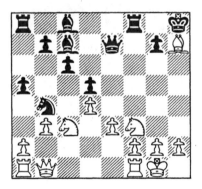

For the price of two pawns Black has active pieces and pressure against White's king. The immediate threat is ...♖xf3 followed by ...♕h4, hitting both h2 and h7.

16 ♘e5 ♗xe5 17 dxe5 ♗g4!

Black must keep his pieces active to justify the sacrifice. After 17...♕xe5 18 ♘e2 ♕h5 19 ♗d3 White – a pawn to the good, remember – gains time to transfer his knight to f4 and, ultimately, perhaps even to g6. The text keeps the pressure on.

18 a3 ♕xe5

Black continues to hold his ground, exploiting the fact that White is tied to the defence of his bishop.

19 axb4 ♕xc3 20 bxa5 ♖xa5 21 ♖xa5 ♕xa5 22 b4?!

The tidy 22 ♕d3 preserves White's lead.

22...♕a3 23 ♗g6 ♖f6 24 ♗d3 ♕c3 25 e4?!

White is being pinned down but this is a little impatient.

25...dxe4 26 ♗xe4 ♕d4! 27 b5! cxb5

27...♗e2 28 bxc6 ♗xf1 29 cxb7 ♕xf2+ 30 ♔h1 and there is no way to stop the pawn.

28 ♕c2 ♕c4

With limited protection for his king Black elects to go into the endgame a pawn down, counting on his passed pawn to offer sufficient counterplay to make the draw.

29 ♕xc4 bxc4 30 ♗xb7 ♗e2?!

This gives White more chances to win the endgame than he deserves. Helping the immediate advance of the c-pawn with 30...♗f5 31 ♖c1 ♖b6! 32 ♗f3 c3 is imperative, although Black is still obliged to play accurately to split the point after 33 ♔f1.

31 ♖e1 ♖d6 32 f4 ♖d2 33 ♔f2 c3! 34 ♔e3 ♗d1 35 ♗f3 ♗c2 36 ♖a1 ♖d3+ 37 ♔e2 ♖d2+ 38 ♔e3 ♖d3+ 39 ♔e2 ♖d2+ 40 ♔e1 ♗f5 41 g4?!

Too eager. White retains some pressure with 41 ♖a5 g6 42 ♖c5 etc.

41...♗e6 42 ♖a8+ ♔h7 43 ♗e4+ g6 44 f5

White has already committed himself to this.

44...gxf5 45 gxf5

45...♖d4?!

Missing an immediate draw with 45...♗d5! 46 f6+ ♗xe4 47 f7 ♗d3!! 48 f8♕ (48 ♖d8 ♖xh2! 49 ♖h8+ ♔g6 50 ♖xh2 ♔xf7 is drawn) 48...♖e2+ 49 ♔f1 (49 ♔d1 c2+ and Black queens with check) 49...♖e8+ 50 ♔f2 ♖xf8+ 51 ♖xf8 and the strong passed pawn

guarantees the draw, just as Black had hoped.
**46 ♗c2 ♗f7 47 ♖a7 ♔g8 48 f6 ♖d8 49
♖c7 ♗d5 50 ♗h7+ ♔h8 51 ♗c2 ♖e8+
52 ♔f2 ♖f8 53 ♖h7+ ♔g8 54 ♖g7+ ♔h8
55 ♖g6 ♖d8 56 ♔e3 ♗f7 57 ♖g7 ♖d2
58 ♗f5 ♖d5 59 ♗d3 ♖d7 60 ♗g6 ♗e6
61 ♖xd7 ♗xd7 62 ♔d3 ♔g8 63 ♔d4
♗e8 64 ♗c2 ♗h5 65 ♔e5 ♔f7 66 ♗b3+
♔f8??**

A terrible mistake that costs the game. Instead a dead draw results from 66...♔g6 67 h4 ♔h6 68 ♔e6 ♔h7 69 ♗c2+ ♔h6! (69...♗g6?? 70 f7) 70 ♔e7 ♗g6 71 ♗xg6 ♔xg6 72 f7 c2 73 f8♕ c1♕ as the defending king blockades the passed pawn.
**67 ♔f5 ♗e2 68 ♗c2 ♔f7 69 h4 ♗c4 70
h5 ♔g8 71 h6 ♗f7 72 ♔e5 ♔h8 73 ♔d4
♔g8 74 ♔xc3 ♔h8 75 ♔d4 ♔g8 76 ♔e5
♔h8 77 ♔d6 ♗c4 78 ♔e7 ♗d5 79 ♗g6**

Of course not 79 f7?? ♗xf7 and the position is a theoretical draw.
**79...♗c4 80 ♗f5 ♗f7 81 ♗e6 ♗h5 82
♗d7! 1-0**

Game 73
Cvitan-Sveshnikov
Tilburg 1993

---

1 d4 d5 2 c4 e6 3 ♘c3 c6 4 e3 ♘d7

One of the two ways Black can delay ...f7-f5 but, unlike 4...♗d6, the light-squared bishop no longer supports f5 in case of an early g2-g4.
5 ♘f3

5 ♗d3 ♘gf6 6 ♘f3 leads to traditional Meran lines but here White cannot play the 6 ♕c2 line, which some players might consider significant.
5...f5!

Now there is no g2-g4.
6 ♗d3 ♗d6 7 ♖b1

White quickly turns to the queenside to try for an initiative, with Black clearly looking for activity on the other flank. The question is who will be first? In this game it is Black, but I do believe that the general strategy em-

ployed by White is a little dubious, and that White must in some way counter Black's offensive.
7...♘gf6 8 b4 a6 9 0-0 0-0 10 a4 ♘e4

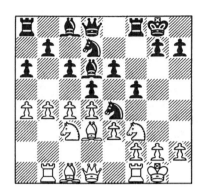

11 ♕b3

A sensible alternative is 11 ♕c2. White chose this square in Kozul-Shirov, Biel 1991, the only difference being that White's bishop stood on e2 instead of d3. Then 11...♖f6 is okay, with similar play to the main game, but Shirov turned to the centre with 11...♕e7. After 12 b5 axb5 13 axb5 c5 14 cxd5 ♘xc3 15 ♕xc3 exd5 16 dxc5 ♘xc5 17 ♖a1 ♘e4 18 ♕b2 White had only a modest edge thanks to his better centre, although 18...♗e6 19 ♖xa8 ♖xa8 20 g3 ♗f7 21 ♕c2 ♕c7! 22 ♕xc7 ♗xc7 23 ♘d4 g6 24 ♗b2 ♔f8 25 ♖c1 ♗b6 saw Black comfortably hold the ending.
11...♖f6!

Black begins his attack at once. With control of the e5-square White can address this offensive more comfortably. This will be covered later in the chapter.
12 b5 axb5 13 axb5 ♖h6

Black's plan on the kingside is certainly direct and easy to conduct.
14 g3

14 h3 gives Black something to aim at after 14...g5.
14...♘df6 15 bxc6 bxc6 16 cxd5 exd5

White has executed his plan but stands worse. In fact the clearance of pawns on the queenside has left the single target on c6, whereas Black's forces point (increasingly) at White's king. Best now is the simple 17 ₩c2 but, unfortunately for White, the thematic continuation chosen presents Black with a winning opportunity.

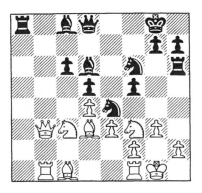

17 ♘e5? ♖b8?!

Returning the favour by allowing White to complicate matters with a queen sacrifice. Simpler is 17...♗xe5! 18 dxe5 ♘c5 19 ₩c2 ♘g4 20 ♗e2 (on 20 h4 Black does not go for any complicated sacrifices but cashes in with the decisive 20...♘xd3 21 ₩xd3 ♘xe5) 20...♘xh2 21 ♖d1 ♘e4.

18 ₩xb8! ♗xb8 19 ♖xb8 ₩c7 20 ♖b3 ♘d7?!

This is passive and makes it harder for Black to realise his advantage. 20...♘c5! 21 dxc5 ₩xe5 is the correct way to deal with the e5-knight.

21 ♘f3 ♘b6 22 ♗b2 ♘c4 23 ♗xc4 dxc4 24 ♖b4

The last few moves have seen White generate promising compensation and the position is no longer so easy to play for Black.

24...c5 25 dxc5 ₩xc5 26 ♖b5 ₩c7 27 ♘d5 ₩d7 28 ♖b8 ♖c6 29 ♖d1 ₩a7?

Mistakes are not difficult to come by under such pressure! From a practical point of view Black's situation has changed dramatically, which might explain why Black missed 29...♖c5!, challenging the troublesome knight. Play might then continue 30 ♘f6+ (30 ♗a3?! ₩a7! 31 ♖xc8+ ♖xc8 32 ♘e7+ ♔f7 33

♘e5+ ♔f6 34 ♘xc8 ₩xa3 is good for Black; White cannot play 35 ♘xc4 in view of 35...₩a2!) 30...♖xf6 31 ♖xd7 ♘xd7 32 ♗d4!, when White fights on, although the task is not easy after 32...♖c7.

30 ♘e5!

Suddenly White is winning.

30...♖c5!

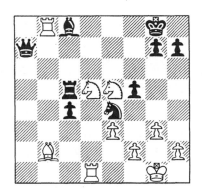

The only chance for survival. Black loses by force after 30...₩xb8 31 ♘e7+! ♔f8 32 ♖d8+ ♔xe7 33 ♘xc6+.

31 ♘b6?

31 ♘f4! ₩e7 32 ♘e6!! wins.

31...h6 32 ♖xc8+

Leading to a forced draw. Also possible is 32 ♘ed7 with a complicated and unclear position after 32...c3! 33 ♗c1! (33 ♘xc8? ₩xb8 34 ♘xb8 cxb2 and the b-pawn is a winner) 33...c2 34 ♖d3. A remarkable draw is 34...₩a5 35 ♔f1 ♔h7 36 ♘f8+ ♔g8 37 ♘fd7 ♔h7 38 ♘f8+.

32...♖xc8 33 ♘xc8 ₩a2 34 ♘e7+ ♔h7 35 ♘5g6 ₩xb2 36 ♘f8+ ½-½

Game 74
Van der Sterren-Piket
Holland 1992

---

1 d4 d5 2 c4 c6 3 ♘f3 e6 4 e3 f5 5 ♗d3 ♘f6 6 0-0 ♗e7

The bishop tends to be better placed on d6, the b8-h2 diagonal offering more prospects and providing Black with some influence over e5. In this game, however, White is more interested in keeping Black out of e4 than using e5.

7 b3 0-0 8 ♗b2

8 ♗a3 is a normal means with which to exploit ...♗e7, and should grant White a minimal advantage.

8...♘e4 9 ♘c3 ♘d7 10 ♘e2 ♕e8 11 ♘d2?!

As we shall see this is not Van der Sterren's day. The text gives Black a chance to take over the initiative, something a player such as Piket does not miss.

11...♗b4!

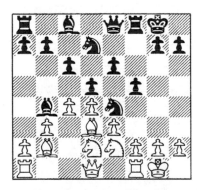

White should now accept his mistake and play 12 ♘f3, but instead he plans to drive Black's pieces away from the centre – forgetting that his own should be developed.

12 ♘b1?! ♘df6

Black is interested only in sending his forces to the kingside.

13 f3 ♘g5 14 ♘bc3 ♗d7 15 a3?!

There is no reason for White to chase the bishop back to d6, from where h2 is under fire. White seems to be paying little attention to the potential weakness of his kingside.

15...♗d6 16 ♕d2 ♕h5

Black's most powerful piece comes into play.

17 ♘f4 ♕h6 18 g3 ♖ae8 19 ♖ae1 ♘f7

Yet again the f7-square is a useful outpost for a knight. Black is now ready to launch an attack, the sheer mass of fire-power within

range of White's king ensuring him a pleasant game. In fact White does not find a way to handle the numerous threats.

20 cxd5?!

The opening of the e-file benefits only Black, while White gets nothing from the c-file. 20 b4!? dxc4 21 ♗xc4 e5 22 dxe5 ♗xe5 is an improvement, with the better game for Black.

20...exd5 21 h4 ♘h5! 22 ♕h2?

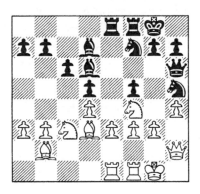

A mistake that is easy to punish. Nonetheless White's compromised pawn structure requires precise defence, and 22 ♘xh5 ♕xh5 23 ♔g2 ♖e7 followed by ...♖fe8 is pretty uncomfortable.

22...♘xg3!!

Tearing apart White's defences. Pawns on e3, f3, g3 and h4 cannot be recommended.

23 ♕xg3 ♖xe3

The point, and a fitting culmination of Black's pressure play thus far. Total domination of the dark squares is just one decisive factor.

24 ♗c1 ♗xf4 25 ♗xe3 ♗xe3+ 26 ♔h1 f4 27 ♕h2 ♗xd4 28 ♘d1 ♘e5 29 ♗c2 ♕h5 30 ♔g2 ♘xf3! 0-1

Game 75
Boensch-Lobron
Graz 1993

---

1 d4 d5 2 c4 e6 3 ♘f3 c6 4 e3 f5 5 ♗e2 ♗d6 6 b3 ♘f6 7 0-0

Playing with the bishop on e2 is a conservative, positional approach in the style of Karpov. White prefers to use the bishop to defend the kingside.

7...♕e7

The normal move as Black need not allow ♗a3. Remember that earlier 7 ♗a3? loses to 7...♗xa3 8 ♘xa3 ♕a5+.

8 ♗b2

White can force the exchange of bishops with 8 a4 a5 9 ♗a3 ♗xa3 10 ♘xa3 but then Black is no worse. One example is Mecking-Panchenko, Linares 1995, when after 10...0-0 11 ♕c2 ♗d7 12 ♘e5 ♗e8 13 cxd5 exd5 14 ♘b1 ♘bd7 15 ♘d3 ♗h5 16 ♗xh5 ♘xh5 17 ♘d2 f4 Black obtained good counterplay.

8...0-0 9 ♘e5!

The mere presence of the knight hinders Black's harmony on the kingside.

9...♗d7

Sending the bishop on the traditional route. For 9...♘bd7 see Speelman-Seirawan, next.

10 ♕c2 ♗e8 11 ♘d2 ♘bd7 12 ♘df3 ♗h5

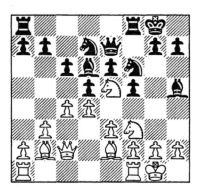

Black has equalized but nothing more. White has the e5-square but Black can jump into e4, and Black has prospects of a dangerous looking kingside expansion. Consequently White looks to the c-file to create a distraction.

13 cxd5 cxd5 14 ♖fc1 a6 15 ♘xd7 ♘xd7 16 ♘e5 ♗xe2 17 ♕xe2 ♖ac8 18

♖c2

Trading pieces reduces the attacking potential of both sides, although Black still has ambitions involving his kingside pawns.

18...♖xc2 19 ♕xc2 ♘f6 20 ♖c1 g5!?

Seizing territory and preventing f2-f4, which would open the g-file and leave d4 (and perhaps even f4) slightly weaker.

21 f3

21 ♕e2 g4, intending 22...♗xe5 23 dxe5 ♘e4, practically forces White to play 22 f3 with a transposition to the game.

21...g4 22 ♕e2 ♕g7 23 fxg4 fxg4 24 ♖f1 h5

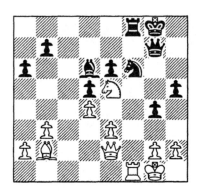

Black has a small advantage due to the great knight he will soon have on e4. Despite this White should be able to defend this position.

25 ♖f4 ♘e4 26 ♕c2 ♖xf4 27 exf4 ♕c7 28 ♕xc7?

The endgame without queens turns out to be very difficult to defend. In fact it might even be lost due to the weakness of f4 and the considerably limited scope of White's pieces. Note that White made nothing of the open c-file.

28...♗xc7 29 ♘d3 ♔f7 30 ♔f1 ♔g6 31 ♔e2 ♔f5 32 ♔e3 h4 33 h3 ♗a5

It is interesting to compare the relative strengths and weaknesses of the bishops, not forgetting the pawn structures.

34 b4 ♗c7 35 ♘e5?

Losing by force in an anyway increasingly

untenable position.

35...♗xe5 36 dxe5 ♘g3 37 ♔d4 ♘e2+ 38 ♔c5 ♘xf4 39 ♔b6 ♘xg2 40 ♗d4 gxh3 41 ♗g1 d4 0-1

Game 76
Speelman-Seirawan
Saint John 1988

---

1 d4 d5 2 ♘f3 c6 3 c4 e6 4 e3 f5 5 ♗e2 ♘f6 6 0-0 ♗d6 7 b3 ♕e7 8 ♗b2 ♘bd7 9 ♘e5!

White responds to ...♘bd7 by occupying e5 anyway. This can be further supported by f2-f4.

9...0-0 10 ♘d2

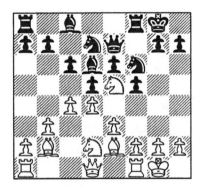

White has an edge as Black has no easy way to develop his queenside. To be considered is 10...a5!? followed by ...♔h8 and gradual improvements on the position. Alternatively there is 10...♘e4 with the idea of 11 f3 ♘g5 and 12...♘f7, either gaining control over e5 or, after 13 f4, playing ...♘f6-e4 and ....♗d7-e8. In conclusion White might claim a small advantage, but certainly no more.

10...g5?!

Understandable but too ambitious, for White is free to react vigorously with his knight already firmly planted on e5.

11 f4! gxf4 12 exf4 ♘e4 13 ♘xe4 fxe4 14 ♕d2

White has play on both flanks.

14...♘f6 15 c5! ♗c7 16 b4 ♗d7 17 a4

♘e8!

In a severely cramped position Black finds the correct plan – relocating the knight on f5.

18 ♖a3 ♘g7 19 ♖h3 ♗e8!? 20 ♗c3 ♗g6?!

20...h5 is preferable according to Speelman.

21 g4! ♗xe5?

Black should bring the other rook into play with 21...♖ad8, waiting to see how White will continue.

22 dxe5 h5

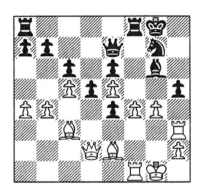

23 f5!

Making sure that the h5-pawn drops without Black being able to take advantage of the f5-square.

23...exf5 24 gxh5 e3?!

Speelman demonstrates that White is winning even after the best defence with the following wonderful line: 24...♗h7 25 ♖g3 ♔h8 26 e6 ♖f6 27 ♖g6!! ♗xg6 28 ♕h6+ ♔g8 29 hxg6 ♘xe6 30 ♖xf5 d4 31 ♗c4 dxc3 32 ♖xf6 ♕xf6 33 ♗xe6+ ♕xe6 34 ♕h7+ ♔f8 35 g7+.

25 ♕xe3 f4 26 ♖xf4 ♗e4 27 e6 ♘f5 28 ♖xf5 ♖xf5 29 ♕h6

Black is now defenceless on the dark squares.

29...♖g5+ 30 ♖g3! ♖xg3+ 31 hxg3 ♕h7

Or 31...♗h7 32 ♗f6 ♕c7 33 ♕g5+ ♔f8 34 h6.

32 ♕f6 ♖e8 33 ♗e5 ♖e7 34 ♕g5+ ♔f8 35 ♗d6 1-0

Game 77
Karpov-Ivanchuk
Tilburg 1993

1 d4 d5 2 c4 e6 3 ♘c3 c6 4 e3 f5 5 f4!?

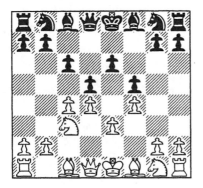

The Karpov variation. It is not particularly dangerous, as we see in this game, but it is without risk to White. Black should not fear the early f2-f4 line unless he is intent on winning. My experience is that you always have your chances in a game so it is important to be ready to take them, in the meantime having positions you enjoy.

5...♘f6 6 ♘f3 ♗e7 7 ♗e2

Facilitating a later capture on e4. However, with the bishop on d3 White has the e2-square for the queen. Ivanchuk-Nogueiras, Lucerne 1993 saw White earn a tiny edge after 7 ♗d3 0-0 8 0-0 b6 9 b3 ♗b7 10 ♗b2 ♘e4 11 ♖c1 ♘d7 12 ♕e2, after which Black did himself no favours by misplacing his rook on h6 over the next two moves.

7...0-0 8 0-0 b6

The most natural form of development. Black can also consider 8...♘e4 9 ♕c2 ♘d7. Then after 10 b3 ♘xc3 11 ♕xc3 ♘f6 12 ♘e5 ♗d7 13 a4 ♘e4 14 ♕d3 White was only marginally ahead in Karpov-Spassky, Leningrad 1974. The alternative 10...♘df6 followed by the usual bishop manoeuvre to h5 has been suggested as an improvement,

with an even position.

9 ♕c2 ♗b7

9...♗a6 achieves nothing as White has the natural 10 ♘e5 to pressure the c6-pawn.

10 cxd5

Waiting with 10 a3 meets with 10...♘e4 because Black is in no hurry to develop his queen's knight as long as there is a chance to put it on c6 (and as long as there are other constructive moves available). After the text the c-file becomes a major focus of attention for both sides.

10...cxd5 11 ♗d2 ♘c6 12 a3 ♘e4 13 ♖fc1 ♖c8 14 ♕d1 ♕d7 15 ♗e1 ♖c7

In answer to 16 ♘b5 Black simply drops back to c8 and continues with ...a7-a6 (with tempo) and ...b6-b5.

16 ♖c2 ♘xc3 17 ♖xc3 ♖fc8 18 ♖ac1 ♗d6 19 ♕a4 ♘b8!

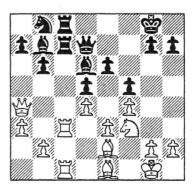

Black volunteers to take the game to a slightly inferior ending, confident that he can defend. The plausible 19...a6 might run into the strong sacrifice 20 ♗xa6!? ♖a8 21 ♗xb7 ♖xa4 22 ♗xc6 ♖xc6 23 ♖xc6, when White will have either play on the 7th rank or a powerful knight on e5.

20 ♕xd7

There is nothing better, e.g. 20 ♕xa7 ♗c6 21 ♕xb6 ♖b7 22 ♕a5 ♖a7 23 ♕b6 ♖b7 with an immediate draw.

20...♘xd7 21 ♖xc7 ♖xc7 22 ♖xc7 ♗xc7 23 ♘g5

White's pieces are better placed but there

are no significant structural problems for Black, nor does Black have problems with his pieces. Consequently the position is not difficult to defend for a player of this calibre.

23...♘f8 24 ♗b5 h6 25 ♘f3 ♘g6 26 h3 ♔f7 27 ♗b4 ♘e7 28 ♘e5+

Ftacnik suggests 28 ♗xe7!? ♔xe7 29 g4 as the only way for White to develop pressure.

28...♗xe5 29 dxe5 ♘c6! 30 ♗c3 ♘b8 31 ♗d3 ♗c6 32 b3 ♘d7 33 ♗d4 ♘c5 34 ♗xc5 bxc5 35 ♗a6 h5 36 g3 g6 37 ♔f2 ♔e7 38 ♔e1 ♔d8 39 a4 ♔c7

The diagram position is not untypical of Stonewall endings. Black's bishop is a match for its opposite number and the kingside pawns are safe.

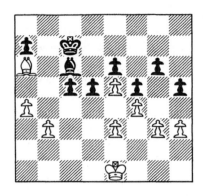

40 a5 ♗b7 41 ♗e2 ♗c6 42 ♔d2 ♗e8 43 ♔c3 ♗d7 44 ♗a6 ♗c6 45 b4 cxb4+ 46 ♔xb4 ♗e8 47 ♔c5 ♗a4 ½-½

Summary

Systems involving e2-e3 are not a threat to the Stonewall player, unless White has already brought his queen's bishop into play, as in Game 68. If White tries something aggressive like g2-g4 (Games 69-70) Black's position is okay, and the game can easily prove more difficult for White to handle than Black. The only strategy for White that fights for an advantage is demonstrated in Speelman's win against Seirawan (Game 76), although I am convinced that this line is not dangerous for Black. Karpov's 5 f4 (Game 77) is a solid idea that aims for no more than a modest edge, thereby affording Black some flexibility.

Because this chapter – unlike the others – consists of games with diverse initial moves/sequences, below is an index in order of available plans. All games include the move **e2-e3**.

Black allows **&f4** – *Game 68*
White plays **g2-g4** *(D)* to challenge the centre – *Games 69-70*
White monitors the e4-square with **&ge2** and **f2-f3** *(D)* – *Game 71*
Black plays ...**&f6** – *Game 72*
White expands on the queenside – *Game 73*
White plays **b2-b3** and **&b2** *(D)* – *Games 74-76*
White plays **f2-f4** – *Game 77*

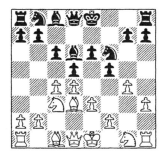

White plays g2-g4

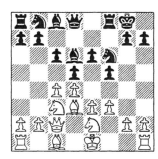

White plays f2-f3

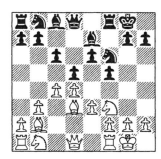

White plays b3 and &b2

INDEX OF COMPLETE GAMES